The Best American
Travel Writing 2017

The Best American Travel Writing™ 2017

Edited with an Introduction
by **Lauren Collins**

Jason Wilson, Series Editor

A Mariner Original

HOUGHTON MIFFLIN HARCOURT

BOSTON • NEW YORK 2017

hmhco.com

ISSN 1530-1516 (print) ISSN 2573-4830 (e-book)
ISBN 978-1-328-74573-6 (print) ISBN 978-1-328-74233-9 (e-book)

Printed in the United States of America
DOC 10 9 8 7 6 5 4 3 2 1

"Cover Story" by Elif Batuman. First published in *The New Yorker*, February 8 and 15, 2016. Copyright © 2016 by Elif Batuman. Reprinted by permission of Elif Batuman.

"My Holy Land Vacation" by Tom Bissell. First published in *Harper's Magazine*, July 2016. Copyright © 2016 by Thomas Carlisle Bissell. Reprinted by permission of the author.

"Chiefing in Cherokee" by Stephanie Elizondo Griest. First published in *Virginia Quarterly Review*, Fall 2016. Copyright © 2016 by Stephanie Elizondo Griest. Reprinted by permission of Stephanie Elizondo Griest.

"Cliffhanger" by Peter Frick-Wright. First published in *Outside*, November 2016. Copyright © 2016 by Peter Frick-Wright. Reprinted by permission of Peter Frick-Wright.

"The Ones Who Left" by Jackie Hedeman. First published in *The Offing*, December 8, 2016. Copyright © 2016 by Jackie Hedeman. Reprinted by permission of Jackie Hedeman.

"The Big Leap" by Leslie Jamison. First published in *AFAR*, July/August 2016. Copyright © 2016 by Leslie Jamison. Reprinted by permission of Leslie Jamison.

"Refugees Hear a Foreign Word: Welcome" by Jodi Kantor and Catrin Einhorn.

Contents

Foreword

IS TRAVEL WRITING DEAD? That's the question the distinguished UK literary magazine *Granta* posed to a dozen or so writers in its Winter 2017 issue. Like so many of these faux-provocative questions ("Is the novel dead?" "Is the cocktail dead?" "Is baseball dying?"), no definitive answer was reached. As Geoff Dyer, who was among the respondents, wrote: "Yes and no. Sort of."

Ian Jack, *Granta*'s former editor, was more blunt: "Travel writing isn't dead. It just isn't what it was."

Much of the discussion dwelled on nomenclature, the idea that the genre's name—"travel writing"—did not adequately capture what it is to write about place in 2017. "So what matters to me is not whether a piece of writing is called travel writing," wrote Mohsin Hamid.

Dyer offered up Miles Davis's work from the 1970s as a possibility. At that time, Davis no longer referred to his music as "jazz" but rather "Directions in Music." Said Dyer, "That's what I'm after: Directions in Writing."

So yes, a generally weird discussion in the pages of *Granta*. Still, the simple fact of the magazine asking the dreaded "Is travel writing dead" question was astonishing enough, and somewhat alarming to those of us who've been ardent readers of both travel writing and *Granta* since the 1980s.

Granta, after all, led a revival of travel writing in the 1980s, advocating for what had become a badly atrophied, nearly moribund genre in the late twentieth century. With Bill Buford as its editor, *Granta* dedicated two special issues to new travel writing, in 1984 and 1989. Legendary travel writers regularly turned up in the magazine's pages: Bruce Chatwin, Colin Thubron, Martha Gellhorn, Jan Morris, Ryszard Kapuściński.

I can't overstate how exciting and freeing it was when I first discovered writers like Chatwin and Kapuściński and Gellhorn and Rebecca West and Ted Conover and Pico Iyer. While I was supposed to be focused on fiction in my graduate creative writing program in the early 1990s, I found my mind drifting toward travel writing. This was still before the rise of so-called creative nonfiction, several years before the mainstreaming of the memoir, and a decade before the emergence of personal blogs. Travel writing, in those days, was not a topic of polite discussion in graduate fiction seminars. (Of course, now we know that Chatwin and Kapuściński introduced quite a bit of fiction into their work.)

In any case, the travel writing published by *Granta* would inspire me, in the mid-1990s, to create my own journal devoted to travel, *Grand Tour,* which lurched along for a few years, then died and went to small-underfunded-literary-magazine heaven. Out of *Grand Tour*'s ashes, however, this Best American anthology emerged. In early 2000, I scoured through the travel stories of 1999 along with our first guest editor, Bill Bryson—one of those travel writers whom I'd first read in *Granta*—to gather our first anthology.

We've been following a similar model now through eighteen editions, spanning 9/11, the endless wars in Iraq and Afghanistan, the lifting of the Cuban travel ban, the Syrian refugee crisis, the presidencies of Bill Clinton, George W. Bush, Barack Obama, and now Donald Trump—chronicling the world as it's been transformed in so many previously unfathomable ways.

Travel itself has also irrevocably changed over that time. Consider what did not exist when we began this anthology eighteen years ago: euro notes and coins, Google Maps, translation apps, Uber, Yelp, "premium economy," boarding passes scanned from iPhones, and TSA "PreCheck." The readers of *The Best American Travel Writing 2000* could wander through security without removing their shoes and belts, toting bottles of liquor stowed in their carry-on baggage, yet they could scarcely have imagined snapping a photo during their flight and posting it to Instagram. Nor could they have envisioned the story about Airbnb in Tokyo that ran in last year's anthology, or the story about an epic misuse of GPS in Iceland that appears in this year's.

This evolution is, of course, the sort of thing that's supposed to happen with travel writing. In my very first foreword, to *The Best American Travel Writing 2000,* I wrote:

> Travel writing is always about a specific moment in time. The writer imbues that moment with everything he or she has read, heard, experienced, and lived, bringing all of his or her talent to bear on it. When focused on that moment, great travel writing can teach us something about the world that no other genre can. Perhaps travel writing's foremost lesson is this: We may never walk this way again, and even if we do, we will never be the same people we are right now. Most important, the world we move through will never be the same place again. This is why travel writing matters.

What's important to remember about travel writing is that it's not just about where one goes, or who makes the trip, or how they travel, or why. It's also about *when* that journey takes place. As I read through the pile of this year's travel writing, it struck me that whoever is assigning travel pieces at many magazines has forgotten that the when is as important as the where, who, how, and why.

To be perfectly candid, there was an alarming dearth of travel stories published in 2016. Lauren Collins, our guest editor, and I faced a challenging pool. I can't say that some version of the question posed by *Granta*—Is travel writing dying?—didn't cross my mind during this year's selection process.

Part of the reason was that, in many publications, precious pages were given over to coverage of the exhausting, maddening, disheartening 2016 presidential campaign. So many of the stories published on place took the form of reports "from Trump Country" or journeys "through Trump's America" or explorations "into the heart of Trump Land." But these stories all felt way too late— like ten or twenty years too late. In 1997, Michael Paterniti wrote an amazing piece for *Esquire,* called "Eating Jack Hooker's Cow," in which he visited Dodge City, Kansas. Reread that piece in 2017 and you'll learn more about why we now find ourselves living in such a divided nation than by reading most of last year's "Trump Country" dispatches.

Paul Theroux once wrote: "The job of the travel writer is to go far and wide, make voluminous notes, and tell the truth. There is immense drudgery in the job. But the book ought to live, and if it is truthful, it ought to be prescient without making predictions."

In 1988, Theroux published *Riding the Iron Rooster,* a travel book about a year he spent riding trains in China, accompanied by a Communist Party bureaucrat. At the time, China was closed to foreigners, and in Theroux's book, he was extremely critical of the country, painting an unflattering portrait of a dull, cynical, ugly place. There are pages and pages of dialogue with young people complaining about the government and government officials complaining about students. "I hated sight-seeing in China," Theroux wrote. "I felt the Chinese hid behind their rebuilt ruins so that no one could look closely at their lives."

Riding the Iron Rooster was attacked by critics for being ungenerous and impolite. Mark Salzman, in a *New York Times* review, insisted that Theroux had drawn conclusions "that don't ring true." Salzman wrote, "More often than not, he is passing judgment on China rather than describing it, all from a very limited perspective. The result is an opinionated, petty and incomplete portrait of that country." Less than a year after that review, the Tiananmen Square massacre occurred, setting off the complex chain of events that ushered forth the contemporary China we now know. With those events in hindsight, someone who now reads *Riding the Iron Rooster* is more likely to see the book as an example of what the best sort of travel writing can reveal.

Perhaps what *Granta* suggests with its "Is travel writing dead?" issue is that the genre reached its high-water mark in the 1980s (not coincidentally when *Granta* was at its own peak). Or perhaps the editors are wondering whether travel writing is outdated or old-fashioned or in need of a fancy, avant-garde, literary "subversion." Whatever the case, these are ridiculous notions. Travel writing has existed longer than most other forms of literature, dating at least to Herodotus in ancient Greece. And travel writing has faced criticism for nearly as long. In the first century AD, the Roman essayist Plutarch was already calling bullshit on Herodotus, accusing him of bias and "calumnious fictions." Maybe the most subversive, experimental "direction in writing" one could actually take is to try one's hand at a classic, traditional first-person travel narrative?

Pico Iyer (guest editor, *The Best American Travel Writing 2004*) was one of the writers who took up *Granta*'s question. I'll let his response stand as mine: "Travel writing isn't dead; it can no more die than curiosity or humanity or the strangeness of the world can die."

The stories included here are, as always, selected from among dozens of pieces in dozens of diverse publications—from mainstream glossies to cutting-edge websites to Sunday newspaper travel sections to literary journals to niche magazines. I've done my best to be fair and representative, and in my opinion the best travel stories from 2016 were forwarded to guest editor Lauren Collins, who made our final selections. Though she and I debated "What is travel writing?" during this selection process, I believe loyal readers of the series will find that the key elements of great travel writing never really change. I'd like to thank Tim Mudie, at Houghton Mifflin, for his usual aplomb in helping to produce this year's outstanding collection, our eighteenth. I hope you enjoy it.

I now begin anew by reading the travel stories published in 2017. As I have for years, I am asking editors and writers to submit the best of whatever it is they define as travel writing—the wider the better. These submissions must be nonfiction, and published in the United States during the 2017 calendar year. They must not be reprints or excerpts from published books. They must include the author's name, date of publication, and publication name, and must be tear sheets, the complete publication, or a clear photocopy of the piece as it originally appeared. I must receive all submissions by January 1, 2018, in order to ensure full consideration for the next collection.

Further, publications that want to make certain their contributions will be considered for the next edition should make sure to include this anthology on their subscription list. Submissions or subscriptions should be sent to: Jason Wilson, Best American Travel Writing, 230 Kings Highway East, Suite 192, Haddonfield, NJ 08033.

JASON WILSON

Introduction

THE BEST DOOR in Paris can be found halfway between the Seine and the Champs de Mars at 29 Avenue Rapp. You don't necessarily see it coming. The block goes Luxembourg Embassy, *épicerie* selling plums in liqueur and candied violets, real estate agency, and then you're standing in front of it: a grand slab of polished oak featuring a six-foot-high phallus. The testes are wrought in glass and iron. Below them, a central panel, in the same materials, forms the shaft. The door handle, in brass, takes the shape of a lizard, which, according to historians, was once a common euphemism for the male sex.

What do you do when, in the midst of an elegant Parisian neighborhood, you stumble across such a thing? Obviously, you stop right in front of it, whip out your phone, and type "penis door" into Google. I did, and became intrigued by the door's creator, the architect Jules Lavirotte, whom a Musée d'Orsay catalog once memorialized as only the "second grand master" of the Parisian Art Nouveau, but the "uncontested master of the erotic and decadent 1900 baroque."

It was a Saturday morning. I was a mile and a half from my apartment, with a list of errands to complete. After about fifteen minutes of browsing, I continued on my way. The next door down housed a rare bookseller, specializing in hunting and gastronomy. The shop was closed, with no sign of when it might reopen. But in the window, halfway obscured by treatises on falconry, I noticed a shiny volume on Lavirotte, cowritten by someone of the same last name. This boded poorly, perhaps, for its objectivity, but well for the inclusion of lots of juicy detail from primary documents and family lore that might help to explain, far better than the Internet, how Lavirotte—sometime during the last years of the reign of Queen Victoria—had managed to erect a bachelorette party of an apartment building in the middle of the seventh arrondissement.

I kept on down the block, but before I made it to the Alfa Romeo dealership on the corner, I'd been pulled by force of curiosity back to number 29. This time, I let my gaze rise, taking in the intricate ceramic sculptures that framed the doorway; the second floor's undulating lintels; the third-floor balustrade; the fourth-floor bow window, supported by a team of sandstone oxen; the fifth-floor loggia, its columns of green malachite tinged with gold; the torch-shaped posts that alternated, on the sixth-floor facade, with feminine statue heads. The more I looked, the more there was. The building appeared to be efflorescing in real time, bursting forth with acanthus leaves, lilies, pineapples. Its walls comprised a bestiary so vivid that it seemed a songbird might vanish, devoured by a pair of tomcats that lurked nearby, if I turned away for a second. I was pretty sure I spotted some other anatomical references too. I needed to get my hands on that book.

If this were a Woody Allen movie, I would have returned again and again to the always-shuttered secondhand bookshop, becoming a habituée of the neighborhood café, where I'd fall madly in love over endless packs of Gauloises (nobody vapes in Woody Allen movies) with a waiter who would clear the night's last tables, take off his apron, cross the street, unlock the *librairie,* and present me with the Jules Lavirotte monograph under the light of the full moon, by which he would elucidate every last quirkily charming detail of the building (in addition to his hospitality job, he has an architecture degree). It's not, so I ordered the book on Amazon and had it by the next day. The front cover featured the door at 29 Avenue Rapp as viewed from the building's foyer. Reprinted on the back cover was Lavirotte's blueprint for an *hotel particulier,* commissioned by a Madame la Comtesse de Montessuy. Even his handwriting seemed playfully concupiscent, with *m*'s that rose and fell like cleavage.

Jules Lavirotte, it turns out, was born in 1864 in Lyon. His father was a notary; his mother, originally from Beaujolais, gave birth to eight sons, of whom he was the second-oldest. Their family picture—stolid *maman,* whiskery *papa, fils* after black-suited *fils* —goes a long way toward suggesting why he might have wanted to get out of town and make a building with some genitals and tropical fruits on it. But perhaps that's just the solemnity of late-nineteenth-century portraiture. Lavirotte's boyhood seems to have been full of larks: descending the Rhône in a barrel, attempting to fly behind a kite, touring France by rickshaw.

When Lavirotte was eighteen, studying at a private *lycée,* he fell in love with an older woman. Jeanne Barbier (née de Montchenu) was twenty-five, the wife of the school's director and the mother of three children. When Monsieur Barbier, a former army lieutenant, found out about the affair, he challenged Lavirotte to a duel. (The younger man avoided the challenge, counting only a hunting rifle in his arsenal.) Not long after that, his mother and father sent him to Paris to live with his older brother, who was there doing an internship, in order to become a notary like his father. Still tortured over the affair, Lavirotte enrolled at the École Nationale Supérieure des Beaux-Arts and, as a means of distracting himself, started studying architecture. In 1895, thirteen years after they'd met, Lavirotte and de Montchenu—having finally obtained a divorce, the terms of which stripped her of custody of her children —were married in a discreet ceremony in Paris.

"I don't see that there's anything immoral or so fantastic about it," Lavirotte wrote to one of his still-disapproving brothers. The situation was clearly painful, but he and Jeanne, a painter, put the scandal behind them and began to pursue a glittering life in the capital. At the age of thirty-one, Lavirotte complained that architecture was an "idiotic profession." He'd "yet to earn a sou." But soon he received his first commission, for a wealthy Frenchwoman's holiday mansion in Chaouat, Tunisia. Built more or less in the Moorish style, it was nothing spectacular. He dared a little more for his next project—an apartment building at 151 Rue de Grenelle —decorating a courtyard fountain with a bullfrog and sneaking a few salamanders onto the front door. But it wasn't until he met the Comtesse de Montessuy, a rich widow, that his imagination, or his ability to indulge it, truly flourished. In rapid succession, she commissioned the *hotel particulier,* and then another residence at

3 Square Rapp. It was there that Lavirotte began to experiment with what would become the Art Nouveau look, playing with asymmetry and using a variety of materials, such as varnished tiles and colored bricks. (Around the same time, Hector Guimard, the undisputed master of the style, created his sinuous canopies for the entryways of the Paris metro.) Even the doorbells were exquisite, with settings wrought in glazed sandstone by the ceramicist Alexandre Bigot.

Lavirotte bought the land for 29 Avenue Rapp from the Comtesse de Montessuy in the summer of 1899. He started construction the next year. Upon its completion, in 1901, the building won the "best facade" prize from the city of Paris. Its decoration doesn't seem to have caused any major outrage, which is amazing when you think about the drama that would likely ensue if someone tried to mount something similar today. The eccentricity of the place, however, seems to have put off tenants. "I think I've rented the ground floor," Lavirotte wrote to a brother. "It's a young Spaniard. He's supposed to come sign the lease tomorrow. I'll believe it when it's done." In 1905, Lavirotte sold his shares back to a partner. The vogue for Art Nouveau passed quickly, and in 1919 the building was sold off to a northern industrialist who wished to invest in depressed Parisian real estate.

Lavirotte went on to build a series of rather sober municipal buildings—a post office, an orphanage—which can still be seen all over France. In 1920, he was injured in a car accident; a year later he contracted typhoid fever. He was sick and suffering for the rest of his life. "Succumbing to her great sadness," according to her son, Jeanne de Montchenu Lavirotte died of a heart attack in 1924. Lavirotte, too frail to work, attempted suicide several times before dying five years later in a nursing home in Lyon.

Above the entryway of 29 Avenue Rapp, the face of a tired-looking woman protrudes from the building's sandstone facade. She has rosebud lips, a long neck, and a tidy hairdo that divaricates into a tangle of ornamental curlicues. Several architectural historians have speculated that she might be Madame Lavirotte. The first time I saw her, I took her presence as a sort of sly provocation, another dirty joke. Now I think that her presence was Lavirotte's testament to love. *Put penises on your doors! Gather your pineapples while you can!* I imagine him wanting to say to the millions of jaded urbanites who've passed by the building over the course of its 116-year existence. In the end, passion will be all you have.

It had never occurred to me to write anything about my interest in Lavirotte. Then I sat down to think about this book, and I realized that his life and career and the way that he inscribed them into the very fabric of one of the world's great cities was, in fact, a travel story. That is, if you changed one variable: where I lived. But why did you have to come to a place from afar in order to notice something about it, to be changed by it, to undertake a pilgrimage? And how far away did that afar have to be? Was a mile and a half far enough? Or what if the trajectory that counted was Lavirotte's —from province to Paris, an irreverent come-hither city of his own invention—rather than my own? The distinction between what we by habit think of as travel stories and the stories that materialize every time we travel, even to the dry cleaners, struck me as arbitrary. It also seemed somewhat outdated, in an age when so many people are constantly in motion, our *to*'s and *from*'s as scrambled as our identities. Travel writing, in 2017, might be thought of simply as writing about space and time.

It was with this more capacious definition in mind that I selected the pieces that appear in the book. In Robert Macfarlane's profile of Merlin Sheldrake, a scientist who studies mycorrhizal fungi, writer and subject go to a place (Epping Forest, Henry VIII's royal hunting ground, now pocked with blast holes from World War II "doodlebug" rockets) and do something cool there (eavesdropping on trees!). Simple as that: travel writing. Randall Kenan proves that home—in his case, the American South—can be as moving as any exotic destination, the shovels and secateurs of the Richmond citizens reclaiming an African American graveyard more memorable than entries on a bucket list. One of the volunteers, a Tony Award–winning actress, shows up at a Saturday morning cleanup in search of a headstone whose inscription, once read, is impossible to forget. "Of all the bustling cities of the American South during the Jim Crow era, Richmond laid claim to one of the nation's largest black middle classes," Kenan writes. "As a result they had the means to memorialize their dead grandly." His story, told with quiet assurance, adds to that work.

Society can be a place too—a flamboyant landscape of sodalities and subcultures. Gwendolyn Knapp's destination is technically Naples, Florida, but she's really taking you straight to the variegated-red-hot center of the world of plumeria enthusiasts. Plumeria, Knapp explains, is a "tropical flowering tree most people associate with Hawaiian leis." Later, she calls them "trees for people like me." The story, I think, is about loneliness and even about class—the failure to grow up and acquire much more than a dozen gaudy, temperamental plants. Stephanie Elizondo Griest, meanwhile, interrogates the fraught history of the practice of "chiefing," by which Cherokee Indians in the mountains of North Carolina pose for pictures in regalia that often doesn't have much to do with their own cultural traditions. "There are three kinds of tourists who visit Cherokee: those who know nothing about Indians; those who think they know everything about Indians; and those who are aware of how little they know about Indians and want to be enlightened," Griest writes, keenly aware of where she's coming from. She uses the road trip to build a bridge between Cherokee and Chicana cultures, writing, "From that day forward, whenever I began another essay about Chicanidad, or wore a rebozo to a reading, I thought of those buskers dancing for tourists on the side of the street. Was I also commoditizing my culture when I performed my identity, or was I offering reverence to my ancestors? Could anything profitable be authentic?" Her insecure narrator invigorates a genre traditionally dominated by heroic accounts of mastery and domination. Saki Knafo's dispatch from the whaling village of Kivalina, Alaska, is less about marine mammals than about human nature.

Sometimes travel is an excuse for a sort of spiritual journey, a way to crystallize thoughts and clarify complicated things. Tagging along on a group tour of the Holy Land, Tom Bissell reflects on fear and tribalism. Elif Batuman contemplates Turkish history, Muslim nationalism, her parents, taxi drivers, Neolithic archaeology, and Michel Houellebecq in a singularly illuminating examination of why a woman might or might not choose to wear a head scarf. Kim Wyatt takes off in a camper van on a "save-your-marriage vacation"; Jackie Hedeman reflects on tragedy and inheritance; Elizabeth Lindsey Rogers, on her own in Taigu, China, grapples with a secret. Leslie Jamison, vacationing at a Belizean resort, is concerned with "a tower that looked like outsize macramé, with hidden passageways and grottoes and cubbies, a concealed stairway and—its pièce de résistance—an interior waterslide," insofar as it involves her transformation into a stepmother. When Wells Tower recounts the sublime hellaciousness of the Great Smoky Mountains National Park, he's writing about being a parent. Part of fulfillment, in travel and in life, is feeling like you have a purpose, even if that's to "pass eight moist, black hours conceiving the proper torment for the Coleman employee" who forgot to warn that a pump wasn't included with your inflatable mattress. The campsite is a physic respite for Tower, who realizes he hasn't checked his phone so little since the day of the birth of his son. "More than one friend told me that their main vacation in August was a vacation from Instagram," Gideon Lewis-Kraus recalls, considering travel photography, "because they'd endured more than enough ostentatious displays of wealth and leisure for one season."

Two thousand sixteen was a year that privileged time over space, history over geography. "This is 2016," we heard, as the shocking events came and came, as though they were an affront more to their era than to the places in which they were happening. Timelessness can be a literary virtue, but I wanted *The Best American Travel Writing 2017* to address the rising isolationism and xenophobia of its moment, as well as the set of political, economic, and environmental crises that have set more than 65 million people, one-third of them refugees, in transit across the globe. I thought it would be stupid to try to talk about travel without acknowledging tightening controls, immigration raids, the refugee ban.

Jodi Kantor and Catrin Einhorn's reporting on the efforts of hockey moms and poker buddies to welcome Syrian refugees to Canada takes measure of the various distances that they must traverse in order to become the "New Canadians" that their hosts would make of them. Even figuring out the correct dosage of Tylenol is a stretch across language and habit. Travel writing has often been the domain of people we think of as "expats" and "globetrotters." But it shouldn't be confined to tales of Americans and Europeans going *to* places. We need immigrants, the people coming *from* somewhere, to help us make sense of both the rest of the world and of our own surroundings. Take the Eritrean defectors whom Alexis Okeowo writes about, or Reggie Ugwu's American family, on whom Nigeria exerts an eternal pull. There's Zarif Khan, aka Hot Tamale Louie, who moved to Sheridan, Wyoming, from the borderlands of Afghanistan and Pakistan in 1909. Kath-

ryn Schulz traces his life to devastating effect, her reckoning of
the ways in which each generation of Americans walls off access
to certain newcomers resonating with the resurgence of "nativist
nostalgia."

Which is not to say that we didn't need escapism. In fact, we
positively craved it. One of the most effective ways to counteract
the impulse to turn inward—the feeling that you didn't have any
curiosity to spare; the temptation, after another terrorist attack, to
never leave home—was to tag along with Peter Frick-Wright on a
mission to solve a famous Bolivian plane crash, or to lose yourself,
along with Tim Parks, in the archive of the Corsinis, a family of
Florentine aristocrats who have installed 4,000 feet of steel shelving in their Tuscan villa to house the papers of their ancestors,
who "[wrote] down everything about themselves and preserv[ed]
everything they wrote." Parks gets to touch paper from the 1400s.
Some documents have been "eaten away by silverfish"; others reveal "tiny cuts made in the sixteenth century to show that the surface had been disinfected against the plague." Joining Ann Mah
for harvesting season in Champagne, where her cheeks turned
pink and her hands turned black, was a deliverance from sitting in
front of my computer, refreshing the news. "One evening, the Polish guys and I sat after dinner and drank the house Champagne,
glass after glass poured from the wine refrigerator in the corner of
the kitchen," Mah writes. "In halting English, they told me about
their children and, as they warmed to the language, waxed enthusiastic about the foods they missed from home." I wish they'd
raised a glass to Jules Lavirotte, who probably would have appreciated it.

LAUREN COLLINS

The Best American
Travel Writing 2017

ELIF BATUMAN

Cover Story

FROM *The New Yorker*

IN 1924, a year after founding the Turkish Republic on the ruins of the Ottoman Empire, Mustafa Kemal Atatürk, the country's new leader, abolished the Ottoman Caliphate, which had been the last remaining Sunni Islamic Caliphate since 1517. Having introduced a secular constitution and a Western-style civil and criminal legal code, Atatürk shut down the dervish lodges and religious schools, abolished polygamy, and introduced civil marriage and a national beauty contest. He granted women the right to vote, to hold property, to become supreme-court justices, and to run for office. The head scarf was discouraged. A notorious 1925 "Hat Law" outlawed the fez and turban; the only acceptable male headgear was a Western-style hat with a brim. The Ottoman Arabic script was replaced by a Latin alphabet, and the language itself was "cleansed" of Arabic and Persian elements.

At the time, my grandparents were either very young or not yet born. Only my mother's father was old enough to remember throwing his fez in the air on the Sultan's birthday. My parents were born into a secular country. They met in Turkey's top medical school, moved to America in the 1970s, and became researchers and professors. Both were, and continue to be, passionate supporters of Atatürk. I grew up hearing that if it hadn't been for Atatürk my grandmother would have been "a covered person" who would have been reliant on a man for her livelihood. Instead, she went to boarding school, wrote a thesis on Balzac, and became a teacher. I felt grateful to Atatürk that my parents were so well educated, that they weren't held back by superstition or religion, that they were true scientists, who taught me how to read when I was three and never doubted that I could become a writer.

My father grew up in Adana, not far from the Syrian border. His family was Alevi—part of Turkey's Shia minority—and one of his earliest memories was waking up to hear his grandfather reciting the Koran in Arabic. My father experienced his first religious doubts at the age of twelve, when he discovered Bergson and Comte in an Adana bookstore, and read that religion was part of a primitive and pre-scientific state of civilization; he has been an atheist since his teens. My mother grew up in Ankara, Atatürk's capital. Her father, one of the civil engineers who helped to modernize Anatolia, was politically a staunch secularist and privately a devout Muslim (though not a proponent of head scarves, which nobody in the family wore). In grade school, my mother read what the Koran said about skeptics—that God would close their eyes and ears—and got so depressed that she didn't get out of bed for two days. Her parents told her that God was more merciful than she thought, and that people who did good would go to Heaven on the Day of Judgment, regardless of what they believed. I have always known my mother as an agnostic, less certain than my father that the universe hadn't been created by some great intelligence. But she would get even more annoyed than my father did when she thought that people were invoking God to do their jobs for them—for example, when she saw a bus with a sticker saying ALLAH PROTECT US.

Both my parents always told me that, in order to be a good person, it was neither necessary nor desirable to believe in God; it was more noble and efficient to do good for disinterested reasons, without thoughts of Heaven. Nothing in the milieu where I grew up, in New Jersey in the eighties and early nineties, contradicted the idea I formed of religion as something unnecessary, unscientific, provincial—essentially, uncool. For a long time, I thought there was an immutable link between coolness and positivism. I thought this was the way of the world. Then came identity politics and, in Turkey, the rise of the Justice and Development Party (AKP), a center-right party with Islamist roots. Its charismatic leader, Recep Tayyip Erdoğan, has been the head of state since 2003, after the AKP won its first landslide victory.

Suddenly, it was the secularists who seemed stodgy: racist, authoritarian, elitist, and slavishly pro-Western. The *Times* started referring to them as "the secular elite." In 2007, the *Times* reported that a protest of the AKP by hundreds of thousands of Turkish secularists was motivated in part by a "fear" of the lifestyles of their more religious compatriots—by "snobbish" complaints that "religious Turks were uneducated and poor" and that "their pesky prayer rugs got underfoot in hospital halls." It's difficult to imagine the *Times* reporting in an equally condescending manner about the elitism of Americans who oppose the Christian right. The Western view of Erdoğan eventually soured, especially after the Gezi protests of 2013; he was criticized for alleged corruption and for increasingly authoritarian tactics toward journalists and opposition parties. But for a number of years all my American liberal friends who had any opinion at all on Turkey were pro-Erdoğan. They thought it had been unsustainable for Turkey to repress and deny its religion for so long—that the people had finally spoken out.

Many spoke warmly of the anthropologist Jenny White, an important scholar of modern Turkey whose book *Muslim Nationalism and the New Turks* characterizes the pro-Atatürk Kemalist culture as one of "militarism, hostility, suspicion, and authoritarianism" rooted in "blood-based Turkish ethnicity." Muslim nationalism, by contrast, has sought to replace "historically embattled Republican borders" with "more flexible Ottoman imperial boundaries" and to "privilege Muslim identity and culture over race." In the AKP-sympathetic worldview, the Ottomans, whom Kemalists had blamed for selling Turkey to the British, enjoyed a vogue as models of enlightened Muslim multiculturalism.

I could see that every slight to Kemalism was a knife in my parents' hearts. For my part, I wasn't sure what to think. Unlike them, I was educated in America. To me, as to most Americans, it seemed a tiny bit weird that nearly every public building in Turkey had a picture of Atatürk on the wall. I also knew that, in order for the Turkish Republic to succeed, millions of people had been obliged to change their language, their clothes, and their way of life, all at once, because Atatürk said so. I knew that people who had been perceived as threats to the state—religious leaders, Marxists, Kurds, Greeks, Armenians—were deported, exiled, imprisoned, tortured, or killed. I knew that, even at the start of the twenty-

first century, there still weren't enough checks on the military, and
that women who wore head scarves were subject to discrimination,
barred from certain jobs and universities.

Furthermore, when I thought about my own family, something
about White's critique of Kemalism felt familiar: the sense of em-
battlement and paranoia. Kemalism, not unlike Zionism, drew
much of its energy from the fact that there could easily have been
no Turkish state. At the end of the First World War, the victorious
Allied powers assumed control over nearly all Anatolia; they divided some of it up into British and French mandates, and parceled
much of the rest out to the Greeks, the Armenians, and the Kurds.
Before Atatürk was a lawmaker, he was a military commander, the
leader of the Turkish War of Independence; and, from a military
perspective, all those people and nations were anti-Turkish (as
were the Arabs, who supported Britain in the First World War).
My parents always dreamed of a post-nationalist world; as a small
child, my mother prayed to Allah every night that the United Nations would be formed and there would be no more countries or
wars. At the same time, I remember being warned as a child that
there were anti-Turkish people in the world, people who held old
grudges and could cause problems. For a while, Erdoğan really did
seem to be trying to counter this kind of adversarial thinking—to
open up business and diplomatic relations with Turkey's neighbors, to lift the taboos on mentioning the "Kurdish issue" and the
Armenian genocide. Under the AKP, a Kurdish-language channel
debuted on Turkish national television; in 2009, Erdoğan went on
the air and expressed good wishes in Kurdish. This would have
been unthinkable a short time earlier.

In 2010, I moved to Istanbul, where I taught at a university and
reported for this magazine for three years. I found that, much like
America, Turkey was polarizing into two camps that were increasingly unable to communicate with each other. There was a new
dichotomy I had never heard of before: the "white Turks" (West-
ernized secular elites in Istanbul and Ankara) versus the "black
Turks" (the pious Muslim middle and lower-middle classes of Anatolia). The black Turks were the underdogs, while the white Turks
were the racists who despised them. Jenny White writes, "The term
'Black Turk' is used by Kemalists to disparage Turks of lower-class
or peasant heritage, who are considered to be uncivilized, patri-

archal, not modern, and mired in Islam, even if they have moved into the middle class." Erdoğan proudly declared that he was a black Turk.

The black and white breakdown was difficult for me to understand. My mother's family—fair-skinned Ankara professionals who once had a chauffeur and a gardener—clearly fit the "white" profile. My father's relatives in Adana were generally less educated and darker-complexioned. His father owned a store that sold textile dye to shepherds. There was a brief time when my father wore a mustache. Yet my father had written the essay in praise of Atatürk in his high school yearbook, his sisters were pro-choice, none of the women in his family wore head scarves except to do housework, and I had never heard any of them express the remotest hint of nostalgia for the Ottoman past. I had heard relatives on both sides of my family worry that, if Atatürk's reforms were undone, Turkey could end up "like Iran." So who were my father's family —also white Turks?

In Istanbul, I became careful about how I talked, careful not to sound—not to *be*—Orientalist or Islamophobic. One evening, while I was hanging out at my apartment with a Turkish friend, our conversation was interrupted by the call to prayer, which was amplified by loudspeakers. In my apartment, as in most points in the city, you could hear the competing calls from several mosques going off at the same time, five times a day. Often, when I was walking around the city, I liked hearing the call to prayer. Some people were really good at it. (My mother had often told me that when her father was a boy he had such a beautiful voice and knew the prayer so well that he would fill in when the regular muezzin was sick.) Still, when I was at home with the windows closed, working or trying to have a conversation, the sound of amplified male voices extolling Islam always felt somehow invasive. "I know I sound like an asshole, but I really get mad sometimes," I confessed to my friend. "Oh, no, are you an Islamophobe?" he said playfully. He advised me to think of the imam as "a singer, like Michael Jackson."

Because I spoke Turkish imperfectly, smiled a lot, and often traveled alone, I got a lot of lectures from men, particularly taxi drivers. Some were secularists; others, those with the most religious paraphernalia in their cars, didn't try to make conversation. That still left many outgoing, casually Muslim drivers who took the time to explain to me how great the head scarf was—how it was "actually a beautiful thing." For a woman to cover her head, they said, was in fact a feminist gesture, because it made clear she was demanding respect. There weren't the same misunderstandings as with a woman whose head was uncovered.

I usually didn't reply, especially if the driver seemed at all excitable, because when those drivers started to argue they would stop watching the road, and a lot of the cabs didn't have seat belts. But once, when a driver pressed me particularly jovially for an opinion, I said something like "I think all women should be respected. It shouldn't depend on their hair."

The driver replied that I was absolutely right, that of course women should be respected, and that the head scarf was the best way for women to remind men of this necessity for respect. Men, after all, were worse than women: they could sometimes forget themselves, and then unfortunate things could happen, "even"— he said in a hushed voice, adding that he didn't like to mention such things in front of me—"even rape."

I replied, in my simplistic Turkish, that to me this sounded like a threat: either cover your head or rape can happen. The driver protested in ornate phrases that nobody was threatening anyone, that to speak of threats in this situation was unfitting, that he could tell from my smiling face that I was a good and trusting person, but that the world was an imperfect place, that some men were less like humans than like animals, and that it was best to send clear signals about what one was or wasn't looking for. Then he left me at the fish restaurant where I was going to meet some literature professors.

If it had been just the two of us in the taxi in a political vacuum, I wouldn't have begrudged the driver his opinions. It was his car and his country, and he was driving me where I wanted to go. I knew that my limited Turkish, which felt like such a handicap, was in his eyes a marker of privilege—a sign that I could afford to travel and live abroad. Often, the second question drivers asked, after the invariable "Where are you from?," was "How much did the plane ticket cost?"

But the cab wasn't in a vacuum; it was in a country where the head of state, whose wife wore a head scarf, repeatedly urged all women to have at least three children, preferably four or five.

Erdoğan opposed abortion, birth control, and cesarean section. He said that Islam had set out a clear position for women, but that you couldn't explain it to feminists, because they "don't accept the concept of motherhood." The longer he stayed in office, the more outspoken he became. In 2014, he went so far as to describe birth control as "treason" designed "to dry up our bloodline." No matter how hard I tried to be tolerant—no matter how sympathetic I felt toward Muslim feminists who didn't want to be "liberated" from the veil, and who felt just as judged by the secularist establishment as secular women felt by the Muslim patriarchy—I could never forgive Erdoğan for saying those things about women. And, because he said them in the name of Islam, I couldn't forgive Islam either.

In the fall of 2011, I traveled to southeastern Anatolia to report on a newly discovered Neolithic site that archaeologists thought might have been the world's first temple. The site, Göbekli Tepe, was near the city of Urfa, a Muslim holy destination, believed to be the birthplace of Abraham. (The town, near the Syrian border, is now one of the points through which foreign fighters pass in order to join ISIS.) I seemed to be the only unaccompanied woman at my hotel. When I told the clerk I was staying for six days, he almost had a heart attack. "Six days?" he repeated. "All by yourself?" When I asked about the hours of the steam bath, he said it was for men only—not just at that time of day but all the time. I took the elevator up to my room, filled with the depressing knowledge that there would be no alcohol in the minibar. All the time I was in Urfa, whenever I saw any member of the hotel staff in the halls or the lobby, I always received the same greeting: "Oh, you're still here?"

I had a hard time finding a taxi to take me to the archaeological site. In the end, the hotel receptionist called a driver he knew: a surly guy with no meter, who charged an exorbitant $55 round trip, and sighed and muttered under his breath the whole way. He didn't answer his phone when I called him to pick me up, and I ended up having to hitchhike. Thinking that life might be easier if I had my own car, I made an appointment for six the next evening at a Europcar location supposedly on Urfa's 749 Street. I got so lost that, by seven, I was still wandering up and down a mysterious stretch of road that seemed to start out as 771 Street and then to become, without any visible change, 764 Street. I had walked sev-

eral times past the same convenience store, catching the attention
of a bread-delivery man.

"Are you looking for something?" the deliveryman asked. I
showed him the address. He showed it to another guy. They debated for a long time whether there was or was not a 749 Street.
A third guy came out of the store and joined in the conversation.
I waited for a few minutes, but it was clear that they were never
going to agree, and, anyway, the Europcar was already closed. I
thanked them for their help and walked back to the city center to
get something to eat.

Most of the restaurants in Urfa had a sign that said FAMILY RES-
TAURANT, meaning there was one room that was for men only and
one "family room," where women were allowed. The one I chose
had its family room on the roof. There were two or three families
sitting up there, with children. The remaining tables were empty.
I sat at a table for four people, in a corner. The families had a lot
of requests, and I was unable to get the waiter's attention. I had
been sitting there for several minutes when I got a phone call from
a friend in Istanbul. When I started talking, in English, two of the
women at a nearby table turned and stared at me, open-mouthed.
I thought that maybe they thought I was being rude for talking on
a cell phone.

"I'll call you back," I told my friend.

Even after I hung up, the women didn't stop staring. I tried
smiling and waving, but they neither waved back nor looked away.
The waiter, who still hadn't taken my order, was standing in a corner gazing up at a ceiling-mounted TV. I gave up and went back
to my hotel room, where I ate tahini rolls while reading about the
Neolithic Revolution.

The main tourist and religious sites in Urfa—an ancient castle,
numerous mosques, a cave where Abraham may have been born
and suckled by a deer for ten years, and a lake of sacred carp believed to mark the spot where Nimrod tried to burn Abraham alive
(God turned the cinders into fish) are all in or around a shady
green park, with fountains and rosebushes. I went there every day
to escape the heat. Women had to wear head scarves at the holy
sites, so I bought one at the market and always kept it in my bag. It
was soft, gauzy, spring green, with a pattern of tiny intricate vines
and leaves.

One day, when I had been visiting Abraham's cave, I forgot to take the scarf off. Walking back through the park, I almost immediately felt that something was different. I passed two beautiful young women in scarves, walking arm-in-arm and laughing about something. When I looked at them, they looked right back into my face and met my eyes, still smiling, as if we were all in the presence of a great joke. I realized that no young women had met my eyes or smiled at me in Urfa till then. As I walked on, I felt a rising sense of freedom, as if for the first time I could look wherever I wanted and not risk receiving a hostile glance. So I kept the scarf on. And then I went back into the city.

This isn't a scientific study; I didn't try it multiple times, or measure anything. All I have is my subjective impression, which is this: walking through the city with a head scarf was a completely different experience. People were *so much nicer.* Nobody looked away when I approached. I felt less jostled; men seemed to step aside, to give me more room. When I went into a store, a man held the door for me, and I realized that it was the first time anyone had reached a door before me without going in first and letting it shut in my face. Most incredibly, when I got to a bus stop shortly after the bus had pulled away, the departing vehicle stopped in the middle of the street, the door opened, and a man reached out his hand to help me in, calling me "sister." It felt amazing. To feel so welcomed and accepted and safe, to be able to look into someone's face and smile, and have the smile returned—it was a wonderful gift.

How long can I keep wearing it? I found myself thinking, as the bus lurched into motion and cars honked around us. The rest of the day? Forever?

I wondered why it hadn't occurred to me sooner to try wearing a head scarf—why nobody ever told me it was something I could do. It wasn't difficult, or expensive. Why should I not cover my head here, if it made the people who lived here feel so much better? Why should I cause needless discomfort to them and to myself? Out of principle? What principle? The principle that women were equal to men? To whom was I communicating that principle? With what degree of success? What if I thought I was communicating one thing but what people understood was something else —what if what they understood was that I disapproved of them and thought their way of life was backward? Did that still count as "communicating"?

I found myself thinking about high heels. High heels were painful, and, for me at least, expensive, because they made walking
more difficult and I ended up taking more taxis. Yet there were
many times when I wore heels to work-related events in New York,
specifically because I felt it made people treat me with more consideration. Why, then, would I refuse to wear a head scarf, which
brought a similar benefit of social acceptance, without the disad-
vantage of impeding my ability to stand or walk?

And yet, when I thought about leaving the scarf on for the rest
of my stay, something about it felt dishonest, almost shameful, as
if I were duping people into being kind to me. Those girls who
smiled into my eyes—they thought I was like them. The guy who
helped me on the bus—he thought I was his sister.

At that point, another thought came to me, a kind of fantasy,
so foreign that I could barely articulate it even to myself: *What if
I really did it?* What if I wore a scarf not as a disguise but somehow for real? I was thirty-four, and I'd been having a lot of doubts
about the direction my life was taking. I had had an abortion the
previous year, with some reluctance, and everything—every minor
defeat, every sign of unfriendliness—still hurt a little extra. I had
never felt so alone, and in a way that seemed suddenly to have
been of my design, as if I had chosen this life without realizing it,
years earlier, when I set out to become a writer. And now a glim-
mer appeared before me of a totally different way of being than
any I had imagined, a life with clear rules and duties that you followed, in exchange for which you were respected and honored
and safe. You had children—not maybe but definitely. You didn't
have to worry that your social value was irrevocably tied to your
sexual value. You had less freedom, true. But what was so great
about freedom? What was so great about being a journalist and going around being a pain in everyone's ass, having people either be
suspicious and mean to you or try to use you for their PR strategy?
Traveling alone, especially as a woman, especially in a patriarchal
culture, can be really stressful. It can make you question the most
basic priorities around which your life is arranged. Like: Why do
I have a job that makes me travel alone? For literature? What's
literature?

These thoughts recently came back to me when I read *Submission*, the latest novel by Michel Houellebecq, a satire set in a 2022

France ruled by democratically elected Islamic moderates. The Islam in *Submission* is largely a fantasy designed, by Houellebecq, to appeal to someone just like Houellebecq, with lavishly funded universities, fantastic meze, freely flowing French and Lebanese wines, and multiple teen wives for every intellectual who converts to Islam. But the political rhetoric of the movement's leader, Mohammed Ben Abbes, is well reasoned and coherent, bearing a certain resemblance to Erdoğan's actual platform, and presented with a frankness and lucidity that made me understand the logic of the AKP in a way I never had before.

Internationally, Ben Abbes seeks to transform Europe into a Mediterranean and North African union of Muslim states: a program similar to the "neo-Islamism" of Ahmet Davutoğlu, the AKP prime minister. Domestically, Ben Abbes supports entrepreneurialism, family businesses, and the free market; socially, he seeks to bolster Muslim education and to encourage women to be stay-at-home mothers, while continuing to tout the supreme value of democratic rule. I had never understood how all these goals were related, or even compatible. How could someone who opposed feminism—who was okay with half the population being less educated than the other half—be in favor of democracy? How could a democratic constitution not be secular? How could it be compatible with any of the Abrahamic faiths, with anything that came out of that cave in Urfa? I had always assumed that Erdoğan was being insincere about something: either he was just pretending to care about democracy or he was just pretending to care about Muslim family values—or, as my relatives said, he was pretending about both democracy and Islam, and the only thing he really cared about was building more shopping malls with Gulf money.

Reading *Submission,* I saw that there is, in fact, a logical consistency in the Islamist moderate free-trade platform. Democracy, like capitalism, is a numbers game, and "family values" is a machine that boosts the population. As one Houellebecq character puts it:

> Couples who follow one of the three religions of the Book and maintain patriarchal values have more children than atheists or agnostics. You see less education among women, less hedonism and individualism. And to a large degree, this belief in transcendence can be passed on genetically. Conversions, or cases where people grow up to reject family values, are statistically insignificant. In the vast majority of cases, people

stick with whatever metaphysical system they grow up in. That's why atheist humanism—the basis of any "pluralist society"—is doomed.

The atheist humanists in Houellebecq's 2022 are doomed, not just to extinction but also to uncoolness. The 1968 movement in Europe, much like the Kemalist revolution in Turkey, was once youthful and countercultural, and then it won, and itself became an old and crumbling establishment. Ben Abbes, Houellebecq writes, gets no trouble from "the last of the *soixante-huitards,* those progressive mummified corpses—extinct in the wider world—who managed to hang on in the citadels of the media." The outnumbered, irrelevant zombies, still naively believing themselves to be the defenders of the downtrodden, are so "paralyzed" by the Muslims' "multicultural background" that they don't even put up a fight.

Houellebecq's narrator, François, is a middle-aged professor of French literature—a specialist in the novels of Joris-Karl Huysmans. Huysmans's *Against Nature* (1884), widely considered a masterpiece of the decadent movement, tells the story of a dissolute aristocrat who devotes his life to aesthetic pursuits, such as eating all-black meals and hanging around with a giant jewel-encrusted tortoise. These activities fail to bring him happiness, even as they seem to exhaust the possibilities of the decadent novel. Huysmans converted to Catholicism after writing *Against Nature.* The parallels between François and Huysmans's hero are clear. François, too, has devoted his life to aesthetic pursuits: reading, watching television, chain-smoking, drinking supermarket wine, and dating undergraduates. He, too, finds these indulgences empty and exhaustible: literature stops seeming interesting, and sex gets more difficult every year. In much the same way that Huysmans converted to Catholicism, François converts to Islam.

When the Muslim government subsidizes a Pléiade edition of Huysmans and commissions François to write an introduction, he does some rereading and realizes, for the first time, that "Huysmans's true subject had been bourgeois happiness, a happiness painfully out of reach for a bachelor." That was all Huysmans ever wanted: not the all-black meals, not the jewel-encrusted turtle, but simply "to have his artist friends over for a pot-au-feu with horse-radish sauce, accompanied by an 'honest' wine and followed by plum brandy and tobacco, with everyone sitting by the stove while the winter winds battered the towers of Saint-Sulpice." Such happiness is "painfully out of reach for a bachelor," even a rich one with servants; it really depends on a wife who can cook and entertain, who can turn a house into a home.

This is the cost of bourgeois happiness, in Houellebecq's Islamic utopia: the independence of women. It's fascinating to see how Houellebecq rises to the challenge of making female domestic enslavement seem palatable in the novel, not just to the Islamo-curious François but also, to some extent, to the women of France. For example, early in the novel, François looks up two of his exes, successful single women in their forties; these scenes suggest, not implausibly, that the penalties of aging, and the psychic toll of dating and singleness, are even harder for women than for men, and that they aren't really balanced out by the joys of a career in, say, wine distribution or pharmaceuticals. François subsequently visits a female ex-colleague who has retired to domestic life pending the Islamization of the university. "To see her bustling around the kitchen in an apron bearing the humorous phrase 'Don't Holler at the Cook—That's the Boss's Job!,' . . . it was hard to believe that just days ago she'd been leading a doctoral seminar on the altogether unusual circumstances surrounding Balzac's corrections to the proofs of *Béatrix*," he observes. "She'd made us tartlets stuffed with ducks' necks and shallots, and they were delicious." In a later passage, set on a train, François contrasts the visible stress of a Muslim businessman, who is having a clearly harrowing phone conversation, with the high spirits of his two teen wives, who are solving puzzles from the newspaper. Under the "Islamic regime," François realizes, women—or "at least the ones pretty enough to attract a rich husband"—live in an eternal childhood, first as children, then as mothers, with just a few years of "sexy underwear" in between: "Obviously they had no autonomy, but as they say in English, *fuck autonomy.*"

Houellebecq's vision of an Islamic state, for all its cartoonishness, has a certain imaginative generosity. He portrays Islam not as a depersonalized creeping menace, or as an ideological last resort to which those disenfranchised by the West may be "vulnerable," but as a system of beliefs that is enormously appealing to many people, many of whom have other options. It's the same realization I reached in Urfa. Nobody has everything; everyone is trading certain things for others.

I didn't wear the scarf again, after that afternoon. I couldn't explain it rationally, but it didn't feel right. I stuck to my original strategy of smiling and ignoring social cues—the American way. "In the vast majority of cases," as a French intellectual once said, "people stick with whatever metaphysical system they grow up in."

In the course of multiple trips to the site, the surly taxi driver gradually opened up, especially after I complimented him on the skill with which he avoided hitting pedestrians at the last possible second. "That was nothing," the driver said, and told me about the time he had managed not to run over an old man who was walking right down the middle of the road as if it were the sidewalk, and who, in response to the driver's honking, simply stood where he was and shouted, "Pretend I'm a tree."

"How can you reason with someone like that?" the driver demanded, adding that when he drove in Urfa he conducted himself according to logic and not according to the traffic laws, because the rate of survival for someone who followed traffic laws had dropped to zero percent.

We pulled up at the hotel. "So you're still with us," the receptionist said, not unhumorously, when I walked in.

"Of course," I replied. "What person who has come to Urfa would ever want to leave?"

TOM BISSELL

My Holy Land Vacation

FROM *Harper's Magazine*

I. Stand with Israel

I LISTEN TO A lot of conservative talk radio. Confident mas-
culine voices telling me the enemy is everywhere and victory is
near—I often find it affirming: there's a reason I don't think that
way. Last spring, many right-wing commentators made much of a
Bloomberg poll that asked Americans, "Are you more sympathetic
to Netanyahu or Obama?" Republicans picked the Israeli prime
minister over their own president, 67 to 16 percent. There was a
lot of affected shock that things had come to this. Rush Limbaugh
said of Netanyahu that he wished "we had this kind of forceful
moral, ethical clarity leading our own country"; Mark Levin described him as "the leader of the free world." For a few days there
I yelled quite a bit in my car.

The one conservative radio show I do find myself enjoying is
hosted by Dennis Prager. At the Thanksgiving dinner of American radio personalities (Limbaugh is your jittery brother-in-law,
Michael Savage is your racist uncle, Hugh Hewitt is Hugh Hewitt)
Dennis Prager is the turkey-carving patriarch trying to keep the
conversation moderately high-minded. While Prager obviously
doesn't like liberals—"The gaps between the left and right on
almost every issue that matters are in fact unbridgeable," he has
said—he often invites them onto his show for debate, which is
rare among right-wing hosts. Yet his gently exasperated take on
the Obama-Netanyahu matchup was among the least charitable:
"Those who do not confront evil resent those who do."

Prager's audience is largely Christian; Prager is a Jew. Over the years I've heard numerous friendly callers tell him, often in thick Southern accents, that he's the first Jew they've ever spoken to. One day last summer, Prager mentioned that he would be heading up something called the Stand with Israel Tour. For a little under $5,000, you could join Prager, and his most devoted listeners, on an all-inclusive guided jaunt across the world's holiest, most contested land. The goal, he said, was to remind Israel of its devoted friends in the United States.

America's religious right hasn't always been enamored of Israel, much less of Jews. Quite a few of the originators of the American Christian fundamentalist movement were unabashed anti-Semites. In 1933, the radio preacher Charles Fuller told his listeners that Jews represented "a wicked and willful rebellion against God"; other early fundamentalist leaders eagerly circulated *The Protocols of the Elders of Zion*. Israel had no friendly harbor in American conservatism for decades; its first real champion in the Oval Office was John F. Kennedy, a Democrat.

In 1981, the Israeli prime minister, Menachem Begin, publicly embraced evangelical Christians, whose stated determination to convert Jews to Christianity had long spooked Israelis. While evangelical religious tourism, and the millions of dollars it injected into Israel's economy, had always been welcome, evangelicals were kept at arm's length politically. Begin was the first to recognize that the Israeli right and American evangelicals shared many common beliefs, from forbidding abortion to maintaining a general suspicion toward the Muslim world. The Christian Coalition, founded in 1989 by the broadcast Baptist Pat Robertson, became invested in the Zionist cause, and by 2002, Tom DeLay, former majority leader of the House of Representatives, commended the group for "standing up for Jews and Jesus." Robertson dwelled darkly on the Palestinian leader Yasir Arafat and his "gang of thugs" as the political emergence of Christian Zionism fused with right-wing Israeli goals. In the early fifth century, St. Jerome resisted the acceptance of Jews with faith in Christ, warning Augustine that "they will not become Christians, but they will make us Jews." Sixteen hundred years later, American evangelicals have become de facto Israelis.

I wanted to more fully understand why conservative politics had become synonymous with no-questions-asked support of Israel, so I asked my beloved partner, Trisha, if she would accompany me on

Prager's tour. This would necessitate leaving our sixteen-month-old daughter with her grandparents for ten days. Trisha was okay with a vacation from parental obligations, but she had some questions: "Will people care I'm not a Republican?" I told her I wasn't sure. "Do I have to pretend to be religious?" Not if you don't want to, I said. "Will I have to get baptized?" I doubted it.

Trisha was in.

II. The Israel Test

Months later, in November, we step out of the elevator and into the lobby of the Leonardo Plaza Hotel in Ashdod, Israel, to catch Prager's tour-opening lecture. We want good seats. But when we arrive, forty-five minutes before go time, we find none. Everybody is already here. The majority of our fellow Stand with Israelites are sixty years of age and older. There are somehow around 450 of us, from a dozen American cities. There are too many Stand with Israelites for one hotel, so our cohort has been spread throughout Ashdod, a coastal city twenty miles north of Gaza and a frequent target of Hamas's rockets in the 2014 Gaza war. I watch our tour group's few latecomers step off their buses, all of them marveling, as I had, at the huge banner draped across the front of the hotel: WELCOME TO THE LAND OF THE BIBLE.

Around me a lot of "Hey you!" reunions are happening, with people remembering faces but not necessarily names from previous Prager tours. (He's done them for more than a decade, leading his listeners everywhere from Israel to Albania to Nova Scotia.) Platters of cookies are attacked. Jugs of mint-flavored water are drained. Everyone wears a lanyard with a laminated name tag attached to it, all branded GENESIS TOURS, the faith-based travel company that's been squiring Christians around Israel since 1990.

We finally find two seats. Trisha starts chatting with the older woman sitting next to her, one of the seventy-eight conservatives from southern California. I hear Trisha tell the woman what she does for a living (actor) and where she lives (the Hollywood Hills), which triggers some intrigued follow-up questions.

Trisha has just violated the cover story we agreed to use while standing with Israel: Trisha would say that she is a stay-at-home mom, which is true, and I would say that I work in the video-game

industry, which is also true. We wouldn't disclose our politics or
other jobs unless asked—we agreed not to lie—and we would
never argue with anyone. We'd listen and observe and try to understand. I'm open to making friends here, and hope I do. A good
way not to do that, however, is to be identified as a crypto-liberal
during our first interaction on our first night in Israel. Trisha
blames her slip on jet lag.

The presentation begins. Prager is introduced by a bald, fit, vel-
vet-voiced Israeli named Reuven Doron, the man on the ground
for Genesis Tours. "We are here for one purpose," Doron tells us.
"We came to stand with Israel." This extracts a few vaguely amenish
sounds from the audience. Doron goes on: "You are our strength,
and our encouragement, and a joy to our hearts."

Eventually Prager himself ambles over to the mic. He is a big
man, around six-foot-four, with fine white corn-silk hair. In his
khaki slacks and open-collar blue-striped shirt, he could be the
provost of a university. (He is, kind of. Prager University—"Free
courses for free minds"—offers a catalog of five-minute online vid-
eos covering a variety of subjects, from anger management to electric cars.) There's a collective titter from the ladies as Prager gets
ready to speak. He has a lot of female admirers here, including his
third wife, a six-foot blond amazon standing in the back. Trisha
will later tell me that she gets why women like Prager, pointing out
that when he smiles his dimpled face adorably resembles that of "a
really wise Muppet."

Prager begins by talking about something he calls the Israel
Test. What is the Israel Test? The Israel Test involves seeing "how
people react to Israel," which is, he says, "about as quick a way you
have to understand their judgment." Meaning, essentially, that if
you ever find fault with Israel, you're horrible. President Obama
fails the Israel Test, even though, in 2012, he sent the single largest military-aid package America has provided the country to date.
John Kerry is an even worse Israel Test failure, Prager tells us, because he often takes a "middle position" on the Israel-Palestine
contretemps, "as if there really wasn't a dark and a light."

Prager continues, "You can't imagine how proud I am of you.
I'm very serious. It means the world to me. To be honest, when
there were these attacks that started a month ago"—more than
a dozen Israelis had been stabbed in the street by Palestinian as-
sailants—"we really didn't know how many people would cancel.

And the answer is almost nobody." I'd written an email to Genesis Tours when the stabbing frequency got bad, wanting to know if the threat of violence had at all altered our itinerary. The "Dear friend" form letter I received in return assured me, "These incidents of Islamic-driven violence are isolated, and thanks to our alert security forces and citizens, they are contained within seconds."

Prager emphasizes that he's not getting paid to be here with us. He also believes that American parents—Christians and Jews alike —should send their children to Israel between high school and college. Why? "The moral compass of the world," he says, "is upside down. If your child can spend time in Israel, and then become clear as to how upside down the world is, they will return to the university *already immunized* against the most morally upside down of all Western institutions, the university."

I listen to Prager's speech with these preconceived views: Israel has a right to exist and to defend itself. Palestinians have been collectively wronged—by Israel, by their leaders, and often by their own actions. The growing religious fundamentalism within Palestinian society, which was once more secular than most of the Arab world, scares the hell out of me. At the same time, I'm sympathetic to the plight of average Palestinians—most of whom are not violently "Islamic-driven" en masse, like those referred to by Genesis Tours. I'm equally sympathetic to the plight of average Israelis— who, contra other accounts, are not mindless bigots. And I realize that, in the past twenty years, there have been at least seventeen full-fledged failures of the peace process, for which there is a surfeit of blame to go around.

Too often, the subject of Israel becomes just another way for Americans to refract their own views of America. Liberals tend to assume that right-wing evangelicals support Israel because of how it fits into their imagined apocalypse: only when God's Chosen People reoccupy the entirety of their biblical territory will the Final Dispensation, the rise of the Antichrist, the Tribulation, the eventual return of Jesus Christ, and his Last Judgment commence. In many ways, the founding of Israel in 1948 was the Woodstock of fundamentalist Christianity. A recent Pew study of Christian fundamentalism found that 63 percent of white evangelicals believe that the creation of a Jewish state in modern times fulfills the supposed biblical prophecy of Jesus's Second Coming. Yet not one evangelical Christian I will meet on tour seems interested in any of that. Rather, the conservative Christian love of Israel that I will encounter, over and over again, seems bound up in a notion of God the Father, who has two children: Israel and the United States. This Israel—not a nation but a wayward brother—lies beyond history, beyond the deaths and wars that made it, beyond the United Nations, beyond the Oslo Accords, beyond any conventional morality. Understand that and you have passed the Israel Test.

III. Black Arrow

The following morning I eat six different kinds of cheese at the buffet breakfast. Later there will be a buffet lunch and a buffet dinner. (Wherever we go in Israel, no matter how remote the place, several tons of warm food will be waiting.) Outside our hotel ten tour buses are lined up; Trisha and I have been assigned Bus Five.

Around 50 percent of Bus Five's occupants wear cross pendants. A few older women have on velvet tracksuits. The men, for the most part, wear boonie hats, T-shirts advertising corporate cruise lines, and red-state suntans. Trisha and I have already made friends with a quiet Quakerish couple who recently finished their Peace Corps tour of duty in Azerbaijan, and with Marty Schoenleber, an evangelical pastor from Illinois who can read the Hebrew Bible and New Testament in their original languages, and who will later lament to me the core problem with overtly Christian fiction, which is that it's usually written by hacks.

As we get rolling, our guide, David Westlund, a bearded and curly-haired man who is in his late fifties but looks a decade younger, introduces himself over the bus PA system. Originally from Minnesota, David has lived in Israel for thirty-five years. Neither he nor his wife is Jewish; eventually, I will learn that he's a devoted Christian. He's as Israeli as an American Christian can get, in that he speaks Hebrew and all his children served in the Israel Defense Forces. When not guiding tours, he works in construction, which has kept him fit. He asks how many of us have been to Israel before. Most of us haven't. "I like first-timers," he says. "They don't know much, and if I make mistakes, they don't catch it." David tells us that he once got a scathing review from a British couple irritated by his "endless prattle." He will keep using that phrase—

"Time for more endless prattle"—throughout the tour. Trisha and I agree: David is the tour guide to have while standing with Israel.

We drive south through the gray, lunar landscape of the Negev Desert, out of which erupts an occasional green blob of habitation. David explains that the flowering and settlement of the Negev has been one of Israel's major environmental accomplishments, much of it traceable to Levi Eshkol, a farmer and water engineer who served as Israel's prime minister in the 1960s. Eshkol likened the national irrigation system to the "veins of a human body." Much of the water that the Negev receives is diverted from the Sea of Galilee, 150 miles north. The events that led to the Six-Day War, in June 1967, began two and a half years earlier, when guerrilla fighters under the command of a thirty-five-year-old Yasir Arafat raided a water pump on the Lebanese border that fed the Negev. Israel's Arab neighbors had long worried that an irrigated Negev would be able to support millions of additional Israelis—an entirely prescient fear.

We pass by a few tidy Jewish settlements, along with others that look like tidy Jewish settlements after five weeks of riots. These are Bedouin villages. Unlike most Arabs in Israel proper, Bedouins serve in the IDF, often as trackers. Thus, David tells us, Israel "bends the law and rules" for Bedouins. Polygamy, for instance, is officially illegal, but Bedouin men are allowed to take multiple wives. (As it happens, Bedouin men sire a spectacular twelve to twenty-five children per male—off the demographic charts—meaning, at this rate, Bedouins will make up a quarter of Israel's Muslim population by 2030.) These and other accommodations by the Israeli government have led to anti-Bedouin sentiment among many Arabs; Hamas, especially, despises Bedouins as rootless traitors.

Someone asks whether Bedouins and Jews could ever live in a village together. David replies by explaining that who lives in what settlement is determined by "the nature of the town," by which he means its existing ethnic makeup. "It's an unwritten rule," he says. "You just stay with your people. Why would you want to go somewhere you know you don't belong?"

Conservatives often point out that Palestinian citizens of Israel enjoy more rights than Palestinian refugees do in neighboring Arab countries, which does not address the negligible rights Jews and other religious minorities enjoy in most Arab nations. But most Arab nations don't claim to be democracies. Israel is a de-

mocracy in which interfaith marriage is illegal. (A couple of weeks
after our tour, Israel's Ministry of Education would ban a novel
from being taught in Israeli schools because it depicted a romance
between a Jewish woman and a Palestinian man. One ministry official explained to the press that young people who read the book
might lose track of the "significance of miscegenation.") Israel's
Arab citizens, who make up more than 20 percent of the population, face entrenched legal obstacles in everything from buying property to receiving equitable funding for their schools and
hospitals. "The worlds separate when you go home," David tells
us, without much relish, "but they come together when you go to
work. Christian, Arab, Jew, Muslim—we all work together." No one
stirs or says a word against this stick-to-your-own logic. Is anyone
uncomfortable? I am, but I also live in the single whitest neighborhood in Los Angeles.

At long last, in the middle of nowhere, Bus Five stops at a palm-
tree-encircled cluster of *Gilligan's Island*–style thatch huts. I over-
hear one guide tell another that the idea for this fake oasis was
ripped off from a similar tourist trap near Jericho: hire fifty Bedouin, lease a herd of camels, make believe it's an ancient desert
settlement, and count the money as the tourist-crammed buses
start rolling in.

When you're part of such a large tour group, everything seems
designed to make you feel like a child. One of our guides blows
his trumpet whenever he wants his group to form up. Another has
stuck a large plastic flower into his backpack so people can pick
him out of a crowd. David, admirably, has forsworn such theater.
As he walks into the fake oasis, he holds up an oversize ping-pong
paddle marked "5," and we obediently follow him to a large tent.
Inside, two long-haired Israeli hippies wearing T. E. Lawrence
robes over blue jeans retell the story of Abraham, who passed this
very way all those years ago, or so we are told.

Off to another tent, thick with the sweet, resinous smell of a
wood fire. Body-size pillows have been scattered around; we re-
cline while a Bedouin boy pours us fire-warmed coffee and tea.
Soon a Bedouin elder named Muhammad enters through the tent
flaps, wearing a robe and keffiyeh, both a bright boiled white, with
a curved dagger tucked into his cloth belt. Muhammad has apparently been prepped on his audience's political sympathies. "We
have to welcome everyone into our tent," he says. "Even Obama."

Before we leave the fake oasis, we're supposed to ride the camels. Twenty-five camels are here, a gastrointestinal symphony of snorting and farting and groaning. I consider Muhammad's parting words to us—"Don't touch the head or the neck. They don't like it"—as a Bedouin guy helps Trisha and me atop a camel. Me: "Do they bite?" Him: "Okay." Me: "Wait. Is this safe?" Him: "Okay." Our camel walks fifty feet and stops. As Bus Five drives away I look back at the fake oasis and see another Bedouin guy with a rake solemnly erasing our footprints from the dust.

We're scheduled to end our day with a visit to an IDF camp on the northern edge of the Gaza Strip. As we pass through the northernmost Israel–Gaza border crossing, I see a massive wall, observation towers, and endless spirals of barbed wire. It could be a piece of dystopian concept art.

We arrive at Camp Iftach, where we're told many of the soldiers stationed here were among the first into Gaza during the 2014 war. When they're not fighting Hamas, the officers of Camp Iftach are a combat-engineer unit. This explains the earthmoving heavy machinery we see all around, including the massive snub-nosed military bulldozer known as the Caterpillar D9. These behemoths, which can withstand multiple mine hits, are used to destroy Hamas's arms-smuggling tunnel network into and out of Gaza. Within Camp Iftach proper, several baby-faced soldiers wave and smile as our bus slides into its parking space.

Most Israelis serve in the IDF. In the 1970s, Saul Bellow marveled at how Israel had become a society both Spartan and Athenian, by which he meant that you saw teenagers in baggy green fatigues with automatic weapons slung casually over their shoulders everywhere you went. Israel is tiny; in Bellow's day its wars happened an hour's drive from where many soldiers grew up. But after two horrifying insurgencies—the Intifadas, with enemies not at the border but clawing from within—Israel's Athenian face has withdrawn. Here, instead, is Sparta—a garrison state, securely walled and tensely patrolled.

We visitors are herded into a dilapidated concrete hangar while a Merkava Mark IV tank—pale green, with loose-paneled armor intended to lessen rocket-propelled-grenade impacts—rolls out in demonstration, churning up dirt and sand while the tourists clap and cheer. A teenager pops out and explains some of its features. It's got a 1,500 horsepower engine (that's five Hondas), a 120mm smooth-bore main gun, three additional machine guns, and a 6omm mortar. The Mark IV's big barrel swings around, hitting the antenna on the stern with a small *twap*, and stops once it's pointing directly at us. Many of us throw up our hands and beg, in jest, "Don't shoot!" A Namer ("leopard") troop carrier rolls out next. It's built low and flat, with a sloped hull and a machine gun on top, which is controlled from inside the vehicle with two joysticks. "Like a video game," someone says. We are adults watching children play in the mud. Another soldier walks out cradling a shiny yellow artillery shell. Big cheers when we're informed that this shell was made in America. Trisha turns to me and asks an eminently reasonable question: "What the fuck are we doing here?"

At dusk, we travel to a nearby site called the Black Arrow Memorial, which honors eight IDF soldiers who lost their lives during a retaliatory incursion into the Gaza Strip in the mid-1950s. Off in the distance are the twinkling yellow-orange lights of Gaza City. In 2005, Israel ended its direct military occupation of Gaza, around the time when the Palestinian Authority, the mouthpiece of the Palestinian people since its founding in 1994, formally renounced violence. In the next year's parliamentary elections, Hamas was voted into power, triggering a Palestinian civil war. A succession of brief but horrendous wars since then have all played out in similar ways: Hamas fires rockets. Israel responds with air strikes. Hundreds and sometimes thousands of Gazans are killed. The international community chides Israel for its tactics. Israel withdraws. The smoke clears. Hamas claims victory. The Gazan people climb atop their rubble piles and applaud.

Israel now enables foreign aid to the Palestinian Authority, to fight Hamas terrorists. Hamas and Fatah, the largest Palestinian political party, might hate each other more than they hate Israel. (Fatah fears that Hamas will trigger another intifada in the West Bank; Hamas fears that Fatah will forcibly end its rule of Gaza.) In recent years, Gaza has given rise to a violent group of Salafis who think that Hamas cares more about Palestinian rights than it does about forging the perfect Islamist society; these Salafis believe that Hamas is not extreme enough.

The most recent Gaza war, in 2014, displaced close to half a million Gazans and killed more than 500 children. After 5,200 Israeli bombardments, the damage was so extensive that the estimated time it will take to rebuild Gaza is two decades. Of course, little construction material is arriving, today or any day soon, thanks to an Israeli and Egyptian blockade that has made Gaza into a twenty-five-mile-long, five-mile-wide penal colony.

At the Black Arrow Memorial, we're told to gather around another young Israeli soldier, who recently finished his third year of service in the IDF. He's dark-haired and bearded, with a long face. "I don't know what percent of the people," he says of the Palestinians he's encountered, "but most of them really want to live in peace." He spent two years in the West Bank, and whenever he encountered young Palestinians throwing rocks at cars, he knew they were young and aimless, "not focused about anything. They're immature." The young soldier pauses, searching for a better English word to describe these Palestinians.

Someone in the crowd suggests, "Thugs!"

The young soldier either ignores or does not hear this. He goes on to say that many Palestinian teenagers have nothing to do *but* throw rocks. He adds, "We don't need to think about all Arabs when they do something wrong, because I know a lot of people from their side want to live in peace."

A collective unease falls over the crowd. You can almost hear the cognitive whir while everyone's brains rewind and replay. The soldier goes on to say that religion factors in too. "The radicals from both sides are taking part, very good part, very big part, and this becomes very, very, very complicated."

A woman—not a Bus Fiver, I'm relieved to report—pushes through the crowd. She's in her forties, and is wearing oversize sunglasses, a puffy winter jacket, yoga pants, and colorful sneakers. "When you refer to radicals from both sides," she says, "you're talking about radicals who teach their children at a very young age to hate the Jews, versus the radicals of the Jewish faith?"

Yes, the young soldier answers.

"But Jews do not do any of that." She begins to gesture in an am-I-going-crazy way. "Somehow you're saying that both have a role to play? Am I understanding that correctly? When the mentality is completely opposite."

The number of Israeli settlers in occupied Arab territory has grown from 230,000 in 1992 to 570,000 in 2015; many of these people are religious fanatics who regard the Palestinians as murid intruders on land promised to them by God. According to one 2015 poll, half of all Jewish Israelis would like to see Palestinian citizens expelled from Israel. Another study found that nearly half of all Jewish Israelis wouldn't want to live in a building with Arabs and wouldn't want their children to attend school with Arabs. The Palestinians are no better; almost half want to continue to use violence against Israel, and 60 percent believe that their goal should be to reclaim the whole of Israel from the Jews. Since 1987, at least 1,600 Israelis have been killed by Palestinians. During the same period, at least 10,000 Palestinians have been killed by Israelis.

The young soldier looks gape-mouthed at his interlocutor. He tries to inform her that many Jews who live in the "complicated areas" of the West Bank raise their children with the same kind of hate.

At this, she throws up her hands. "Respectfully, no," she says. "Respectfully, *no*."

A man near Trisha mutters, "If Dennis Prager were here he'd rip that guy a new asshole." With the crowd now against him, the young soldier stands silently, gripping his microphone. Another soldier steps in, takes the mic, and says, "Maybe there's a small language issue here and let's move on, yes?"

I walk back to the lookout point. In the distance I see a sputtering red dot, out of which twirls a corkscrew of smoke. In Gaza City something is on fire.

IV. *"Mercy Is Kind of Punched Out of Me"*

A century ago, Caesarea, the first-century Roman capital of Judaea, was controlled by the Ottoman Empire, the last caliphate. Important archaeological sites—relics of Palestine's non-Islamic history—were left entombed beneath sand dunes. Sitting in Caesarea's restored theater, Trisha and I sit in pinprick rain and wait for another Dennis Prager lecture to begin. Not terribly far away, the caliphate reenactors of the Islamic State are busy destroying every pre- and non-Islamic artifact they can find.

We have a good view of the remaining bits of Caesarea from our seats: the foundation of the seaside Herodian palace, the track of an old hippodrome, the outline of a royal pool, rings of worn sandstone and pitted marble. I'm reading aloud to Trisha passages about ancient Caesarea from Josephus's *Jewish War*—how King Herod built its harbor in a spot "as awkward as could be"; how the statue of Herod's benefactor, Caesar, was "no whit inferior to the Olympian Zeus which it was intended to resemble." A couple rows ahead of us, someone is reading Ben Carson's autobiography, *Gifted Hands;* a dozen others have copies of Dennis Prager's book, *The Ten Commandments: Still the Best Moral Code.*

Prager himself appears, wearing a sport coat, his shoulders gray with damp. The guy reading Ben Carson looks up. "The emperor has arrived," he says. Meanwhile, two dozen people from another Christian tour group are singing in the theater's wings, their voices dreamlike, as rainfall patters on the marble around them. Once again, Reuven Doron from Genesis Tours introduces Prager. By now, the drizzle has almost stopped, and Doron says that this is proof that "God loves Dennis Prager."

Prager tells us about his university days as a twenty-one-year-old student of Russian, buying copies of *Pravda* from a Forty-Second Street newsstand. One day, someone from the Israeli government contacted him and asked him to travel to the Soviet Union to smuggle in Hebrew Bibles and prayer shawls. "It was somewhat dangerous," he says. "I was sent because I knew Hebrew and Russian." He emerged with names of Jews who wanted to leave the USSR, and then began to deliver lectures on Soviet Jewry. He describes this as "the beginning of my public life."

He would speak around four times a week. "Almost every synagogue in the United States—for that matter, Australia, France, anywhere in the free world—had a sign: SAVE SOVIET JEWRY. To my shock, no church had a sign, SAVE SOVIET CHRISTIANS ... More Christians were being killed by the Soviet government than Jews were. So why weren't there SAVE SOVIET CHRISTIANS signs but there were SAVE SOVIET JEWRY signs? Because Jews are a people, whereas Christians are a religion."

According to Prager, this helps explain why, even today, there is little collective outcry for the Christians being murdered by the Islamic State in Syria, Iraq, and elsewhere. "I don't know why Christians aren't going crazy over the decimation of Christians in the Middle East," Prager says. "*I'm* going crazy over the decimation of Christians in the Middle East." I have another explanation: those being targeted are all Middle Eastern Christians who belong to sects—Syrian Orthodox, Maronite, Chaldean—so conceptually unfamiliar to Western Christians that they may as well be Muslims.

The rest of Prager's speech concerns Judaism's convergences

with its sister faith Christianity. He affirms that Jews are the Chosen People, while "Christians are doing God's work." He doesn't understand the Christian ideation of Jesus, he confesses, but, he says, "I am closer to a Christian who shares my faith and God and the Bible and my values than to a Jew who doesn't. We're doing God's work together. Who is right? We'll find out."

Back on the bus to Nazareth, a largely Arab area, where we're having lunch in an old immigrant-detention center that's been converted into a hotel. We ascend a twisty-turny road to see hillsides awash in trash. Someone asks David, "Why is every Arab town we see filled with garbage?" Another person wants to know: "How'd the Arabs get Nazareth?" David explains that Jews never lived in great numbers in Nazareth; it was always an Arab town, built up by Arabs for Christian tourists. "It's not like Arabs took it from the Jews," David says. No one appears satisfied by this.

The hotel conference room is filled with silver platters of food. Trisha and I sit with some Bus Fivers, all of whom are discussing Matt Bevin's recent election as the governor of Kentucky—thanks in part to his campaign promise of gutting Obamacare. We have a Kentuckian at the table with us, a self-avowed Tea Partyer, his voice so deep and resonant it could split wood. Despite his strong anti-moocher convictions, he returns from his dessert run with enough pastries for everybody, which is more than I thought to do.

My fellow Stand with Israelites say things like, "These people need the Prince of Peace." They say, "I'll have to pray on that one." They are warm and funny. They talk about the foster children they've raised, the people they've helped lift out of meth-induced darkness. A man describes a young friend who lost his wife to cancer as a "trophy of grace." Another describes his regrets about homeschooling his children, which, he worries aloud, may have damaged their ability to socialize. In that unguarded moment, as he stares at his plate, I find myself wanting to share my own anxieties about parenting.

After lunch, we head for a kibbutz on the Lebanese border. We ride through the changeful topography of the Galilean high country. One minute it's gorgeous valleys, then extinct volcanoes, then parched hills, then Crusader castles, then papyrus groves, then half-hidden dirt roads, then aqueducts with hundred-inch pipes, then Druze villages. It's the first century, it's the twelfth century, it's November 2015. The questions my fellow Bus Fivers ask of David are getting more wide-ranging. At one point David is fielding inquiries about Mexican immigration in America and his personal feelings on the European Union. Finally, he admits that guides are discouraged from discussing politics and religion. At this he laughs, as that's pretty much all he talks about.

We're now moving along the Naphtali Ridge, a world of sky and evergreens and maize-colored stones aglow in sunlight. The valley directly beneath us is Lebanese territory: here are the cedars of Lebanon. Syria is just to the east. David points out Syria. We all look toward Syria. David redirects our attention back toward Lebanon. We all look toward Lebanon. It's like we're on safari: "To your right, the beastly hordes of the Islamic State. On your left, Hezbollah." Between Israeli and Lebanese territory is a big, mean double fence; shots have been fired across the patrol road that runs through it as recently as 2010. The village we're approaching, Adaisseh, along with much of southern Lebanon, used to be predominantly Christian. Israel occupied the area until 2000, and in the past decade, it has become Hezbollah's turf. David points to a tiny outpost on a distant hill on the Israeli side of the border and tells us that his son was stationed there while serving in the IDF. He describes how he used to stop there, along his tour route, to drop off cookies.

We arrive at Misgav Am: THE KIBBUTZ AT THE END OF THE WORLD, according to its welcome sign. It is famous as kibbutzim go, founded in 1945, two years before the state of Israel itself, by members of the Haganah, an underground militia. Three military-intelligence units are found within its walls. The people who live here aren't freewheeling kibbutzniks making artisanal soap, like you'd find down near the Dead Sea, but rough-edged farmers living within tossing distance of a Hezbollah grenade.

We're greeted by a Misgav Am old-timer whose huge gray beard, as thick as it is wide, suggests Yosemite Sam in his senescence. He tells us, "Those of us who live up here, I tell everybody—and you'll forgive me if I insult anyone, it's not on purpose—we're Israeli rednecks." This particular Israeli Redneck was born in Cleveland and moved to Israel in 1961, "after I decided I was wasting my life." He's fought for Israel "in four and a half wars. I was with the paratroopers in the liberation of Jerusalem in 1967. We had fifty percent casualties." As a result, he says, "Mercy is kind of punched out of me. I have no love for my enemies, and I have no problem shooting them. I take a little white pill in the morning. It keeps me level, and I sleep real good every night." This gets a big laugh from the audience.

He is unapologetic about the fact that territory was taken from Palestinians. To say outright that Jewish fighters ethnically cleansed historically Palestinian land remains taboo in Israeli society, even though a number of historians—Benny Morris, Tom Segev, Ari Shavit—have found documents in the state archives that admit as much. (The diary of Zionist leader Theodor Herzl, which dates before the founding of Israel, contains plans to expel Arabs from Arab land and the belief that "we are not obliged to state the limits of our state.") Netanyahu tightened access to the national archives before any more embarrassing documents could be discovered. According to the Israeli Redneck, though, "Possession is ten-tenths of the law around here. If you can hold it, it's yours."

He continues his speech. "The people in the Hezbollah are committed," he tells us. "The Palestinians are committed. Some may want peace. Some may not. It doesn't matter, but they're committed to the destruction of Israel one way or another." He adds, "In this part of the world there's no such thing as innocent civilians. There's combatants and noncombatants. Nobody's innocent except children. Children are always innocent."

During the question-and-answer period, the Israeli Redneck is asked if he would consider running for president. (Yes, we're now deeply within a peculiar American epoch: those who claim they want liberty search only for Cincinnatus.) He smiles. "I'd be willing to be king," he says. Someone then asks about the extermination of Israel's enemies. "Believe me," he replies, "if we were China or Russia or the United States or somebody, there wouldn't be a Palestinian problem and there wouldn't be a Hezbollah problem. They'd just turn their army loose and that's it."

I excuse myself and stroll outside. I notice that someone else has also walked out early: Pastor Marty. He tells me that he was troubled by the violence of the Israeli Redneck's speech. I tell Pastor Marty that I don't fault a man who's fought in four wars for sounding like a lunatic. What bothers me is the way people were applauding him.

Pastor Marty tells me that he blames increasing partisan belligerence on talk radio and Facebook—the way they allow us to "vent sideways," as he calls it, in our little simpatico cocoons. The tiniest disagreements get amplified—from sharing and liking and retweeting—until they're all anyone hears. When was the last time, he asks, that anyone was forced to have a civil discussion with someone who thought differently?

The Israeli Redneck has finished speaking. Stand with Israelites are streaming out, laughing and raving about what they just heard. Two of our tour guides walk past us. One says to the other, "That's totally how I wanna talk, but I'd lose my license."

V. The Occupation of Bus Five

Our daily itinerary is now established. Get a barbarically early wake-up call, overeat at the buffet breakfast, ride a bus, meet Israeli soldiers, ride a bus, overeat at the buffet lunch, hear a lecture, use the phrase "I need a vacation from my vacation" ironically, ride a bus, see some sights, meet more Israeli soldiers, ride a bus, use the phrase "I need a vacation from my vacation" unironically, check into a new hotel, overeat at the buffet dinner, hit the mattress like a lumberjacked tree.

We're in Tiberias now, it's just after sunrise, and Trisha and I trade yawns on the lakeside dock of our hotel. The Sea of Galilee sloshes unseen beneath a layer of fog. As a couple are telling us about how, in the middle of the night, they sneaked down here and went swimming, the sky suddenly clears and what cinematographers call God rays blast erumpent through parting clouds.

The plan, once we're picked up by a boat, is to sail into the middle of the Sea of Galilee, participate in what has been ominously described as a "ceremony," and cross over to the northern bank, where we'll visit famous New Testament sites. I'd been looking forward to hanging out with Pastor Marty while touring Galilee, but he and half our contingent set off for the day with Dennis Prager to visit Safed, the birthplace of Jewish mysticism. "I have two advanced degrees in ancient history," Marty said. "I'll live without seeing Capernaum."

The awaited boats finally pull up to the hotel dock. Hulking and wooden, they're designed to resemble first-century Galilean fishing vessels, intact remains of which have been excavated from the sea's muck. Most of our boats have apostolic names; the boat Trisha and I board is called *Matthew*. Rows of white plastic chairs line the deck. Every member of our boat's crew is wearing a white T-shirt that reads I'VE SAILED ON THE SEA OF GALILEE. These sailors (their website is jesusboats.com) have an apparent lock on trans-Galilee travel: from where we float I count more than a dozen in-transit Jesus boats, all filled to the gunwales with members of at least three different tours.

While we drift away from the western shore, "How Great Thou Art" is blasting over our boat's loudspeakers. It's as catchy as Rodgers and Hammerstein. Dozens of people are singing along as Tiberias disappears behind us. Others are doing the mellow rocking-out thing sometimes seen in evangelical megachurches: eyes shut, swaying to the music, a single hand raised as though to wash some celestial window. One person is crying, then two, then ten. Some of these people saved for years to afford this trip, for the chance to sail over Christianity's ground zero.

All the Genesis Tours–booked Jesus boats meet in the middle of the sea, whereupon they're lashed together by men of unsmiling industriousness and dexterous knot-making skills. The people on one boat are taking pictures of the people who are taking pictures of them on the other boat. The mood of peaceful singing and swaying from five minutes ago is gone. Laughter, callouts, selfies —it feels like a booze cruise without the booze. We relax in our seats. Reuven Doron gets on the *Matthew* boat's microphone and tells us how special this morning is, how special this lake is. He's proud of us, he says. Then all the *Matthew* boat guys begin to raise the American flag.

We're asked to stand and face the back of the boat. A loudspeaker is right next to us, so I hear static first, followed by a drumroll. "The Star-Spangled Banner" begins to play. When it's over, up goes the Israeli flag, followed by Israel's national anthem. Hearing the two songs side by side is instructive. One anthem, militaristic and silly, emerged from a single battle in a war whose origins only a professional historian could explain. The other, harrowing and heartbroken, emerged from exile. It might be the least triumphalist national anthem on earth. Almost everyone is crying by the end.

Doron tells us, "Thank God we can fly the American and Israeli flags together this morning. May this bond endure forever." He talks about Ezekiel 38 and its "northern nations" prophecy. According to the common evangelical interpretation, fighters from a five-nation confederacy (including one army on horseback) will attack Israel, ushering in the End Times. "It's a difficult passage," Doron says, understating things quite a bit. "A difficult prophecy. But let them come. They've come before. It never works." He holds up his Bible and gives it an affirmative shake. "It *will* never work, because God wrote this book." Throughout our tour we've been told, over and over, how dearly Israel needs our support, how endangered it is by monstrous forces. Yet at the same time, we've been told, just as frequently, that Israel cannot lose, because it is protected by God.

We disembark on the other side of the sea. David leads us to the Mount of Beatitudes. Beside a small, dark-stoned Byzantine-style church, he reads to us from Jesus's Sermon on the Mount in the Gospel According to Matthew. People I've watched applaud the suggestion of gunning down Palestinian teenage rock-throwers are now nodding in agreement to the blessedness of the meek, the merciful, and the peacemakers. When David finishes, he holds up his Bible and says, "Jesus calls us to attain something we can never really attain." He looks around. "This is all temporary. All of this. Everything we can't see is permanent."

An hour later, we're standing on the Sea of Galilee's gravel beach, behind the Church of the Primacy of St. Peter. In the last chapter of the Gospel of John, Jesus, Peter, and other disciples eat breakfast together shortly after Jesus's resurrection. According to local lore, this is the spot where that meal took place. Unfortunately, the shoreline remains thick with haze. Several people, needing no prompting, remove their shoes and socks, roll up their pants to reveal knobbly old-person knees, and wade into the foggy water. In the sea, everyone looks big and childlike. Fellow travelers I have not yet seen smile are smiling, including the man who so perfectly resembles Rupert Murdoch that I've begun to suspect he is Rupert Murdoch.

We end our day at the Jordan River, which is frankly not much of a river. Trisha and I find our way to a large observation deck that looks down onto a popular baptismal site. The shoreline—all wild viny drapery—more closely resembles the sculpted scenery of a Disneyland log-flume ride than indigenous vegetation. Nearby is a bulletin-board hall of fame, on which we see photos of various post-baptism celebrities in drenched white T-shirts: Oliver North, Whitney Houston, Mike Huckabee. There's also a photo of the actor James Van Der Beek not getting baptized, but rather chilling on the viewing platform, which seems like a very James Van Der Beek thing to do at the Jordan River.

As we walk along the deck, a group baptism is getting under way below us. The baptizees, all in white gowns, silently descend a stairway. One after another, each person is dunked. The proceedings are quick; it's an assembly line. Standing by me on the viewing platform is an older man from my tour, shaking his head. He's one of the few among us to consistently step back from group prayer, and can always be relied on to say, "Oh, come *on*," when someone complains about having to walk uphill. He seems to me less a conservative than someone who's sick to death of everyone's whiny bullshit. This is the type of conservative I could very much see myself becoming one day, if I ever became a conservative.

"Getting baptized?" I ask him.

He chuckles. "Nah," he says as the baptizees below us hug and weep. "Had it done. Think it worked."

That night we have dinner in our new hotel in Jerusalem. Afterward, on the way to our room, Trisha and I run into our guide, David. "Goodbye, guys," he says. We keep walking and tell him we'll see him tomorrow. "No," he says. "*Goodbye.*"

We stop. It turns out that, only ten minutes ago, a Genesis Tours representative took David aside and told him that everyone on Bus Five got together, voted, and cast him out as our guide. I assure David that there's been no such vote as far as I'm aware, which seems to cheer him up a bit. After David announces that he's going to his room to call his wife, Trisha and I gather together all the Bus Fivers we can find. Not one of them has heard of any secret vote to ditch David.

Together we confront the nearest Genesis Tours lackey, who is sitting behind the official Genesis Tours information station in the hotel lobby. The kid's job (he looks twenty-one) appears to be to ensure that our most elderly Stand with Israelites don't get lost between the dining hall and the elevator. We pour recrimination on the poor guy for a while; the phrase "travesty of justice" is used. The representative remains irritatingly poised: "Thank you for bringing this to our attention, but there were several complaints." Our group breaks away, huddles up, and assembles a short list of the likeliest anti-David complainers.

Another Genesis Tours representative is spotted trying to tiptoe past us in the lobby; we fall upon her like locusts. As leader pro tempore of the insurrection, I try to appear calm and steadfast, knowing full well that I'm backed up by a dozen peppery American conservatives. I am in the middle of patiently explaining why we, as a group, believe David's firing was unjust, when someone bellows, "You're *ruining* my vacation!"

We all turn to find Roger, a large, courtly Southerner. All I know of Roger is that he believes he can prove that the Gospels were originally written in Aramaic rather than Greek. He always sits up front on Bus Five, near David, and asks by far the most questions of anyone in our cohort. The face of this hitherto kind, gentle man is now trembling with anger.

I try to de-escalate the situation, but the Genesis Tours representative talks right past me, telling Roger that he's being rude and aggressive. Roger demands a full and immediate refund. The Genesis Tours woman has heard enough, tells us there's nothing she can do, and storms away. We haunt the lobby for another hour or so, pestering all who will listen, but eventually the word comes down: David's removal from Bus Five is final.

The next morning, at breakfast, a bunch of us decide that more conspiring will only hurt David and his chances of future employment. The guide community in Israel is small; the more we complain, the more likely it is that news of this incident will spread, potentially tarring David as a problematic tour leader. As we eat scrambled eggs and sip apple juice, we laugh in recollection of our anger the night before and congratulate ourselves on our newfound emotional maturity. Supply-side logic is trotted out: *It's not our place to tell Genesis Tours who they can't fire. They have a right, as business owners, to do what's best for their business.* We're living again in a reasonable, if depressing, adult world. "The best thing we can do for David," I find myself saying, "is give him a generous tip and let him know we support him."

Then Roger sidles up to our table. He's wearing a neon-green polo shirt, his hair is still wet from his shower, and he's breathing like a bear that just tore apart an animal carcass. I invite Roger to sit. He declines, so I stand and take him aside to explain the group's thinking. Roger—head atilt, eyes focused—listens carefully.

"So," he says when I'm done, "your suggestion is surrender. To give up. Am I correct in that understanding? You wanna wimp out and enjoy your vacation—no offense—instead of doing the right thing. That's what *you* all have decided to do. Let me know if I'm mischaracterizing this. Again, no offense. It's okay if that's what you all want." And here Roger's voice begins to rise: "Because my opinion is *revolt*." He throws his arms out—the classic demagogue pantomime of the world's last reasonable man. "Why are we here again? To stand with Israel. If we don't stand for David, we're just like those Americans who don't stand with Israel."

Is this why conservatives so often win and liberals so often lose? Roger is a man who still believes the world can and must be bent to his will.

"Okay," I say to Roger. "So what's your plan?"

Roger, who obviously spent the night thinking through a plan, answers quickly: "We occupy the bus. Take over."

We all head out to Bus Five, with Roger leading the way. Walking right behind him, I say, "You realize you're basically a Bolshevik right now, right?"

"Works for me," Roger says, not breaking stride.

Bus Five has two doors; we quickly set up a loyalty checkpoint at both. "I refuse to share a bus with someone who complained about David," Roger says. As the remaining Bus Fivers board, they will be interrogated. If they admit that they objected to David, they will be encouraged either to renounce their disapproval or to find a seat on another bus. Checkpoints, loyalty tests, Maoist self-criticism—I point out that these are overtly left-wing tactics. "Hey," someone says, "it works for liberals! Let's make it work for us!"

Unfortunately, our plan quickly breaks down in its particulars. No one passing through Roger's (objectively terrifying) loyalty checkpoints is willing to admit that they complained about David. The couple that always kvetches about walking, for instance, who've been identified by multiple sources as members of the anti-David faction, lie to Roger's face. No, they say. They never complained. Roger allows them onto the bus, only to be informed of their real views once they're aboard. "I'll deal with them later," he says, flustered. Soon gossip begins to move through our group with sinister fluidity; people are silently thumbing toward others whose backs are to them and mouthing "Complained!" One elderly woman says to Roger, "I heard we have a liberal in the group." Trisha and I share a glance. "I don't know anything about that!" Roger cries.

A snooty rich woman upon whom fancy scarves and sunglasses are exhibited daily approaches the bus with her rigorously silent husband. We all know for a fact (don't we?) that they complained about David, multiple times. To her credit, the woman confesses, but she assures Roger that she didn't want David to get fired. Roger thanks her for her honesty and asks if she will now stand with the group, Roger, and Israel to ensure David's return. She and her husband stare at Roger while sweat drips down his face. "Yes," she says quietly.

By now most of the other Genesis Tours buses have left the hotel and begun the day's itinerary; several members of the anti-David faction have joined those buses. Our revolution began with amity and optimism, but now it feels misshapen with anger and resentment. I realize that if someone tries to push past Roger to get on Bus Five, I am prepared to restrain that person, using force if I have to. Pastor Marty is now beside me, saying that while he's typically inclined to play peacemaker, in this case an injustice has been done.

A petition is drawn up and signed by twenty of us, thirty of us, and soon forty of us, despite there being only forty-six passengers on Bus Five. One guy taps me on the shoulder and reveals with a snicker that he signed Bill Clinton's name to our petition. I smack my forehead and point out that if our petition is going to be taken seriously, we need it to be legitimate. The man, grasping the enormity of his blunder, bites his lip, chases down the petition holder, and violently scratches Bill Clinton's name from the document.

We've occupied Bus Five for more than an hour, by which point we've won our Palestinian bus driver to the cause: he has promised that he will not go anywhere without David. But no one from Genesis Tours has come out to speak with us. I take Roger aside, praising his leadership. However, I tell him, we'll need to instigate a showdown with Genesis Tours if we want to bring this to an end. Roger shakes my hand and gives me his blessing. I rush off to the hotel lobby and find several Genesis Tours representatives speaking excitedly into their cell phones.

A company emissary returns with me to Bus Five and listens as Roger enumerates our demands. They are (a) the expulsion from Bus Five of all who complained about David, followed by (b) David's reinstatement as Bus Five's rightful guide. Any failure to meet these demands will necessitate a complete and total refund of our package tour's costs. The emissary runs a hand across his bald head, makes a few agitated calls, and promptly disappears.

It's hard to be certain what happens next. Several of us have begun to argue about strategy. Others are upset that we will probably not get to see all the scheduled sites today. Roger, for some reason, heads off to the hotel. With Roger gone, I feel lost and dispirited. I wonder if I ever really believed in the movement so much as I did in the man. Ten minutes later, he reappears, his hands stuffed glumly in his pockets. When he's within twenty feet of us, though, Roger smiles beneath watery, exhausted eyes. "David's coming back!" he says. We cheer. We applaud. Roger falls into the arms of another Bus Fiver and says through tears that he can barely talk. "I'm just glad it didn't end in violence," I hear someone say.

Fifteen minutes later, a red-eyed David boards Bus Five wearing his official tour-guide headset. He is greeted with a series of ovations. In a lull between rounds of applause, David tells us he slept only two hours the night before. I realize, and I can't be the only one, that we've perhaps made David's life significantly more complicated. Maybe he just wanted to go home?

VI. Tribes

A few days later, the end of our tour approaching, we board Bus Five to be warned that the coming day will be "emotional." This is code for our imminent visit to Yad Vashem, Jerusalem's Holocaust memorial.

I've visited half a dozen Holocaust museums around the world. I weep every time, never knowing whom I pity more: those who died, or those who did not. I weep, too, pondering the apathy that allowed a regime and its quislings to murder 6 million Jews. Clearly a great number of Europeans did not much care whether the Jews were exterminated; Theodor Herzl recognized as much in France four decades before the Holocaust began, and there modern Zionism begins. What most upsets me, though, is thinking about those who *did* care that Jews were being exterminated —and did nothing. I picture myself in Germany, in 1939, with Trisha, sitting in our kitchen while we feed our daughter. We hear scuffling next door in the apartment of our Jewish neighbors. We know what's happening and why. I know if I say anything I'll be killed, possibly before my daughter's eyes. So what do I do? I cover my daughter's ears.

Wandering the concrete pyramidal hallways of Yad Vashem, you can quickly understand why Israel's security fears are so overriding, even with the most dominant military force in the region protecting it and the world's last remaining superpower supporting it. Thousands of its citizens can recall an entire continent colluding to rid itself of even the most assimilated and accomplished Jews. This gnawing, passed-down, tribal fear is what holds together an increasingly fractious Israeli society, just as Palestinian society —comprising Muslim and Christian, Israeli citizen and occupied subject—is held together by its tribally shared anger and humiliation at Jewish hands.

Looking at more displays within the Hall of Remembrance, however, you can also begin to see how this commonality breaks down. Israel has violated international law, sure, but not like this. Israel has committed wartime atrocities, yes, but not like this. The Palestinians have suffered, undeniably, but not like this.

Critics of the Jewish state often allege that Israel uses the Holocaust as both sword and shield; they view talk of avoiding another Holocaust as preposterous fearmongering. But at Yad Vashem, you'll find room after room filled with photos of thousands of Jewish families who could not have imagined the first Holocaust. Whether the assailed, protectionist mentality inculcated by that experience is a reasonable reaction or a delusion is beside the point. Whatever else it is, this mentality is probably ineradicable in our lifetimes.

It occurs to me, while Trisha drifts away to watch an old Nazi propaganda film, that this sense of potential extinguishment is the link between Israelis and American conservatives. Israelis respond to what has happened; American conservatives respond to what they fear will happen. Both are losing. Israel's democracy crumbles under the pressure of occupation without end, and white conservatives' cultural supremacy breaks apart under the pressure of rapidly changing demographics. In the face of these challenges, both attempted a short-term fix: harnessing the political power of a fanatically religious base of support. The demotic anger political elites believed they could wield in pursuit of their goals came to control the agenda, and now there's no way out. I think of something I'd heard a fellow Bus Fiver say: "I bought a couple Israeli flags—so people'll know where my heart's at."

Inside the Hall of Remembrance, I stop at a display devoted to the principal of a Hebrew school in Warsaw, who wrote avidly in his diary right up to the beginning of the liquidation of the Warsaw ghetto. "Anyone who could see the expulsion from Warsaw with his own eyes would have his heart broken," reads an entry from that final night. "The children, in particular, rend the heavens with their cries." His last line is: "If my life ends, what will become of my diary?" On the museum card it says he went to Treblinka the next day.

I walk into Yad Vashem's Children's Memorial. It's so dark you can barely see the person standing in front of you. Flickering within the oceanic black are tiny lights—flames, seemingly millions of them, reflected doubly and triply in the mirrors that line the way through. A voice reads the names and ages—"Akiva Broner, twelve. Eva Gruenwald, four"—of the 1.5 million children killed during the Holocaust. The memorial, by design, simulates how the Holocaust felt from a child's point of view: lost, confused, instinctively reaching out to strangers, and following a distant point of light. This experience feels a certain way to me, as a parent. Having a child causes one seismic internal shift: you feel less like someone else's culmination and more like a single, modest link in a chain of continuance. The lights all around me are a million and a half broken links, and I try to imagine that—to imagine dying, separated from Trisha and my daughter, not knowing where they are or how badly they're suffering. A worse fate there cannot be, and yet every name that's read aloud is one more instance of it.

In the darkness, my hand comes to rest on solid wood. I push open the familiar gate and a gush of light breaks across me. I'm standing on our stone patio in Los Angeles. My daughter is sitting on the flagstones, looking up into the tree outside her bedroom window, where the owl that keeps her awake at night lives. Trisha and I go to her and become the thing that we are—a tribe, in miniature.

Here are the people, I sometimes fear, for whom I would do or justify anything.

Chiefing in Cherokee

FROM *Virginia Quarterly Review*

BY THE TIME we rolled into Cherokee, North Carolina, Nick and I had been crisscrossing the country for three months straight, scouting for stories for an educational website called the Odyssey. Because it was the year 2000—that is, when cell phones were mostly used for urgent matters—we had filled our endless road hours with conversation. But neither of us said a word as we cruised down Tsali Boulevard, the town's main strip. We just stared and shuddered.

Practically every storefront sign featured a Native American rendered in caricature above a business name like MIZ-CHIEF, SUNDANCER CRAFTS, or REDSKIN MOTEL. Store pillars had been carved and painted as totem poles. Teepees crested the rooftops. Souvenir shops advertised two-for-one dream catchers. Mannequins dressed in warbonnets were posed mid-wave in the windows. Nick and I had traveled here to research Andrew Jackson's forced relocation, in 1836, of the Cherokee from their ancestral lands to territories out west. At least 4,000 Cherokee died from hunger and exposure along the way. We wanted to learn how the tribe had processed this tragedy, how they explained it to their children. Indigenous Disneyland wasn't what we'd had in mind.

Up ahead, a billboard touted LIVE INDIAN DANCERS in a tawdry font. Nick pulled over so we could join a flock of tourists gathered around a teepee propped on the side of the road. Two men wearing elaborately feathered headdresses were midway through a performance. The younger one was playing a drum; the elder was telling a story about the *Titanic*. Too many people had crowded into the life raft, he said. They were sinking. Three brave men needed to make the ultimate sacrifice. A French man shouted, "Vive la France!" and jumped overboard. Then a Brit yelled, "Long live the Queen!" and jumped overboard. Finally, a Cherokee stood up. He looked around at all of the passengers and said, "Remember the Trail of Tears!" Then he grabbed a white boy and threw *him* overboard.

I laughed. The white tourists did too. Nick, an Oglala Lakota Sioux from the Pine Ridge Nation in South Dakota, did not, which altered how I might otherwise have reacted to the next joke, and the one after that. Again and again the storyteller mocked his audience, and again and again they chuckled on cue. I didn't know what to make of this. Were these jokes undermining the significance of the tribe's calamities or intensifying them? And was laughing a sign of our complicity, or was it a strange way of seeking karmic forgiveness for the atrocities that some of our ancestors had committed against theirs?

No time to contemplate: Live Indian Dancing had begun. The storyteller took over the drum and started chanting while his younger partner stepped into the center of the circle of listeners. He wore regalia—war paint, dozens of beaded necklaces, a headdress and bustle made of turkey feathers—over faded Levi's and sneakers. For about a minute, he shuffled his feet and bobbed his bustle as the tourists took pictures. When he bowed, the storyteller passed around a basket, which the audience filled with bills and coins.

I had witnessed touristic practices ranging from the questionable to the degrading the world over, but this struck me as something dangerously complex. Self-exploitation? I turned to Nick for guidance, as he was my de facto barometer for what was morally acceptable in Native America. He clenched his jaw in anger.

When the last tourist departed, we marched over to the performers. Though just nineteen years old, Nick had inherited formidable oratorical skills from his grandfather (who provided legal counsel for the American Indian Movement) and mother (who won the 1993 Goldman Environmental Prize), so he did our talking. One by one, he ticked off every instance of cultural misappropriation we had encountered there: how, historically, the Cherokee had never lived in teepees, raised totem poles, or performed the Sun Dance, and how they had certainly never worn that style of headdress. What gave these men the right to profit from traditions not their own?

The storyteller shook his tip basket. He fed his kids with this money, he said. White people, they didn't know anything about Indians. He was educating them.

"How are you doing that? You are totally misrepresenting your history."

He looked Nick in the eye. "You say you're Lakota, eh? Do you speak the language? Do you know the dances and the ceremonies? I do. But I don't do them here. They're too sacred."

And just like that, our righteous indignation fizzled. No, Nick did not speak Lakota—for the same reason that I, a Chicana from South Texas, did not speak Spanish. Our elders had suffered so much discrimination for using their mother tongues that they'd declined to pass them on to us. Although Nick and I had been hired by the Odyssey to represent our communities, we couldn't actually talk with many of our elders. What, then, gave us the right to question these men? They knew their culture, which was more than we could say about our own.

Sensing that he'd hit a nerve, the storyteller invited Nick to sit with him, then picked up a drum and started singing. After a while, Nick joined in. They sang song after song together, until the next flock of tourists arrived. When the storyteller rose from the bench to open a new show, we slinked away.

In the year that followed, I drove more than 45,000 miles across the United States with Nick and other colleagues. Nothing affected me like that Cherokee trip. From that day forward, whenever I began another essay about Chicanidad, or wore a rebozo to a reading, I thought of those buskers dancing for tourists on the side of the street. Was I also commoditizing my culture when I performed my identity, or was I offering reverence to my ancestors? Could anything profitable be authentic? Did any of this matter if you were simply trying to survive?

About a year ago, I returned to Cherokee to continue the conversation that had troubled me since that first visit. The timing was auspicious: The town was celebrating its 103rd annual fair, a five-day homecoming festival complete with parades, stickball matches, a Ferris wheel, and a late-night "Pretty Legs" contest featuring scantily clad men in drag. Along Tsali Boulevard, all the teepees were gone, swept from the rooftops and plucked off the streets. The Old Squaw Moccasin Shop had been replaced by a string of upscale stores promoting "authentic Cherokee crafts." Only one or two bonneted mannequins were left.

These changes were yet another instance of the remarkable agility of the Eastern Band of Cherokee Indians. This nation was founded by some of the hundreds of Cherokee who escaped Jackson's death march by fleeing into the mountains, as well as by those who'd been granted the right to stay through treaties. In the 1870s, they bought back their ancestral territory from the U.S. government, via a land trust called the Qualla Boundary. White outsiders arrived a few decades later, looking to invest in baskets and blowguns. Sensing an opportunity, the white-run Bureau of Indian Affairs organized the tribe's first fair in 1912, which drew even more visitors. Once the Great Smoky Mountains National Park and the Blue Ridge Parkway opened in the 1930s, cabals of federal, state, and county officials, local businessmen, and a handful of Eastern Cherokee decided to capitalize on the tribe's heritage.

First came an outdoor theatrical production called *Unto These Hills* that, according to an early promo, dramatized "the epic clash of the red man and the white man," from colonization to the Trail of Tears. The show reeled in more than 100,000 spectators during its 1950 inaugural season, and has run every summer since. Next came the Oconaluftee Indian Village, where historical reenactors portrayed daily life circa 1759 for clusters of camera-wielding tourists.

Competition started brewing on the other side of the Smokies when Tennessee towns like Gatlinburg and Pigeon Forge began to hype up their own heritage. White, middle-class families came in droves for the moonshine stills, wax museums, and attractions like Rebel Railroad (now Dollywood), which at the time offered train rides culminating in "wild Indian attacks." Refusing to be outdone, the Eastern Band sanctioned Frontier Land, a Wild West theme park that also featured Indian raids. By the early 1960s, the town of Cherokee was awash with tomahawk shops, campgrounds lined with teepees, petting zoos where kids could play tic-tac-toe with roosters, and round-the-clock Live Indian Dancing. Whereas earlier ventures like the Oconaluftee Village aimed for historical accuracy, these newer businesses touted the Hollywood version of the American Indian. Totem poles abounded. Not only did this satisfy tourists, it enabled the Eastern Band to keep their real traditions private and therefore sacred. Once the Red Power civil rights movement elevated Native consciousness in the late 1960s, however, more and more Eastern Cherokee questioned the persona the tribe had put forward, worried about the psychic harm it could cause. Tourism also changed, with heritage seekers wanting to learn more, say, about their great-great-grandma rumored to have been a Cherokee princess.

Then, in the eighties, air travel became more affordable, triggering a nationwide decline in family road trips that parched the tribe's economy. The time had come for reinvention. In 1997, the Eastern Band launched their most ambitious transformation yet: On the grounds where Frontier Land once stood, they erected Harrah's Cherokee, North Carolina's first casino. Suddenly, the Eastern Band had the cash flow not only to fortify their infrastructure—education, health care, housing, public safety—but to revamp their image as well. The Museum of the Cherokee Indian underwent a $3.5 million renovation the following year. In 2006, the tribe hired a Kiowa playwright, Hanay Geiogamah, to revise *Unto These Hills* according to Native storytelling traditions and to write better roles for community members. (The original script was composed by a white graduate student at the University of North Carolina.) A few years later, the tribal government began offering incentives to local businesses to more accurately represent Cherokee culture. This explained the dearth of teepees along Tsali Boulevard, replaced by new facades hewn of wood and stone.

Vintage Cherokee lives on, though, in the buskers who pose for tourist photographs. Known locally as "chiefing," this profession dates back to 1930, when a souvenir shop called Lloyd's asked its employees to stand outside in their regalia to draw in customers. After Polaroid popularized instant cameras in the late 1940s, some Eastern Cherokee (as well as members of other tribes) began dressing up and standing along the thoroughfare, beckoning motorists to stop for photos. The first buskers saw a direct correlation between the ostentation of their outfits and how much tourists tipped them, so they abandoned the modest, traditional dress of the Cherokee in favor of the splendid warbonnets of the Plains Indians. Although chiefing soon became one of the town's biggest attractions—one busker, Henry "Chief Henry" Lambert, claimed to be "The World's Most Photographed Indian" after posing by his roadside teepee for almost six decades—it was also one of the most controversial, with some members challenging the profession's dignity. Over the years, the tribal government has tried curtailing the practice through increasingly stringent regulations, allowing only enrolled members to chief inside the Qualla Boundary, requiring annual permits, and, most recently, restricting busking to a handful of three-sided huts equipped with a raised stage, a ceiling fan, and benches. Anyone caught busking outside these huts can be slapped with fines, even arrested.

At 9:00 a.m. all the huts around town were still empty. Over by the Museum of the Cherokee Indian, two members of Cherokee Friends—the museum's ambassadorial wing—stood in a shady alcove, knapping flint and whittling wood. Both men had shaved their heads smooth except for short ponytails at their napes. The younger of the two was wearing jeans and a black T-shirt; the other, who introduced himself as Sonny Ledford Usquetsiwo, wore a belted white trade shirt over red leggings. They both wore metal bands around their wrists and coin-sized gauges in their earlobes. "The reason we are here is to answer questions," Usquetsiwo said grandly, drawing out each vowel in Appalachian fashion. "Here, we are in our culture 24/7."

I complimented his regalia, and he nodded, rubbing the red-and-black engravings that covered his arms. "My markings, it is earned. It is not a fad. I'm not just going to the tattoo parlor and getting it done. It is between me and the elders. They are called warrior marks. Real warriors give us that status because we are fighting for our culture. Lots of what is written about us is wrong, like the way we look. You see us on the Internet, but that's Plains Indians, not us."

I asked Usquetsiwo whether chiefing had contributed to the public's misperception of his tribe. He stared at me for a moment before resuming his flint work. "Gradually, they are easing them out. In a way I agree with [chiefing] because I know the people who do it. Yet another way I don't because they are using warbonnets of another tribe. Our elders will not let us stand on the side of the street trying to get people to take a picture for a tip. We have been told, 'We don't want to see you out there.'"

At that, the younger man, Mike Crowe, looked up. "My dad chiefed on the side of the road, didn't he?" he asked.

Usquetsiwo nodded.

"They do what they had to do," Crowe said. "It was a smaller job market then. They just tried to make cash to feed themselves. This day and age, I'd rather see them take the time to research our people and give an authentic view. If they are trying to make an honest living, I can't be mad at that."

Usquetsiwo's diplomacy was one of many examples of how the Eastern Cherokee practice what's called a "harmony ethic," which values consensus and not causing offense. I'd learned about it in the time between my visits here, and noticed how it manifested not just in the people but in the attractions too. The Museum of the Cherokee Indian, for instance, is said to be one of the first in the United States to require visitors to contemplate human suffering. And certainly its mural of the Trail of Tears—of families trudging through snow in mournfully blue strokes—was proof that there is no painless way to tell the story of Native American displacement. But I sensed, too, how the harmony ethic tempered other displays, like one about Cherokee firepower, where a placard listed various excuses as to why the colonists had traded weapons to the Cherokee that were "cheaply made, required special shot, and broke easily" before landing on what made the most sense—namely that "the colonists did not want the Indians to have equal firepower." A timeline of the Cherokee school system, meanwhile, spared you from the horrors of a century and a half of "Indian residential schools"—during which 100,000 indigenous children were forced to attend Christian boarding schools, where they were beaten for speaking their mother tongues and berated for professing their traditional beliefs—by solely noting how, in the 1930s, American public opinion shifted to support the idea that "removing five and six year olds from their families was inhumane." This was, in essence, a museum about an attempted genocide, but you couldn't tell from its rhetorical restraint.

I found a more wrenching experience at the Cherokee Bear Zoo. For decades, animals played a large role in Cherokee tourism in the form of trained-chicken acts and pose-with-a-bear-cub stands, most of which have been phased out. One of the zoos in Cherokee, Chief Saunooke's Bear Park, was shuttered in 2013 af-

ter the USDA fined it $20,000 for deplorable conditions. Tribal
elders have sued the Cherokee Bear Zoo as well, contending it
violates the Endangered Species Act. (A court ruled otherwise in
March 2016, but a PETA campaign against the zoo continues.)

At the entrance were the sounds of more prerecorded flutes
and a vendor selling paper trays arranged with apple slices, a
piece of white bread, and a leaf of iceberg lettuce. I sidestepped
a trash can with a sign that read DON'T SPIT IN THE BUCKET,
then peered over the railing. Twenty feet below, bears paced inside tiny concrete pits. Black bears, brown bears—nine in all. The
closest one, a grizzly, was standing on his hind legs and staring up
at a couple of kids with cell phones. "Lookit!" one shouted, laughing and snapping a photo before dropping an apple slice into the
bear's open mouth. The animal's teeth were jagged and yellow.
His mate stretched out beside a stack of tires that held aloft a log
topped by an overturned garbage can. A few feet away, a dripping
pipe replenished a tub of water. That was it, in terms of amenities:
no plants or grass or even dirt. The kids tossed down a lettuce leaf
that alighted by the paw of the prostrate bear, which batted at it
listlessly while they laughed and took her photo.

By noon, the streets had filled with fairgoers, but the huts were
still empty. On Paint Town Road, I noticed a tattoo parlor flanked
by a two-story fiberglass Indian wearing half a headdress and white
streaks on his cheeks. I walked inside. A bald man with a goatee
looked up from behind the counter. I confessed that I'd driven
300 miles to meet some roadside chiefs but hadn't found one yet.

"I did it when I was ten," he offered, adjusting his glasses. "I
tanned a lot better then."

His name was Robin Lambert, and he hailed from three generations of chiefs: his grandfather, his uncle, and he and his brother
all busked at one point or another—his uncle, in fact, was none
other than Chief Henry. Was it true that the famed showman had
put five kids through college by chiefing? Indeed it was, Lambert
said, and not only that, but one of those sons—Patrick Lambert
—had just been elected "real chief," or the Principal Chief of the
Eastern Band, by a landslide last month.

"So, I guess that makes you an advocate?"

"When you go to Disney, you want to see Mickey Mouse. When
you come here, you want to see Indians," he said with a shrug.

Lambert stepped out from behind the counter. His arms, legs, and neck were so intricately tattooed that I couldn't help asking which mark had come first. An eagle, he said, but it got covered a while back. His clients, Native and white alike, tended to request animals, feathers, or portraits of Indians. But not every request was honored. "[White] people will come in and say their great-grand-mother is Cherokee and they want a tribal seal, but I won't do it," Lambert said. "Some will get offended, but then I'll tell them that to do that, I'd need to make markings on their face. And then they'll say no." Lambert didn't do this out of rudeness; for many tribes, refusal is a political stance, a way of asserting sovereignty. Here in Cherokee, it can even trump harmony.

Down by the Burger King, I met Mark Hollis Stover Jr., another legacy roadside chief, whose great-grandfather, grandfather, and mother had all been in the business. A tall and slender man, Sto-ver wore an orange ribbon shirt topped by a breastplate of beads shaped like elk bones. An otter pelt was slung across his back and his head was crowned with a "porky roach" (a headdress bristling with porcupine and deer hair). He'd just opened his hut for busi-ness and was still arranging beaded bracelets for sale, but he took a moment to tell his story. He grew up in Atlanta—"the only Indian I knew," he said—then "got in a little bit of trouble" before mov-ing to Cherokee and finding his passion: dancing. A champion in the Men's Southern Strait Dance on the powwow circuit, Stover said he enjoyed chiefing because it allowed him to live by his art. "That's all I want to do, is dance."

The hardest part of his profession was, as he put it, the "stu-pid questions. They gawk at you. They say *woh-woh-woh*," he said, padding his palm against his mouth. "They ask, 'Are you a real Indian?' They think we still live in teepees." He tried to view these annoyances as opportunities. "I get to educate ignorant people who watch TV all day. Kids come up all scared of me, and I show them my jewelry and say, 'If you take a picture with me, you can pick a piece.' They see we are just like everybody else."

Listening to Stover, it seemed the Eastern Band's biggest ob-stacle to promoting a more accurate view of their culture might be that their fabricated attributes had become tradition in and of themselves. When *Unto These Hills* made its revisionist debut, for instance, some community members protested, saying they liked the old version better, despite its inaccuracies. And if a roadside chief was donning the same style of porky roach that three generations of family members wore before him, couldn't he legitimately claim it as part of his heritage? I shared this notion with Stover. He thought about it for a moment.

"I am just doing what I can to keep it alive," he said.

Unto These Hills had closed for the season by the time I arrived, but the Oconaluftee Indian Village, an expanse of woods and streams and cabins that recreated eighteenth-century Cherokee life (pizza-and-hot-dog kiosk notwithstanding), was still open. Six hundred schoolchildren were somewhere on the premises, observing live dioramas, blowgun demonstrations, and basket weaving. Smoke curled from a hearth. Women pounded corn into meal. Men in leggings sharpened metal tools. An accompanying placard epitomized diplomacy: "Cherokee had a cure for every sickness and disease known until the introduction of smallpox," as if the disease miraculously appeared on its own before annihilating 90 percent of the first Americans.

The village's central feature was a ceremonial square marked by low walls of sand. The surrounding bleachers were named after the seven clans: Bird, Blue, Deer, Long Hair, Paint, Wild Potato, and Wolf. A performance was under way; every seat was taken. Historical reenactors danced until the ringleader gave the cue, whereupon they hopped up and down and said, "ribbit." The spectators, mostly schoolchildren, shrieked with delight. "This hurts me worse than it hurts you," the ringleader joked before speeding up his chants, making the dancers hop in double time. Afterward, he stressed that the Frog Dance we'd just witnessed was a social dance, not a ceremonial one. As with most Cherokee traditions, the latter were too sacred to share with outsiders.

Once the show ended, I joined the children mothing around the ringleader, whose name was Freddy. Like the Cherokee Friends at the museum, he'd shaved his head bald but for a ponytail at the nape and had decorated his earlobes with gauges. A pair of bear paws dangled from his neck. Such striking features were likely why he was emblazoned on postcards sold across town, but he also radiated a luminous kindness.

Finally the crowd cleared out, which gave Freddy and me a chance to talk. I learned that he was the first in his family to graduate not just high school but college, and that he'd chosen the University of North Carolina because, when he was a boy, he found a Tar Heels raincoat in a box of clothes that a church had sent. He told me that he loved making art (mostly stone and wood work, but abstract art too); that some of his family were "bad on drugs" but that his grandparents had "stayed me straight." He also said that October 17 was his last day here, because he had stomach cancer, and he would soon be undergoing chemotherapy treatment. "You can't rely on Cherokee Hospital," he said evenly. "There are no doctors there." Freddy was twenty-five years old.

Other reenactors gathered around. I asked them how they liked working at the village. Quite a bit, they said, though one grumbled about his wife greeting him in the morning with, "You going to go play Indian today?" They agreed that the hardest part was answering the same questions day in and day out: Where are the teepees? Do you have a car? Do you have a house? Where is the reservation? Missing from this list were, of course, the equally insipid questions I myself was asking. For there are three kinds of tourists who visit Cherokee: those who know nothing about Indians; those who think they know everything about Indians; and those who are aware of how little they know about Indians and want to be enlightened. What impressed me about the Eastern Band was how patient they were with us. Granted, they have an economic incentive to be tolerant, but so do plenty of other tribes, and I couldn't think of another one that offered visitors half as many opportunities for connection. True, these interactions were highly contrived, but hopefully we were learning a little more about one another than if we'd all just stayed at home.

At one point a blond, blue-eyed boy raced up to a wall of sand and kicked it, causing a mini-avalanche. "Please don't touch that mound!" a reenactor shouted, rushing over. The child darted away but was soon dragged back by his father. "Say you're sorry," he demanded, pushing the child at the reenactor's feet.

Bending down on one knee, the reenactor looked the little boy in the eye and explained how the sand "is like the walls of our church. Would you want me going into your church and breaking something? No, you wouldn't, because it is your sacred space. The way our people would traditionally handle something like this is, the mom and dad would be held responsible. They would be tied to a post. I know you are really young, but that is why I am telling you this. I want you to respect things."

The father gripped his son by the top of the head and led him away. As they disappeared around the corner, he smacked him.

However jarring it felt to exit an eighteenth-century Indian village and, twelve minutes later, saunter inside an Indian casino, the two are arguably equally authentic. Games of chance have long roots in Native America. (Some European travelogues describe tribes throwing bones for horses and weapons.) Ever since the Seminoles initiated Hollywood Bingo in Florida, in 1979, tribes have opened more than 470 gaming establishments nationwide—businesses that generated nearly $30 billion in revenue in 2015. Yet gambling has been contentious for many nations. In 1989, the Mohawk Nation of Akwesasne nearly erupted into a civil war over the issue, with car bombings and shoot-outs that left two men dead. The consensus among the Eastern Cherokee I met was this: They appreciated their dividend checks—which lately had been averaging $12,000 per member per year—and benefits like attending any college in the world entirely on the tribe's dime. Yet they regretted how the casino had transformed their community from a family destination into a gambling haven. Nonetheless, the Eastern Band had recently opened a second casino, near Murphy, North Carolina.

The casino in Cherokee was posh but not flagrantly so, which seemed appropriate given the local poverty rate (around 25 percent). The entire complex boasted a twenty-one-story hotel and a 3,000-seat event center, but kept the outdoor fountains and flashing lights to a minimum. The ringing, pinging machines on the lower level were mostly operated by an elderly crowd, an alarming number of whom were using oxygen tanks. Middle-aged players, many of them in sunglasses, packed the high-stakes poker tables on the second floor. The only Cherokee-specific item I could find anywhere was in the back of a gift shop, where a cabinet displayed the same kind of beaded bracelets that Stover sold, only for $50 instead of $5. At Swarovski, I saw a crystal that seemed buffalo-shaped, but when I asked the attendant, she pointed at its tiny bell and called it a cow.

On the way out, however, I noticed a massive Cherokee tribal seal hanging in the grand entrance. Something about it reminded me of a dazzling moment in 2006 when Seminoles dressed in traditional patchwork announced from a Times Square marquee that they had just acquired Hard Rock International for $965 million. "Our ancestors sold Manhattan for trinkets," one quipped. "We're going to buy Manhattan back, one burger at a time."

That weekend in Cherokee, there were roadside chiefs performing the Hoop Dance, the Fancy Dance, and the Friendship Dance beside a stuffed buffalo named Bill. There were roadside chiefs juggling the needs of twenty tourists at once—some who wanted their kid's face painted, some who wanted a photograph, and all of whom wanted to see Live Indian Dancing and to know when did it start and was there time to run to the restroom first.

Most memorable was the chief in his early forties who presided over the hut by the post office. His name was Mike Grant. A compact man, he had painted his face black from his eyes down and slung a deerskin over his shirt. A fox pelt crested his head, its furry face inches above his own. He was busily displaying tomahawks while his partner, Tony Walkingstick, painted his own face green behind a drum.

"I want to project different periods of time, and not be like a powwow chicken having a seizure on a dance field," Grant said with a low drawl. "We try to bring back the original. Gourd dances. Rattles. Our historical society doesn't want us to bring it back because it is too sacred, but horse feathers! How are the young supposed to learn their culture?" His grandfather was Lakota, he added, and he hoped to bring their ceremonial dances down to Cherokee someday.

"Isn't that controversial?" I asked.

With a grin, he pointed to a nearby Ford F-150, where a Confederate flag strung on a pole dangled out of the truck bed. "We have family who died under them colors. We fly that flag proudly."

Indeed, a white Cherokee chief named William Holland Thomas led the 69th North Carolina Regiment of the Confederate Army, and many of his infantry were fellow Cherokee (who owned more black slaves than any other tribe). Although the rebel flag is flown by just a fringe group these days, I saw several during my visit—stitched on a teenager's denim jacket, plastered on a Cadillac, even used as the backdrop of a giant dream catcher hanging in a store.

Grant introduced me to his sons. The ten-year-old wore a deerskin, while the twelve-year-old sported a T-shirt depicting a potbel-

lied crocodile that said SEND MORE YANKEES THE LAST ONES
TASTED GREAT. Both were absorbed in the same cell phone.
Grant explained that chiefing was a big part of their homeschooling, since they could learn singing, dancing, and culture "all in
one fell swoop." "They make all these knives and tomahawks for
sale," he said. "They owe me four dollars or five dollars for cutting
and a little more for materials, and not only do they learn culture,
but math and business."

At that, the sky released a downpour, sending a dozen tourists
in brightly colored ponchos scurrying into the hut. Grant glanced
over at Walkingstick, who had just donned a *gustoweh*—the feathered headgear traditionally associated with the Haudenosaunee
(Iroquois) Confederacy—and announced that the show would
now begin. No photos would be allowed during the opening ceremony because "we want you to witness with this"—he touched his
eyes—"and feel it with this"—he touched his heart.

Walkingstick popped in a CD of wooden-flute music, lit a prayer
bowl, and scattered a handful of tobacco atop the drum. As soon
as he played it, more tourists entered the hut, cell phones raised
and recording. He asked for blessings "for babies . . . for veterans . . . for Leonard Peltier." The deerskin-clad son was called
up and given two eagle feathers. Grasping one in each hand, the
boy soared around the hut in bare feet, raising the feathers sky-
ward in each of the four cardinal directions. Then he grabbed a
tomahawk and stomped about, his torso parallel to the ground,
his head turning side to side. I had no idea what—if any—of this
was traditionally Cherokee, but I did know that, for nearly three-
quarters of a century, the United States and Canada outlawed most
Native ceremonies. Those that survived were conducted in secret
by Indians willing to risk imprisonment.

A few songs later, Walkingstick rose to his feet. Scanning the
crowd, he delivered a monologue about "Our Holocaust," sharing how "there were 3,500 who were never captured, killed off, or
conquered by the white man. We are their descendants. My relatives, my clan, our nation, we have never been tamed." Across from
me sat a man wearing overalls and a backward baseball cap that
said MOONSHINE. His eyes welled with emotion. The woman beside me also looked transfixed, leaning forward on her knee-high
moccasins. She later told me she lived six hours away but visited
Cherokee whenever she could to learn more about her heritage.

"We kinda reached the middle part of the show," Grant said. "We are not paid by any entity. We will just pass the donation basket." One by one, the tourists shook his hand and filled his basket. They seemed satisfied for having witnessed something "Indian," and Grant and Walkingstick seemed satisfied for getting compensated.

I left Cherokee feeling as conflicted as ever about the ramifications of capitalizing on a culture. Yet I was reminded that, as preoccupations go, this one was mighty privileged, right up there with worrying about whether your touristic experience was authentic or not. Such matters generally become pressing only after a community has been freed from such crises as devastatingly high rates of domestic violence, unemployment, alcohol and drug addiction, and youth suicide—all of which ravage much of Native America today. Perhaps the most authentic thing to witness in Cherokee is how—despite their catastrophic losses during the Trail of Tears; despite their centuries-long struggles to retain their land, status, and dignity—the Eastern Band has managed not only to survive but to thrive, thanks in part to their willingness to reinvent themselves as needed. Indeed, their readiness to share so much with their former tormentors might be one of the most radical acts of forgiveness I know.

Cliffhanger

FROM *Outside*

BY THE TIME it crashed, Eastern Air Lines Flight 980 would have been just about ready to land. Beverage carts stowed, seat backs upright, tray tables locked. The twenty-nine people on board would have just heard the engines change pitch and felt the nose dip slightly, seat belts tugging at their stomachs.

One imagines a focused cockpit. Pilot Larry Campbell was responsible for the safety of everyone on the flight, and this was just his second landing in the Bolivian city of La Paz. Copilot Ken Rhodes was a straightforward military man. No foolishness, especially when descending through a mountain valley in bad weather. Sitting behind both, flight engineer Mark Bird was a retired fighter jock. In the Air Force, he was known for buzzing the tower and other hijinks, but he'd joined Miami-based Eastern only a few months before, and during a tricky approach in the middle of a thunderstorm would not have been the moment to chime in.

On January 1, 1985, the mostly empty Boeing 727 was headed from Asunción, Paraguay, to Miami, with stopovers in Bolivia and Ecuador. Landing in La Paz was always difficult. Ground controllers there had no radar—and what navigational equipment they did have was spotty—so they relied on the cockpit crew to track their own position.

At 13,325 feet, El Alto International, which serves La Paz, is the highest international airport in the world. The air is so thin that planes land at 200 miles per hour because they would fall out of the sky at the usual 140. Air brakes find less purchase here, so the runway is more than twice the normal length. The airport is so high that, as the plane dropped toward La Paz, the pilots would have worn oxygen masks until they reached the gate, per FAA regulations. Passengers would have felt the altitude's effects as the cabin depressurized: increased heart rate, deeper breaths, fuzzy thoughts.

The last anyone heard from the jet was at 8:38 p.m. Eastern time. According to ground controllers, the flight was about thirty miles from the airport and cruising on track at roughly 20,000 feet. It was cleared to descend to 18,000 feet when it plowed straight into a mountain.

Mount Illimani, a 21,122-foot mass of rocks and glaciers rising from the eastern edge of Bolivia's Altiplano region, towers over La Paz. The Andean mountain is so textured by ridgelines, high peaks, and shadows that, viewed from the city, it seems to move and change shape throughout the day.

Flight 980 hit nose first on the back side of Illimani, just below the summit. It probably cartwheeled forward, the fuselage bursting and splattering across the mountain like a dry snowball hitting a tree. Nearby villagers said it shook the whole valley. The airport's radio registered only a single click.

It took a full day to locate the wreckage. Once the Bolivian air force saw it on the peak, it mobilized a team to get to the crash site, but a storm had dumped several feet of snow, and avalanches turned them back. The Bolivian team was soon followed by representatives of the U.S. embassy in La Paz and those from the National Transportation Safety Board (NTSB) and the Air Line Pilots Association (ALPA), the two organizations responsible for investigating crashes by U.S. airlines. But none of them were acclimatized enough to do any climbing. The agencies asked to borrow a high-altitude helicopter from Peru, but Bolivia wouldn't allow it inside the country.

"The Bolivian government did not want the world to know that the Peruvians had a better helicopter than they did," says Bud Leppard, chairman of the ALPA Accident Analysis Board, who departed for La Paz immediately after hearing about the crash. Eventually permission was granted, and Leppard devised a plan to reach the crash site by jumping off the helicopter as it flew above the ground at 21,000 feet, then skiing down to the plane. Better judgment prevailed when he realized that the chopper couldn't hover at that altitude.

Sikorsky Aircraft shipped an experimental high-altitude helicopter to Bolivia that could drop Leppard off at the crash site, but the mechanics sent to reassemble it were so altitude-sick upon landing in La Paz that several days passed before they could do any work. When they did get it flying, bad weather at the summit kept everyone in the chopper.

One Bolivian climber, Bernardo Guarachi, apparently made it up to the wreckage on foot two days after the crash but then said almost nothing about his findings. When the Bolivian government filed an official—but inconclusive—crash report a year later, Guarachi wasn't named in it. It was unclear who'd sent him in the first place.

Two months after the crash, in March 1985, a private expedition of Bolivian alpinists commissioned by Ray Valdes, an Eastern flight engineer who would have been on board if he hadn't swapped shifts, successfully navigated the treacherous mix of rock and ice. The small team encountered wreckage and luggage, but they couldn't locate the plane's black box. Stranger than that, no one found any bodies at the crash site. Or blood.

Another private expedition went up in July 1985, followed by NTSB investigators in October, but neither was able to spend more than a single day at the crash site.

In all, at least five expeditions have climbed Illimani in search of the wreckage over the past thirty years. None of them found any bodies or flight recorders, nor could anybody establish what brought down the plane. Officially, it was designated a "controlled flight into terrain," which means it couldn't be blamed on a bird strike or an engine malfunction or hijackers. The NTSB ultimately filed its own report to supplement the Bolivian one, but it came to the same flat conclusion: the plane was destroyed because it ran into a mountain.

As time passed, however, details emerged that invited speculation among South American journalists, the families of the victims, and anyone else still following the story. The flight crashed because of an equipment malfunction; no, the crew was new to the route and flying in bad weather; no, the Paraguayan mafia blew it up because the country's richest man was on board; no, Eastern Air Lines was running drugs; no, it was an attempted political assassination—someone took down the flight to get at the U.S. ambassador to Paraguay, Arthur Davis, who was supposed to be aboard but changed his plans at the last minute.

The thing is, even the more outlandish theories had some ring of truth. Five members of Paraguay's prominent Matalón family, who built an empire selling home appliances, were on the flight. The wife of the U.S. ambassador to Paraguay—Marian Davis, who had continued on without her husband—died in the crash. In 1986, a criminal indictment against twenty-two Eastern baggage handlers revealed that, for three years, the airline had indeed been used to deliver weekly shipments of 300 pounds of cocaine from South America to Miami. (Eastern declared bankruptcy in 1989 and dissolved in 1991.)

So the mystery deepened. Theories festered and grew. Where were the flight recorders? Where were the bodies?

One of the more comprehensive explanations came from George Jehn, a former Eastern pilot who published a 2014 book about the crash called *Final Destination: Disaster*. In it he theorizes that a bomb went off, depressurized the plane, and sucked all the bodies out of the cabin. Then he speculates that either Eastern or the NTSB hired Bernardo Guarachi to get rid of the flight recorders as a way of halting further inquiry into the crash, for fear that a full investigation would have revealed that the airline was running drugs for President Ronald Reagan. It's a convoluted plot, too farfetched to take seriously, but seductive as hell to those looking to explain the inexplicable.

"Not one body, not one body part, no bloodstains. Why not?" Jehn said when we spoke in May. "It's the single greatest aviation mystery of the twentieth century."

But the case of Flight 980 is about as cold as they come. Any remaining clues have been locked in the ice of a Bolivian glacier for decades. Trying to solve it would combine the dangers of high-altitude mountaineering with the long odds of treasure hunting—a losing hand almost every time. So here's another question worth asking: what sort of foolhardy seeker suddenly takes an interest in a thirty-year-old plane crash?

Dan Futrell is an affable, loud, heart-on-his-sleeve kind of guy. Impulsive. Persistent. In college he was the Gonzaga bulldog mascot

at basketball games, dancing and making costumed mischief during time-outs. After graduating in 2007, he served two tours in
Iraq. He completed Army Ranger School but decided to move on
to civilian life. Now thirty-three, he manages people and spread-
sheets for an Internet company in Boston, where he lives.

To say that he misses the physical challenge of soldiering is an
understatement, but that's his preface when you ask him what
kicked off his interest in the crash. Since leaving the Army, he's
made a habit of regularly scheduling sufferfests—he once took
aim at all seven peaks in New England named after presidents
and bagged them in one day. A little more than a year ago, he
stumbled across a Wikipedia list of unrecovered flight recorders.
Next to Eastern Air Lines Flight 980, the article listed "inaccessible
terrain" as the reason the flight recorders had never been found.

"Challenge accepted," he wrote on his blog.

Isaac Stoner, Dan's roommate, was the first to hear his let's-
go-find-it sales pitch. Though they've known each other only two
years, they act and argue like brothers. But where Dan has dark
hair, weary eyes, and an expressive face with many angles, Isaac has
the blond hair and classically handsome features of a small-market
news anchor. Dan is spontaneous and emotional; Isaac is calm and
analytical. After the Army, Dan attended grad school at Harvard;
Isaac worked in biotech and then went to MIT.

Finding the box sounded pretty good to Isaac. And it took priority over their other screwball ideas, like running a marathon in a
suit or attempting to set the world record in the pieathlon, a 3.14-
mile race in which you eat a whole pie.

Most people still tracking this plane crash have deeply personal,
often tragic reasons to care about it but very little capacity for travel
and risk. Dan and Isaac had no reason but the adventure. They
had no sponsorships, benefactors, or Kickstarter funding—just a
crazy plan, a bit of money in the bank, and two weeks' vacation.

The first step was to divvy up the responsibilities. Dan was in
charge of learning about the crash and its history, figuring out
where to start searching, and blogging about the trip. Isaac re-
searched the altitude, weather, skills they'd need to learn, and con-
tingencies if things didn't go smoothly—in short, he was tasked
with keeping them alive.

They embarked on a five-month training plan that consisted of
running stairs at the Harvard football stadium and sleeping in a

Hypoxico altitude-simulation tent. Four weeks before wheels up, a friend of a friend sent me a link to their blog and relayed that they'd be happy to have me along. Two days later, I was on the phone ordering my own altitude tent.

Our primary search area was not the crash site itself, but a roughly one-square-mile patch of glacial moraine 3,000 feet below it. Flight 980 hit a saddle on the south side of Illimani, near the top, and for the past thirty-one years plane parts have been sliding down the mountain in icefalls, plunging over a cliff, and then slowly grinding downhill toward a glacier at the bottom.

The Bolivian summer and fall of 2016 (the Northern Hemisphere's winter and spring) had been warm and rainy, and we were told that the glacier had melted far up the mountain. The moraine —and the wreckage—was more exposed than ever. We planned to spend four days searching the debris field at about 16,000 feet, then another searching the original crash site at 19,600 feet.

Which is how we find ourselves standing amid a heap of rental gear in a climbing shop in La Paz, three days after leaving the U.S. Off to one side, I'm nauseous and dizzy from climbing a single flight of stairs. We're at 13,000 feet, but to me it feels like the summit of Everest. Isaac says it looks like I got hit by a large bus. He says he got hit by a smaller one.

Meanwhile, our climbing guide, Robert Rauch, has fallen asleep in his camping chair. Fifty-nine years old, born in Germany but living in Bolivia for the past twenty years, Robert has pioneered more than a hundred routes in the country, including three on Illimani's south side. His house has an entire room devoted to equipment for different kinds of pull-ups. He does not own a couch. Dan calls him "the most interesting guide in the world."

Rauch had taken an interest in the crash as well. He'd traveled through the debris field while scouting routes on Illimani and thought that a concerted, methodical search of the area might turn up the recorders and bodies. "The whole area will lie in front of us like a Google map," he'd written in an email.

A few minutes later, our expedition's cook, Jose Lazo, shows up. He's Aymara—one of Bolivia's indigenous peoples—and he and Robert are soon telling stories about the time Jose was chased by a bear, the time Robert was chased by a condor, the time an angry mob chased the two of them out of Jose's village and they fled 300 miles in seven days, crossing jungles and alligator-infested rivers to get back to La Paz. Dan calls him "the most interesting cook in the world."

Back in the store, Isaac is trying to convince Dan to rent warmer snow pants; Dan is rolling his eyes. Robert is down to his skivvies, having dropped trou in the middle of the shop to rub his sore left knee with an herbal balm he bought on the street.

I'm still feeling queasy, resting on a box of something or other, when a climber with a man bun sits next to me and says that a week of wind sprints before we start will help me adapt to the altitude.

"When do you leave?" he asks.

"Tomorrow morning."

To get to Mount Illimani, we tie our bags to the roof of a rented Land Cruiser and tell the driver to head south from La Paz, following the Irpavi River all the way down to 3,000 feet, where the air feels soupy and rich and our pulses finally find the low side of seventy. I feel remarkably better. Then we cross the river and drive to 12,000.

At least it's a rest day. Our only responsibility is riding in a car and then unloading our overstuffed backpacks and duffel bags at Mesa Khala, an abandoned tungsten mine at 15,400 feet that's a forty-five-minute hike from the lower debris field. As we drive up the other side of the steep valley, past an active uranium mine, we round a corner and see fifty yards of impassable rock blocking the road.

"What if we just drive faster?" Dan says.

We're still two miles and about 3,000 vertical feet below our base camp at Mesa Khala, and we're going to have to hike it. So much for the rest day.

Dan and Robert walk to the uranium mine and return ten minutes later.

"*Cinco* porters-o," Dan tells us, exhausting his knowledge of Spanish. "They'll carry our shit-o. Up the mountain-o."

This is great news, except we packed like we were driving all the way to base camp, so even five porters won't be enough. "This is how Livingstone traveled," Isaac says, surveying the explosion of gear as we hastily jettison nonessential items—candy, notebooks, an extra stove, more candy—to send back in the 4x4.

The ascent doesn't kill us, but it tries. Jose sets the route, and it turns out that Aymara-style climbing consists of walking straight up the fall line. By the halfway point, I'm resting every few steps.

Four hours later, we've covered the two miles to Mesa Khala. Setting up camp among the ruins, we find plane parts that locals must have brought to the mine from the debris field. Scrutinizing and discussing each one in detail, we're transfixed, as if this random piece of aluminum tubing or that tiny drive shaft or the mechanism from an inflatable life vest might shed light on what brought down the aircraft.

The next morning, we hike to the steep glacial moraine that marks the edge of the debris field and find more parts on the ridge. It's exciting. This is exactly what Dan and Isaac spent five months imagining a Bolivian mystery adventure would be like — scattered clues leading to a search area laid out in front of them like a Google map.

In fact, it was only recently that this trip went from being a simple treasure hunt to something heavier, a story about tangible grief and unexplainable loss. Only recently did they meet Stacey Greer.

Greer has a few very specific memories of her dad, flight engineer Mark Bird. Talking on his radio. Eskimo kisses. The two of them snuggling in his recliner. She was three years old when the plane crashed.

"My mom didn't really talk about it a lot," Greer told me when I called her at her home in Fort Benning, Georgia, a few weeks before we left for Bolivia. "She just said that he had been in a plane crash. As a kid, your imagination runs wild. You always ask yourself, Why couldn't he just jump out of the plane? Crazy stuff like that."

She didn't fully understand what had happened until she watched the video of his memorial service as a teenager.

"It was just my dad's flight helmet and a picture of him. It clicked," she said. "There was no casket. There was no body."

In the past few years, Greer, now thirty-four, has started questioning the official narrative that the crash site was too difficult and dangerous to reach. She read George Jehn's book and contacted him by email; he sent her a link to Dan and Isaac's blog. A former Army nurse who met her husband in Iraq, she forged a quick connection with Dan, who was also in the Army and raised by a single parent.

But where Dan carefully avoids any mention of conspiracy, favoring a more straightforward interpretation of the crash, Greer seems to have embraced the idea.

"It's the only plane crash that has never been properly investigated by the NTSB," she said. "And then a few years later, Eastern goes under."

In total, Flight 980 carried nineteen passengers and ten crew. Eight were Americans, five of whom worked for Eastern, and seven were Paraguayans, five of whom were part of the Matalón family. There were also nine Korean passengers and five Chilean flight attendants.

With seating for 189 passengers, the crash could have been far more deadly, and Greer never heard from any of the other families. To her it felt like everything was immediately swept under the rug. The missing bodies aren't so much a mystery as a sign that the general public stopped caring.

"People need closure," she said. "Imagine one of your family members on the mountain for years, and their body has been frozen over and over and over again."

Robert finds the first body part. It's a femur, roughly fourteen inches long and so dry that it's almost mummified. You can see skin, muscle, and fat still attached.

"That's pretty gruesome," Dan says. "It just sheared right off in the crash."

Encased in ice for more than a quarter-century, the bone likely spent several years sliding down the mountain from the crash site, several seconds falling over a 3,000-foot cliff, and—judging by the milky white marrow still visible inside the bone and its location at the base of a rapidly melting glacier—perhaps only months in the sun before being found by us. It's 1:00 p.m. on our first day of searching.

"Shall we say some words?" Isaac asks.

Sure, but no one can really think of anything.

"Shall we bury it?" Dan says.

They dig a small grave, stacking rocks as a marker. Not long after, we find another bone—probably a tibia. Then, a few feet away, cervical vertebrae with frayed nerves still visible down the spinal column.

As we search, the temperature swings wildly between T-shirt

weather in the sun and down-jacket weather in the shade. Every hour or so, a massive block of ice—possibly carrying more plane parts—drops off the saddle and roars toward us before disintegrating into a sugary white cloud.

Our plan was to walk a precise and thorough grid. But the search area is longer and thinner than we anticipated, a lifeless alpine moraine filled with boulder gardens and ice fields, walled off on three sides by vertical rock. Sixty-foot-tall glacier fragments and ten-foot-deep canyons force us off our pattern. So instead we spend the morning scrambling between pieces of wreckage on our own, congregating whenever anyone finds something interesting.

This happens quite a bit. There are plane parts everywhere. First we discover pieces of fuselage and a jet engine, then wiring and toggle switches and seat belts and children's shoes. Then Robert finds a black plastic box.

"That's a black box," Isaac says when Robert holds it up. "Not *the* black box."

We see an astonishing number of contraband crocodile and snake skins, which were probably being smuggled to Miami to be made into black-market goods like shoes and handbags.

Dan gets on the radio to tell us that he found a roll of magnetic tape. "This is either from one of the black boxes," he says, "or it has a great 1985 movie on it."

Isaac and Dan also both find a few chunks of orange metal, which is exciting because—despite the name—flight recorders are painted international orange to help investigators locate them. But the pieces seem too trashed to have come from supposedly indestructible boxes.

Most planes carry two flight recorders: the cockpit voice recorder, which documents conversation among the pilots and the engineer, and the flight-data recorder, which notes the status of the plane's mechanical systems several times per second.

Current specifications require that a flight recorder's metal case be capable of withstanding temperatures of 2,000 degrees, underwater depths of 20,000 feet, and impacts up to 3,400 times the force of gravity. To hit these marks, the outer shell is made from a blend of titanium and steel. It also must have an underwater locator beacon that emits a ping for thirty days.

These standards weren't so rigorous and uniform in 1985, and we couldn't nail down which type of recorders were on Flight 980, in part because the airline has been shuttered for twenty-seven years. Most of Eastern's planes used a model of flight recorder manufactured by Fairchild that recorded via magnetic tape. But not all of them. So aside from the color, we aren't really sure what the black box will look like.

Dan is adamant that the orange metal pieces are part of the flight recorders—but they're aluminum, not titanium or steel. The metal must be a piece of something else on the plane; the tape could just be a home video, stashed in luggage. It feels like our discoveries have only prompted more questions: What happened on all those other expeditions? Why didn't they find any body parts? And could you believe all those snakeskins?

In La Paz, the theories surrounding Flight 980 have less to do with missing bodies and cover-ups and more with the dubious rumor that Enrique Matalón—then the richest man in Paraguay—supposedly carried $20 million on board in a duffel bag.

In 2006, a Bolivian climbing guide named Roberto Gomez got wind that plane parts were turning up in the glacier below the crash site. If the wreckage was turning up, he thought there might also be a bag of money. Gomez and his team spent three days searching the glacier.

"The strangest thing we found was lizard skins," Gomez says when we meet in his office in La Paz. "But it was a really sad scene, because we found a lot of children's clothes, and many pictures."

As Gomez tells his story, it's clear that the Bolivian and American versions of this mystery diverge fairly quickly. The only place they overlap is at the beginning, when Bernardo Guarachi made it to the crash site and then clammed up about what he saw there.

In his book, George Jehn has a lot of questions for Guarachi. "Was he paid? If so, who paid him?" he writes. "What was his specific mission? What did he discover? Did he take pictures? Did he see or recover the recorders? Why didn't the NTSB demand answers to these important questions?"

Oddly, though, Jehn never actually attempted to find Guarachi, even though he's a fairly prominent climbing guide in Bolivia and is open to being interviewed when I contact him.

Born in Bolivia but raised in Chile, Guarachi returned to La Paz to look for work when he was nineteen. After being taken in by a more experienced guide in Bolivia, he went to Germany for formal training as a mountaineer and came home looking to make his name. He introduced himself at various organizations and said he was available if they ever needed help in the mountains.

He tells me that a man named Royce Fichte from the U.S. embassy contacted him after a Bolivian plane spotted the wreckage of Flight 980 the day after the crash. They met at the airport on short notice—Guarachi didn't even have time to grab a camera—and took a helicopter toward the mountain. By the time they arrived at Puente Roto, a base camp on the west side, there were already teams assembling from the Red Cross and the Bolivian military.

The team stayed there that night, and the next day Guarachi and two assistants climbed to the crash site while Fichte stayed behind. Partway up, someone on the radio told them to turn around —he wasn't sure who it was—but Guarachi insisted and finally got permission to keep going. After climbing to the saddle beyond the summit, he could tell they were getting close from the overpowering smell of jet fuel, but he couldn't see the plane. It was only during a tiny break in the weather that he caught a glimpse and hiked over.

There was wreckage scattered everywhere. The team found open suitcases, papers from the cockpit, crocodile skins, and shoes. Fichte had described where the flight recorders should be, but everything was a mess.

"When you went to the crash site, did you see body parts?" I ask him.

"No bodies," he says. "Not even a finger. But there was blood. The plane hit the mountain dead-on. Everything disintegrated."

They slept at the crash site and the next day got word that they would be resupplied from the air and possibly joined by another investigator, who would drop out of a high-altitude helicopter on skis—probably Bud Leppard. But during test runs, the maneuvers were deemed too dangerous, and the supplies never came. Guarachi and his team had to descend.

On the way back down, they saw footprints at their previous camp. They had been followed, but whoever it was didn't continue to the crash site. They just stopped at the camp and left.

"I don't think their intention was to rescue us or see what happened to the plane," Guarachi says. "They were monitoring us."

At base camp, Guarachi's team was detained by the Bolivian military, separated, and taken to three different tents.

"They searched us all," Guarachi says. "My backpack, even our clothing. They got us naked."

He told them that all he'd found were plane parts and snake-skins. They were taken by helicopter to the airport and interrogated again. The official Bolivian crash report states that there were no bodies or blood, but Guarachi says that's because he was too scared to talk about what he saw.

"One of the men threatened me," Guarachi says. "He said, 'Careful telling anyone about this. I will ruin you.'"

We start higher on the search field the next day, marching with purpose toward the glacier. Yesterday it felt like the plane parts were in better shape the higher we climbed, so we start by searching the melting ice itself. Soon we're finding wheels, pistons, switches, hydraulics, another engine, life jackets, an oxygen tank, cables, alligator skins, and tangled clusters of wires.

Dan and Robert find a piece of metal lodged in ice, chip it out, and then decide not to do that again—there's not enough oxygen up here to swing a pickax around. By midmorning we're all thoroughly exhausted, and the novelty of new plane parts has worn off. Back at camp, it felt sort of miraculous to discover wreckage on a mountain, like each piece deserved our attention. But here, in the newly melted ice, there's an almost comical number of parts.

"I think something happened here," Isaac deadpans.

"Maybe a plane crash of some kind?" Dan responds.

You can hardly sit and rest without finding something aviation-related in the rocks at your feet. Jose and Robert find a pilot's jacket half buried in the glacier and start digging it out. Twenty minutes later, I find the cabin's altimeter.

On the way back to our packs for lunch, Isaac spots a lump of green cloth tied off with thick white yarn and begins to unwrap it.

"I hope it's not a body part," Isaac says, embracing the gallows humor that has become a mainstay of the trip. "No body, no body, no body . . ."

I point out that it's more likely to be cocaine.

"Cocaine!" Isaac says, comically hopeful. "Cocaine, cocaine, cocaine!"

It isn't cocaine. It's a brick of papers in a ziplock bag. And a

1985 Baltimore Orioles schedule. And a plastic toy. And some crayons. And pages from a diary?

Oh. No way. This belongs to Judith Kelly.

In July 1985, Judith Kelly made the second private expedition to the crash site. Her husband, William Kelly, had been director of the Peace Corps in Paraguay and was on Flight 980, headed back to the U.S. When the NTSB's immediate response was stymied by weather and logistics, Kelly began preparing for her own trip.

She devoted three months to getting in shape, took a mountaineering course in Alaska, and then went to Bolivia. Kelly declined to be interviewed for this article, but she told her story to George Jehn. In his book, Jehn describes how she met with NTSB investigator Jack Young, who died in 2005. Young reportedly told her to move on and put the loss behind her.

"Perhaps you could say that to someone with a broken arm or leg," she told Jehn. "But not a broken heart."

Kelly took a few weeks to acclimatize in Bolivia before hiring Bernardo Guarachi to take her up the mountain. They arrived at the wreckage on July 5, and Kelly spent a day reading letters she had written to her husband since the crash. She had also collected letters from the family of other victims. When she was done, she wrapped the package and buried it in the snow, where it began the same slow descent as the plane parts.

Back home, Kelly lobbied Eastern to conduct a more thorough investigation. She'd reached the crash site without any problems, she argued, so there was no reason not to send another team. When that failed, she appeared on the *Today* show and said the same thing.

A few days later, the NTSB announced an expedition, which embarked in October 1985, after the Bolivian winter, with logistical support from the Bolivian Red Cross. According to a report by lead investigator Gregory Feith, the mission was nearly its own disaster. It describes how, on the first night, porters delivered their supplies to the wrong base camp. When the two parties did connect, they found that the porters had brought tents for only four of the seven people and no stoves or fuel.

"We were able to melt enough snow to make one pot of cold noodle soup that allowed each of us one cup," Feith wrote.

One investigator developed signs of pulmonary edema—a life-threatening accumulation of fluid in the lungs—and had to descend the next morning; another developed altitude sickness at the crash site. Feith's team spent a day digging through deep snow around the plane and located the portion of the tail where the flight recorders should have been but weren't.

It would be decades before anyone went looking for them again.

After finding so much—wreckage, body parts, Judith Kelly's memorial—Isaac starts to think that the flight recorders have to be here somewhere.

"A couple days ago, I would have told you—I think I did tell you—that I don't really care about finding the black box," he says. "But I find myself becoming more and more obsessed."

The next day, Dan is low-energy, but Isaac's on fire, scrambling around the debris field trying to cover it all. We crawl through glacier ice melted into curious spires. We hop over crevasses and peer into glacial caves, because we've exhausted all the safest places to search.

"Have you found it yet?" Dan and Isaac ask each other every few minutes.

"No, but I'm about to," the other invariably responds.

At one point, Dan finds a human neck with what looks like a dog tag embedded in the flesh. But when he digs the metal out, it turns out to be just another piece of aluminum. "I was hoping I could get an ID," Dan says. "But this unlucky guy just took some plane metal straight to the neck."

By midday we're beat. Isaac walks 150 yards to his gear and barely makes it back to the group; Dan sits down next to an engine. I can't stand without feeling like I've stepped onto a merry-go-round. We give up. Jose and Robert head back to camp to start dinner; Dan and Isaac say they just want to search a little longer.

But instead of searching, they start digging up a metal beam angled out of the ground. When I ask them why, Isaac says, "I don't know, I just started digging."

Just as we're beginning to accept that we've failed, that we still don't know whether the flight recorders were stolen or destroyed or maybe still covered in ice, that we've given up and will have nothing to tell Stacey Greer and George Jehn and all the other people who are still following the crash . . . Just as we're coming to terms with all that, something amazing happens: Isaac finds the cockpit voice recorder.

It's on the ground, ten steps from where we ate lunch, a chunk of smashed metal sitting orange side down in the rocks. Isaac picks it up. Dan comes over to examine it.

There's a wiring harness on one end, with a group of cables leading inside, labeled CKPT VO RCDR. It's bright orange, crushed almost beyond recognition. Like many recorders manufactured before the mid-eighties, its outer shell is made of aluminum.

"This is it, this is the black box," Isaac says.

We've been finding pieces of it—of both flight recorders—the entire time.

When we get back to La Paz, Dan and Isaac call Stacey Greer. "Why didn't anyone find it before?" she says. "It just feels like there are so many unanswered questions."

Indeed. Why didn't anyone find the flight recorders on the first, second, or third expeditions? Who threatened Bernardo Guarachi and why? Who was smuggling reptile skins to Miami? What brought the plane down in the first place?

Flying home, we thought we still might have a shot at answering the last one. We had that roll of magnetic tape Dan found on the first day of searching. And based on nothing more than photos we could find online, it looked pretty similar to what would have been inside a flight recorder.

Before we found anything, the plan had been to turn all notable materials over to the U.S. embassy in La Paz. But with orange metal in hand, giving them to a bureaucrat seemed like a good way to get them locked away forever.

When Dan and Isaac got home, they told a friend who had worked at the FAA about what they'd found, and he said, "I just hope you didn't bring it home."

By taking the flight recorders and tape back to the U.S., they discovered, they had violated Annex 13 of the Convention on International Civil Aviation, a document that lays out the rules for international air travel. It says that wherever a plane crashes, that country is in charge of the investigation. Moving evidence to a different nation could be seen as undermining that authority.

The NTSB told Dan and Isaac that the Bolivian government

would have to request the agency's assistance before it could get involved, and it's the only agency with equipment to analyze the tape.

Unfortunately, relations between Bolivia and the U.S. are pretty frosty. In 2008, Bolivian president Evo Morales accused both the U.S. ambassador to Bolivia and the Drug Enforcement Administration of plotting a coup and expelled them from the country. Then, in 2013, Morales's personal plane was forced to land in Austria because of a rumor that Edward Snowden was on board. Morales was so mad he threatened to close the U.S. embassy.

I tried reaching out to retired crash investigators at Boeing and to various aviation museums, hoping that someone might help us figure out whether the tape was from the black box, but no one would touch it until the legal situation was resolved. Meanwhile, we couldn't get any answers out of La Paz or the Bolivian embassy in Washington. From June to September of 2016, we made phone calls that weren't returned, sent emails that weren't acknowledged, and mailed certified letters that went unanswered.

"This surprises me not one iota," George Jehn wrote in an email when I sent him an update. "It's like that crash is toxic. Nobody wants to go near it."

Conspiracies breed in the spaces between solid facts, and unless the NTSB decides to further strain diplomatic ties with Bolivia or gets permission to look at the tape and finds usable information —and both scenarios seem pretty unlikely—there will always be gaps in the story of Flight 980. But when you're solving mysteries, the simplest explanation tends to be the right one. After we got back from Bolivia, we knew that Guarachi didn't steal the flight recorders and that a bomb didn't suck all the bodies from the plane before it hit the mountain. As we reevaluated the facts about the flight, a plausible story began to emerge.

The descent into La Paz, for example, was even more difficult than we first realized. In addition to the lack of radar at the airport, language problems sometimes plagued communication between flight crews and controllers on the ground. When Eastern purchased the routes to South America, it issued a memo warning pilots to exercise a "dose of pilot type skepticism" when in contact with the tower. There was little training on how to do this, however. Before going into La Paz, the captain was required only to watch a video about the landing. Then, on his first trip, a check pilot—someone who had flown the route before—would ride in the cockpit.

Flight 980 crashed on what would have been pilot Larry Campbell's second landing in La Paz. Check captain Joseph Loseth was aboard but had been seated in first class.

What's more, the navigation technology at Campbell's disposal was rudimentary. Nine months after the crash, Don McClure, the chairman of the ALPA's accident-investigation board, was part of a separate inquiry into the overall safety of flying in South America. His report details a number of shortcomings, particularly with an onboard navigation system called Omega. He noted that on flights between Paraguay and Bolivia, the system steered aircraft four miles off course in the direction of Mount Illimani—though this alone wouldn't have caused Flight 980's impact.

Meanwhile, the aircraft's other navigation system, called VOR for very high frequency omnidirectional range, relied on localized radio transmitters that told pilots only where the beacons were, not where the plane was.

"All the navigation facilities on this route are so weak and unreliable that there is no good way to cross-check the Omega," McClure wrote. Even if the pilots suspected that they were off course, it would have been impossible to verify.

Maybe none of this would have mattered if there wasn't also a storm southeast of the airport. Maybe a more experienced crew would have gone south around that storm instead of north, toward Illimani. (Or maybe not—other airlines had maps of the valley with terrain hazards labeled prominently, but Eastern didn't.) We can speculate that the storm, combined with lackluster navigation equipment, inexperience, and bad luck, led Flight 980 straight into the side of Illimani, but it's still conjecture. Instead of case closed, it's case slightly less open.

Or maybe that's missing the real point. In July, Stacey Greer was in Boston for a week of classes and met up with Dan to talk about the expedition and look at pictures of the debris field. He also brought a couple of small plane parts and gave them to her.

"This is my dad, right here," Stacey said as Dan clunked the pieces down on the table. "This is the closest thing I have to the last time I saw him."

When her young kids called at bedtime, she had them talk with "the man who found Grandpa's plane." Then she and Dan called her mom, Mark Bird's widow.

"Do you have any idea what happened?" she asked.

"We have lots of ideas," Dan said. "The problem is we're no better than anyone else at picking the right one."

But now that there's evidence of the bodies and flight recorders, and any notions of mysterious journeys to the summit have been dispelled, the questions we're left with seem much less nefarious.

Did a storm push the flight off course, or was it a problem with the navigation systems? Did the cockpit crew spot the mountain and try to make a frantic emergency turn? Or were they calmly pulling on the oxygen masks that they would have worn all the way to the gate? Were they sitting in nervous silence as lightning flashed around them and weather beat at the cockpit? Or was Mark Bird wishing everyone a happy new year and telling a joke? If his voice is on the magnetic tape sitting in Dan and Isaac's kitchen, will anyone ever hear it?

The Ones Who Left

FROM *The Offing*

DAD AND I climb off the tram and land in a puddle. I am hunched under a creaking, insubstantial umbrella. Dad keeps the hood of his raincoat up. It is an hour before we are due at dinner and we are wandering through a quiet Amsterdam neighborhood looking for Hans Hedeman-Kalker's house.

I am there to hold the umbrella while my dad stands on the sidewalk and consults damp Google Maps printouts, old school. He planned our days in the Netherlands around nine such printouts. He did his research back in Kansas, ordering the chaos of barely familiar names.

By the time we find the house, the rain has subsided and a hush has fallen over this corner of the city. Amsterdam, under rain and far from tourist coffee shops, is as sweet-smelling as a city can be. Jacob Obrecht Straat is a brick-lined street with brick houses and dripping shade trees. The buildings are all Art Deco right angles, pristine facades with white trim. Number 53, when we approach it, is just like the rest.

We stand in front of it in silence for a few seconds. We don't ring the doorbell or knock. Hans Hedeman-Kalker doesn't live there anymore. She hasn't lived there, or anywhere, since 1942 when she was taken from her home and sent off to Auschwitz to be killed.

"Should we take a picture?" Dad asks.

"Would that be weird?"

We stand a little longer.

We're not on the kind of pilgrimage that ends at a wall or a well

or a shrine. Until relatively recently, we hadn't heard of most of
the stops on our journey. We aren't even sure if these Hedemans
are related to us. But I have quit my job in Chicago and I am
home for the summer, and my belongings are sitting in the basement of my parents' house awaiting a move to Columbus in the
fall, and when will I be able to do something like this again: drop
everything and leave with my dad?

"I'm going to take a picture," says Dad.

I hold up a piece of paper with Hans Hedeman-Kalker's name
written on it. It serves at first as a practical marker; when we get
back home and we're showing the pictures to Mom, we'll be able
to tell her who lived where without consulting one of Dad's many
notecards. With time these sheets of paper transform into something different, some well-meaning, incomplete digital memorial.

But this is the first picture, and I feel uncomfortable, unexpectedly teary and a little silly, standing there with my rain-spattered
half sheet. Maybe it's the weather, or the silence, or the weight of
our project beginning to sink in. I wonder whether we are memo-
rializing these Hedemans for selfish reasons. We're German, they
were Dutch. Our Hedemans were Protestant, the Dutch Hedemans were Jewish. In Germany, our name ended with an extra *n*.
In the Netherlands, it's been Hedeman all along.

We didn't expect to be stopped in our tracks like this. Behind
the camera, I can see that Dad, too, is moved. He's gone bright
red. His jaw is working. We don't share a name with our ancestors.
We share a name with Hans Hedeman-Kalker, and the others on
Dad's list. We are going to visit every single place on the list and
repeat these motions because maybe no one else is.

A car horn sounds on a nearby street and jolts us both into action. I notice it has begun to rain again and I unfurl my umbrella.
"It's a beautiful street," says Dad, and we leave it.

Over dinner, I ask Dad to tell the story again, the story that explains how we got the idea to come to the Netherlands on the trail
of the Dutch Hedemans. The story has its limitations. It doesn't
fully explain what we're doing here, or how to begin to understand our need.

"I was in Berlin," he begins.

Envision him: my dad, gray-haired, tall, and slouching, loud
talker and fast walker, walking fast all over Berlin, a place he hasn't

visited since before the wall fell. He is there to visit a friend and has a few hours to himself, so he traces the wall's foundations, marvels at a seamless unification, and eventually wanders his way into the Memorial to the Murdered Jews of Europe. Underground, in the information center, he finds a row of monitors where visitors may search for victims' names. Curious, he types in the name Hedemann and is unsurprised when the search yields no results. It is a weekday and the museum is deserted with no one else waiting for a turn, so Dad makes another search. On a whim, he types in Hedeman.

The names come immediately. They cover the screen.

Alfred Hedeman, Born 19 Nov 1877, Lived Almelo, Netherlands, Died 15 Mar 1945 Midden-Europa. Debora Julia Hedeman, Born 8 Aug 1901, Lived Ootmarsum, Netherlands, Died 9 Apr 1943 Sobibor. Hanme Hedeman, Born 3 Jun 1920, Lived The Hague, Netherlands, Died 31 Jul 1944 Auschwitz. Hartog Hedeman, Born 26 Apr 1866, Lived Ootmarsum, Netherlands, Died 26 Mar 1943 Sobibor. Hugo Hedeman, Born 18 Oct 1891, Lived Almelo, Netherlands, Died 12 Oct 1944 Auschwitz. Johan Herman Hedeman, Born 20 Mar 1896, Lived Zwolle, Netherlands, Died 30 Apr 1943 Sobibor. Joost Hedeman, Born 26 Oct 1917, Lived Enschede, Netherlands, Died 28 Sep 1942 Monowitz. Julia Estella Hedeman, Born 18 Jun 1925, Lived Rotterdam, Netherlands, Died 30 Sep 1942 Auschwitz. Sophie Celine Hedeman, Born 20 Jul 1920, Lived Enschede, Netherlands, Died 12 Oct 1944 Auschwitz. Hans Hedeman-Kalker, Born 20 Mar 1918, Lived Amsterdam, Netherlands, Died 28 Sep 1942 Auschwitz. Johanna Hedeman-Rosendaal, Born 1 May 1891, Lived Enschede, Netherlands, Died 12 Oct 1944 Auschwitz. Selma Hedeman-Stofkooper, Born 17 Sep 1894, Lived Enschede, Netherlands, Died 7 May 1943 Sobibor. Bertha Hedeman-Zilversmit, Born 2 Mar 1862, Lived Hengelo, Netherlands, Died 9 Apr 1943 Sobibor.

Dad stares at the monitor. There is his own name, John, Johan in Dutch. There is someone with his niece's name, Julia. And there is his own precious, unusual last name, confounder of German teachers the world over: "What does Hedeman mean?" we ask them. "I don't know," they reply. "Nothing. It doesn't mean anything."

At dinner, in Amsterdam, Dad takes a sip of his beer. "This felt completely different from finding out about that rodeo rider, Tuff

Hedeman. That was cool. This was something else. I'm not sure if I still feel this way, but standing at that monitor I kept thinking, 'We're related. We have to be related.'"

My thinking vacillates more or less on the hour. I wasn't in Berlin. The only list of names I've seen is the list my dad made, and I first came face to face with it not in a cold and underground memorial but in the fluorescent glare of my cubicle in Chicago, a Jimmy John's sandwich halfway to my mouth. I got chills, but they were chills of interest, of a project sighted.

I want us to be related, and that wanting troubles me. We are laying claim to dead strangers. It is a peculiar kind of wishful thinking, to wish oneself related to the violently murdered, and sitting opposite Dad in an Amsterdam restaurant, I try to believe I'm here for any reason beyond the story I'll be able to tell when I get home.

Other people do genealogy. Ruth Hedeman combed over immigration documents and shipboard manifests, birth certificates and death certificates and marriage certificates. She was my great-grandfather's niece, and she kept everything in a file, and the file sat in Baltimore until some other, later Hedeman photocopied the contents and shared a version with families of Hedemans across the country.

This was not a burdensome task. Our family, my family, the John-and-Anne D.-and-Jackie Hedeman family, is the only family of Hedemans to live more than twenty miles from the Inner Harbor. Marooned (or so the rest of the Hedemans would have it) in the middle of the country, we are anomalies. Hedemans are drawn to water, despite the fact that they (we) are long and uncoordinated and prone to seasickness. Hedemans are drawn to boardwalks and seafood and bottle cap poker chips. They are drawn *downy oshun* even when they live close enough to smell the salt over the beltway. Their skin burns before it tans and they retreat for afternoon naps and televised baseball. They love the Orioles. They love each other.

According to Ruth Hedeman's research, we are who we are because Hermann Heinrich Hedemann, formerly of Badbergen, Germany, stepped off the boat in Baltimore and changed his name to Henry Hedeman. Henry left Badbergen in the early 1820s. Hedemanns who stayed in Germany would have fought in the Austro-

Prussian War, in the Franco-Prussian War, in World War I, and in
World War II. In Baltimore, my grandfather, born in 1901, was too
young for the First World War and too old for the second. In Germany, a Hedeman his age, with some small portion of his eventual
genetic makeup, might have taken part in both. Because Henry
left Germany, the Hedemans—my Hedemans, the Hedemans who
show in my face and my attitude and my disproportionately tiny
wrists—were spared participation in a traumatic war, or two, or
four, but they (we) were also spared complicity in the deaths of the
Dutch Hedemans who share our name.

But they (we) also arrived in Maryland, a slaveholding state, and
while Ruth Hedeman's genealogical research is silent on the subject of what Henry Hedeman's family got up to in the years leading
up to the Civil War, I think I would have heard if they were aboli-
tionists. I know that Henry Hedeman died in 1843, and was buried
in the German cemetery, which was bulldozed thirty years later to
make room for Johns Hopkins Hospital. One hundred years after
Henry Hedeman was buried, Johns Hopkins was where first my
uncle, and then my dad, was born.

A word about Hedeman Luck. I think we were the first to put a
name to the phenomenon, "we" being John-and-Anne D.-and-
Jackie, a unit which, definitely to outsiders and sometimes even to
ourselves, appears to be the perfect distillation of Hedeman Luck.

Hedeman Luck might not actually be luck. Or it might not
always be luck. Hedeman Luck provides us with parking spaces
near the front, with deals on prom dresses, with fascinating conversation partners, with all the trappings of right-place-right-time.
Hedeman Luck has also been extended to explain the sequence of
events by which my parents—both scholarship kids, my mother in
the second coeducated class and not yet even a Hedeman—managed to find each other within a week of being on the same college
campus. Although there, on that campus, or maybe before arriving there, Hedeman Luck starts to look like Hedeman Privilege.
Certainly by the time I arrived on that same college campus thirty-
three years after my parents left it, luck played an increasingly in-
significant role in getting me there. Yet that is what we continue to
call it, the process-or-phenomenon by which things go well for us.

Luck: that washing of hands.

Let's say it was Hedeman Luck that propelled Henry Hedeman

out of Badbergen, onto the boat in Germany, and off the boat again in Baltimore. Ridiculous, perhaps, a stretch, but Hedeman Luck is an easier sell than gauzy fate. Hedeman Luck is the reason why, when Dad and I drive to Badbergen, Germany, and immediately find the World War I Memorial, we can stand beside it and examine it and not find a single name we recognize.

This side trip to Badbergen is a journey of confirmation. We don't want to read Hedemann on the memorial, and we don't expect to, and standing in the rain, examining a standing, stone soldier, I am forced to admit the truth to myself. I want to be related to the Dutch Hedemans, it is to further let my family off the hook. "Look," I could say, "I know we landed in a slave state, and I know we got along and had intact families and moved to the suburbs and dabbled in the Ivy League and survived, but . . ." But that sentence is unfinishable, an offensive tally sheet of wrongs and rights. Long-dead relatives, far-removed, do nothing to change the hash marks accumulated during a happy childhood and a serene adolescence and a burgeoning successful adulthood, and attempting to claim Hans Hedeman-Kalker to offset my own good fortune does violence to her memory. Better to admit to Hedeman Luck, and use it for something other than parking spaces. Better to stop spinning my wheels.

We travel to the Netherlands in search of strange Hedemans, but Badbergen is where we spend our last day, across the German border and a short drive from where we have been staying. We drive to Badbergen in our red, rented Fiat 500 and I am sneezing, fully stuffed up, run-down after days of searching. Nonetheless, I am still in charge of navigation, so I unwrap a cough drop and unfold the road map.

The Dutch Hedemans, those who never made it to Amsterdam or The Hague, clustered in the eastern part of the country, so the placement of Badbergen could be another stroke of Hedeman Luck, or it could be a piece of the shared name puzzle, or it could be both. The Hedemans and the Hedemanns lived in such close proximity that radio stations on both sides of the border overlap frequencies in bursts of Dutch-German static.

The map I hold in my lap during the drive to Badbergen is only the beginning of proof, but I examine it as if examining could bring the towns even closer together, bring our pilgrimage into sharper focus. Looking at the map, for the first time I feel comfortable voicing the possibility that at one point, perhaps a long, long, long time ago, we may have been the same family.

I say as much to Dad. "It's just so close. That can't be a coincidence."

"Geography is destiny," he says. Maybe it's supposed to be a reply. Maybe it's just something that's been rolling around in his head.

We have been to Johann Herman Hedeman's apartment building in the shadow of Amsterdam's Olympic Stadium. We have been to the site of Hartog Hedeman's last address, now an industrial high-rise decorated with Chinese characters in The Hague. Also in The Hague, we stopped and saw Hannie Hedeman's home on a quiet street overlooking a shaded park. In Ootmarsum, a tiny, beautiful town full of British tourists, we located the place where Rosetta Rijna Godshalk-Hedeman used to live. In Almelo, we took pictures in Hedemanplein, a square named after Hugo Hedeman, a textile merchant. In Enshede, we lingered outside Hugo, Johanna, Sophie, and Joost Hedeman's house. Sophie was my age when she was murdered. Now the church next door uses their house for community outreach. On a commercial strip not far away, we glanced up at the second-floor apartment of Selma Hedeman-Stofkooper. In Oldenzaal, we found where Bertha Hedeman-Zilversmit lived with her daughter, Debora Julia Hedeman. In Oldenzaal's City Hall, which sits on the site of a long-gone synagogue, we read Bertha's and Debora's names on a plaque commemorating the town's murdered Jews. It is the only such plaque we found.

We have no addresses for Badbergen, so our first stop is the Protestant church. That is where we find the World War I memorial, and the slightly smaller World War II memorial, hidden away in a corner of the church's graveyard. We read the memorials, and find nothing. It is raining again, and I am clutching a wet tissue, and for the first time on this trip I want to go home. We've seen the town, I think to myself. The Hedemanns left. That's the whole point. There's nothing to see. Those other places, those actual addresses, those views are where our project had meaning, not here in a muddy graveyard in an empty town.

But Dad has begun to walk up and down the rows of graves and so I join him. We are looking for pre-1820s headstones, but it seems pretty clear to me that the majority of these graves are from the latter half of the twentieth century. If there are older graves, they are unmarked, or they are somewhere else, maybe moved like Henry Hedeman's had been moved to make way for Johns Hopkins. Maybe, like him, the long-ago German Hedemanns rested under unmarked turf, undisturbed and unaware of everything going on above them. Still, we continue up and down the rows, in my case now mostly on autopilot, and we have covered almost the entire graveyard when Dad shouts.

And there it is, a shiny, marble headstone, apparently new but without a date. The branches of a holly bush obscure the words until Dad pulls them back. FAMILIE HEDEMANN, it reads. HILDA VEHSLAGE. URSULA CHRISTL. There are no other names, and no other graves.

Back in the Netherlands, in the hush of the darkened Oldenzaal City Hall lobby and on the bold, blue Hedemanplein street sign in Almelo, we saw our name, Hedeman, no second *n*, and we feel abstract sadness, imprecise connection, blanket curiosity. Here, in Badbergen, there are Hedemanns buried under the ground we stand on. They are our relatives. Their ancestors stayed when ours left. They weathered those things we congratulate ourselves on having dodged. And, even if they risked best-case acts of disobedience, or muttered behind closed doors, they still sat across the border as Hedeman after Dutch Hedeman was taken from their home and killed.

"Somebody stayed," I said, my cold and my wet Kleenex and my frustration forgotten.

"Yeah," said Dad. "Look. We found them."

There is a piece of the family history where Hedeman Luck either fails, or proves itself.

When Dad was seven years old, his father, who was spared both world wars, died of a brain aneurysm while sitting downstairs and watching *Wagon Train*. For weeks, Dad kept catching glimpses of him coming home from work down the alley, only to have the vision resolve itself into a different person, a younger man, a neighbor woman. My uncle, admitted to Wharton, turned Penn down and settled on the University of Baltimore, which kept him close to home and, to hear everyone but him tell it, abbreviated his potential. My grandmother, a nurse, worked around the clock to keep life running: Christmas, Easter, trips *downy oshun*.

When Dad was in junior high, my grandmother asked him to apply for a scholarship to McDonogh, one of Baltimore's premier boarding schools. Dad didn't want to trade his home "steps from Memorial Stadium" for a dorm full of entitled suburbanites, but my grandmother played on his vanity. "I bet you can't pass the entrance exam," she said. "I dare you to try." He passed. He was accepted. He went to McDonogh, where he made the kind of connections and got the kind of education that, in 1968, was what got you into Princeton. He went to Princeton. In his junior year, my mom arrived on campus.

When Dad was drafted to serve in Vietnam, one of his McDonogh connections got him into the National Guard, and another Hedeman was spared another war. Mom and Dad got married. Years later—years enough to allow for a dissertation and a professorship and two new jobs—I was born, healthy and right on time.

And on and on and on. Hedeman Luck admits tragedy. Hedeman Luck does not preclude choice, or the shaping of a story, but it acknowledges those forked-road moments, when events could have gone one way and instead turned toward the sun. My uncle, who stayed in Baltimore, lost Wharton but he gained a family and he kept crabs with Old Bay and the taste of the sea. My dad, who left Baltimore, returns and his accent is gone but he still knows every street. Even I visit Baltimore and am reminded just how much the city feels right, familiar.

But Baltimore is a secondhand home, and Germany is just another country, and I am where I am, and who I am, because of the ones who left. My life admits what they did and didn't have to do to get me here.

We drive away from Badbergen, stopping once we pass back into the Netherlands to take a picture of a windmill. From the parking lot, where our Fiat is the only car, we climb the hill to the windmill under a new wave of misty rain. I am back to sneezing, and all the tea I have been drinking to combat my cold has begun to have an effect. I glance around and contemplate the merits of squatting behind one of the scrubby bushes.

"I don't know what this adds up to," says Dad. He isn't talking about the windmill. "I guess in the back of my head I thought we'd come to the Netherlands and magically find something out."

I know what he means, although I can't quite believe either of us was ever so naive as to think we'd be granted that moment after so little effort, that after Googling a few things and booking a plane ticket, we'd arrive to a sign telling us, "Yes, John and Jackie Hedeman, yes, this, too, is your family. And this is what it means."

"Maybe if we did more research," I say. "Like, genealogical research."

"Maybe."

The windmill rotates lackadaisically, splattering rain with each pass. A barely noticeable fog tones down the intense redness of our Fiat at the bottom of the hill. A Dutch Master could have painted the whole scene.

Dad speaks again. "Even if I found out we weren't related to those Hedemans, I'd probably still feel the same way I felt when I first saw that list. I keep thinking about what it means to share a name."

Dad may as well ask what it means to be a family, an equally unanswerable question, although the asking makes me realize how glad I am that I came to be here, with him.

For the two of us, here, on the top of a hill in the Netherlands, sharing a name means climbing back down to our car and driving back to our bed and breakfast. It means waking up early the next day to return the car to Amsterdam and catching a cab to the airport. It means flying back to the United States and telling my mom the story and preparing a slide show to take with us the next time we visit Baltimore.

Look, we'll say. Look what we saw. There, and there, and there. Hedemans lived there.

The Big Leap

FROM *AFAR*

THE FLIGHT WAS fifteen minutes to San Pedro Town, in a fourteen-seat Cessna over crystalline waters, with the sky impossibly close at our shoulders and our life jackets folded into pockets at our knees. My husband, Charles, said the duct-taped sun visor over the pilot's seat looked like something from a '75 Chevy Vega. My daughter, Lily, tugged my sleeve and told me, nearly breathless, that we'd just gone *inside* a cloud. She was almost six and three-quarters, the salad days of six and a half receding behind us faster than the pink plush snake she'd begged for at the Belize City airport gift shop.

We'd spent the night in Houston, an unexpected layover after we missed our first flight from La Guardia because we didn't have a copy of Lily's mother's death certificate. You see, Lily is not my daughter by birth. She is simply the daughter I am helping to raise —as if *simply* could ever apply to her loss, or our family, or any family; as if you could control everything, or even really anything, about taking a six-year-old to an island 1,800 miles away. Travel is ultimately a series of intentional disruptions, and we found that our disruptions had been disrupted.

But now Ambergris Caye was appearing under us: its shimmering mangrove swamp and the long brown fingers of its jetties. We saw an unfinished spiral staircase made of concrete twisting into the sky. A small motorboat met us at the docks in San Pedro, where dark frigate birds hovered over the water as if suspended by strings, waiting for fishermen to clean their catch so they could dive for the scraps. The boat took us up the coast—salt wind in our faces—until we reached our resort, Coco Beach, an imposing flotilla of villas facing the ocean, their eerie prefab splendor like a record skipping in place: *villa, villa, villa.*

The resort's buildings, all peach stucco and crimson tiled roofs, flanked a terraced honeycomb of swimming pools, circled by saun-tering iguanas and urgently plural: a hot tub enclosed by a warm tub enclosed by a cool pool, a shallow moat around the swim-up bar. All this was just the *first* pool, actually. The second was a mas-sive lima bean that held a faux-rock centerpiece Lily would come to call "the rock-jumping valley," a tower that looked like outsize macramé, with hidden passageways and grottoes and cubbies, a concealed stairway, and—its pièce de résistance—an interior wa-terslide. If you've never paid this kind of attention to a pool fea-ture, then you've never traveled with a child.

Our hotel represented everything I hated about travel in the developing world: soulless luxury divorced from its context, profits funneled abroad. I had been to Central America before. As a six-teen-year-old, full of good intentions, I'd joined a service trip to a small Costa Rican village in the foothills of Chirripó, the country's tallest mountain. I'd stayed with a family and spent a month laying a concrete path between the main dirt road and the church. The only thing worse than my Spanish was my ability to mix concrete, and it became clear that my "service" was really an experience I had purchased—or my parents had. At twenty-three, I'd spent a summer in Nicaragua, teaching at a two-room schoolhouse out-side Granada and drinking my body weight in rum. In each case I had felt the limits of what I was doing—the fraught complexities of being a privileged do-gooder sojourning somewhere beautiful and impoverished—but at least I'd been doing something besides turning money into pleasure. I'd turned it into memories of altru-ism and unremembered nights of drunkenness. Those days had been restless and messy but also committed, however naively, to something besides my own enjoyment.

This trip to Belize, though, was committed to little but the delib-erate and ruthless pursuit of pleasure. Its only selflessness existed within the bounds of our own family: Charles and I were more committed to Lily's enjoyment than our own. I was still getting the hang of being a mom when we went to Belize. I'd been mar-ried to Charles for six months and had known his daughter just over a year. (Things had moved fast.) Lily and I had bonded from the start, which surprised me because I'd never spent time with kids or found myself particularly drawn to them. But she had been calling me "Mommy" for half a year, and I'd started seeing the world differently as I moved through it with her. Manhattan was suddenly full of playgrounds that had been invisible to me before, and crowded subway stations were suddenly places that could swallow a tiny body whole. The world felt full of more danger, more wonder, and less freedom.

We'd been through a huge year—a new marriage, a move to a new apartment, a newly forged motherhood—and it felt good to think that I might be able to give something to our family, some experience of giddy, visceral beauty. But it was the first trip I'd ever planned for all three of us, and I struggled with the fear that I'd do something wrong, something that betrayed my total misunderstanding of a child's needs or that suggested I was placing my needs or desires above hers. So I found myself planning a different kind of trip from any I'd ever taken before. Our double-pooled resort, our swim-up bar, our balcony—these felt like an insurance policy I badly needed.

Actually, we didn't have just one balcony—we had two. Our front deck overlooked a life-size chess set; our back deck perched above a construction site of stray lumber and debris piled onto a dirt yard, rebar gaping out of concrete shells. Something was being built here. On Ambergris Caye, it seemed as though something was being built everywhere. This is nothing new. Foreign interests have shaped the land now called Belize since the sixteenth century. English and Spanish are both widely spoken because the two colonial forces vied for control of its resources. The Spaniards were the ones who first stole the land from the Mayas, but the British kept doggedly going after its lumber anyway. It had other things too: sugar, bananas, oil. But these days the primary resource is beauty, and the main commodity is pleasure itself.

Our first night, we decided to rent a golf cart and drive it into town. I asked for directions and was told, "There is only one road. Take a left."

The golf cart had a half-drunk can of Belikin, Belize's local beer, in its cupholder and an accelerator you had to pump into compliance. It maxed out at something just shy of fifteen miles per hour. I loved it. I loved the wind in my hair and the lagoon to our right glimmering in the sunset, the liquid roots of mangroves curling into the water. We braked for thick ropes laid as makeshift speed bumps. We passed teenagers on bikes wearing decade-old NBA jerseys. We passed fruit stands with banana bunches hanging like bats in the shadows.

We stopped for dinner at a little roadside bar a mile out of town. Boat buoys hung from its thatched roof, Christmas lights looped around palm trunks, an old rusty anchor lay abandoned in the ferns. There was an empty birdcage with a tray full of peanuts and feathers caught in the wire, but no parrot in sight. The crescent moon was sharp, glowing pale, and the sky was like a naked version of our sky back home—as if its skin had been peeled away to show more stars.

We misted ourselves in an organic rose geranium bug spray made by a nonprofit that was offering a prize for the best photograph of the spray in an exotic locale. Lily was thrilled with this mission, a gauntlet thrown down at her small sandaled feet, and we would photograph this bug spray *everywhere*, like a tiny inanimate runway model in a series of photo shoots. We started right there at the bar, tucking it into a hammock behind a rotting fishing net. We ate coconut curry and pork chops that had been smoked in coconut shells. We heard a woman get in trouble for ordering a Red Stripe instead of a Belikin.

On the ride home, we picked up a hitchhiker—an old woman carrying groceries back home to a place called the Reggae Shack, a rusty trailer with light seeping like fluid from its seams. I spotted the silhouettes of scorpions crossing the highway, their raised tails black and regal in our golf-cart headlights.

By day, each day, we adventured. I rode in the copilot's seat of another tiny Cessna, with the pilot's orange soda at my knee and his flip-phone resting on the throttle between us. We flew over a rum distillery that rose like a metal pagoda from the green fields of cane. It had been owned, we were told, by a workers' union—which had been bought out recently by a company based in Florida.

We took a boat upriver to the Maya ruins at Lamanai, passing Mennonite farmers in overalls on break from building a massive barge for their sugar crops. (Sugar had long been Belize's biggest industry until tourism surpassed it.) We pulled over to the riverbank to pee. *Where's the bathroom?* Lily asked, expecting a building.

I taught her how to pee in the woods, as my mom had taught me. Our guide, Antonio, paused to hand out bananas to a group of boys harvesting ironwood. He pointed out sleeping sac-winged bats flattened like furry brown pancakes against the trunk of a dead tree. He gave us the full scoop on pretty much every plant in sight—the strangler fig, the elephant-ear tree, and the give-and-take palm with spines that inflict nasty cuts and sap that soothes and disinfects them. When Lily got tired and her mood started creeping toward meltdown, we brought out the bug spray for art shots: Bug Spray on the Royal Mayan Ball Court; Bug Spray in the Ruined Bedrooms of the Royal Palace; Bug Spray and the Carving of Lord Smoking Shell.

Also, we snorkeled. We snorkeled like nobody's business, though of course it *was* business, for everyone involved. We snorkeled with de-fogging dish soap in our goggles and greed in our hearts. We wanted to spot everything. I heard someone say *octopus* and felt my rubber flippers twitch with resolve. At Hol Chan, we snorkeled over little brains of coral and past a turtle munching on patches of sea grass, its shell an intricate jigsaw of lacquered puzzle pieces. We snorkeled over a wrecked supply barge that had become its own ecosystem, fish like slips of quicksilver darting in and out of the ragged mouths where rust had eaten through the metal. We jumped into the water with great urgency to snorkel with manatees. ("You've got to get on your flippers and GO!" our guide yelled.) We snorkeled with sharks, the water rippling and frothing around their muscled bodies—fifteen of them fighting for the bloody chum our captain, Giovanni, was tossing off the back of the boat. From her perch, Lily reminded everyone, *These are the nice sharks.* She said it several times, a kind of mantra.

Lily loved snorkeling the first time, then things went downhill. The water got choppier, her snorkel kept filling with saltwater. By the end of the trip, her dislike for snorkeling had become an identity statement. Weeks later, when people asked about the trip, she'd answer by saying how much fun she had "except for snorkeling." She'd say, "I'll never go snorkeling again." I felt her pleasure in this insistence—she had preferences. Traveling offers us the chance to constitute ourselves with taste: what we love and what we don't. I fought the impulse to say, *But you liked it the first time,* because I could recognize in that impulse the need for her tastes to be my tastes, and I wanted to fight the imposition.

What Lily *did* love was our afternoon on Bajo Caye, where we stopped for lunch one day. It was a tiny strip of sand the size of a football field, the bathroom just a shack over the sea, a wooden bench inside cut with an oval of perfect blue. Lily wondered how the fish felt about our peeing in their ocean. She teamed up with a little boy to solve the mystery of an abandoned shack that had a half-built solar panel lying on its defunct stove, a hammock in its tiny loft, a T-shirt full of Oreo cookies on the sandy floorboards. Lily went around collecting clues: There was a parrot on the island. The parrot liked Oreos.

Captain Giovanni told me he used to be a deep-sea diver and would dive the atolls off the coast, Turneffe and Glover's Reef. He used to do "crazy things"—he once dove to 285 feet—until his mom heard about how extreme his dives had gotten and made him promise to stop. Now that he was a father, she told him, things had to be different. He said he'd made that promise and kept it —he hadn't gone diving since. He told me this story as if to say, *You know how it goes.* Strangers always assume that Lily and I are mother and daughter because she calls me Mommy and our hair is the same wavy brown. We are both dramatic gesticulators and constant question askers. But it still surprises me to be—now, suddenly —the mother of a six-year-old. I feel perched at the edge of failure in each moment. This is nothing unusual. Every parent feels this way. It's just that if I fail, I am failing another woman's child and my own child at once.

In town, we ate lamb curry and lobster tacos piled with radish and corn, big stewed chunks of meat drizzled with lime. We ate chicken *salbute* on deep-fried tortillas and *crema de calabaza*—a squash soup with crushed seeds sprinkled on top—and *tamalitos de chaya,* moist tamales full of island spinach. We ordered pork *pibil* and coconut chipotle fish. We scarfed tiny stewed plums like they were candy. We ate little balls of coconut and ginger called *dulce de coco.* We drank *café de olla*—a local coffee that tasted like cinnamon. No matter where we were, Lily asked for chicken fingers.

Our hotel might have represented everything I loathed about travel, but it was also *ours*—ours as we kept returning to the wrong villa (they all looked the same), ours as we played Clue and ate our morning bananas, ours as we built one of the first stories we'd shared as a family. Lily eventually faced down her nerves to jump off the rock-jumping valley, to let it earn its name. She climbed up the stairs, came back down, uncertain, pumped her fist in the air —"I can *do* this"—went back up, and finally jumped. The triumph of the moment was palpable. The rock tower was a monstrosity, the resort a touristic obscenity, but it was also *fun* to swim there, and it brought Lily joy. It made me think of Marianne Moore's notion of poetry having "imaginary gardens with real toads in them." Lily's bliss was something real inside the absurd theater of those fake rocks. There were real iguanas strolling the imaginary gardens of the hospitality machine.

For me, the manicured features of our resort challenged my sense of self, or angered the ghosts of prior selves: the self who'd mixed concrete (terribly), the self who'd taught second-graders (with a hangover), the versions of me that slept in beds skittering with cockroaches and ate tamales by candlelight when the power went out. What was that self doing in this villa, with a daughter, trying to decide between balconies?

Lily, on the other hand, loved our hotel but felt uncertain about the rest of Belize. She told me she didn't like going on the golf cart because the rest of the island was creepy. The national flag scared her because it showed two men holding an ax and a bat. I worried that by choosing our hotel I'd done exactly the opposite of what I wanted to do—which was to make her feel comfortable in a strange place—and had instead polarized this place into a familiar world she loved and an unfamiliar world she didn't.

But I learned something from how Lily traveled as well. She got excited about the parts of traveling that I could easily dismiss as packaging around the actual "experience." She loved putting our laptops into bins on the baggage belt at airport security. She adored the water taxi, those bursts of spray when it smacked the choppy water. "This. Is. Awesome," she said, giving each word its own moment. She defeated the notion of child as ego extension. She wasn't a sculpture we shaped from clay, an incarnation of our vision for what she should be. She was beautifully and inevitably *herself*—an engine of curiosity running on peanut butter and watermelon juice. And her dance card was booked with glorious business: solving the mystery of an abandoned shack, hurling herself off a pile of fabricated rocks, organizing a moonlit search for mermaids in the moat around the swim-up bar. What grace for all of us that she was more than a collection of our desires for what she might be—that her curiosity glowed on its own terms, always.

Standing in the customs line at Houston, on our trip back, an agent gave us the wrong information about which forms we needed and a burly American guy standing in front of us tried to commiserate: "There's a reason some people work minimum wage jobs," he said. He understood the world as a place where some people deserve five-day Belizean vacations and other people deserve to provide the human labor that makes them possible—that all of this is as it should be. Taking care of a child made it easier to forget my privilege, or somehow justify it, because I *felt* selfless—attending to her needs, trying to make her world possible and pleasurable. Because I still felt uncertain of my motherhood in every way, all this felt virtuous. But our obligations as parents don't displace our obligations to strangers, and the act of caring for a child doesn't obscure the inequalities that emerge with clarity whenever Westerners arrive in the developing world—hungry for its beauty, for its difference, for its coral reefs and ancient temples.

We left our money in Belize—where much of it went back to U.S. real estate developers—and we left our tips in the hands of men who delivered us to regal manatees and shipwrecks covered in coral. We fed our daughter chicken fingers in the land of coconut chipotle snapper. We leapt from the grip of our guilt and landed in the deep end of the swimming pool, where her bliss at chasing mermaids was one truth and the construction workers beyond our balcony were another—the truth of joy and the truth of profit—and neither truth ever canceled the other.

JODI KANTOR AND CATRIN EINHORN

Refugees Hear a Foreign Word: Welcome

FROM *The New York Times*

TORONTO — One frigid day in February, Kerry McLorg drove to an airport hotel here to pick up a family of Syrian refugees. She was cautious by nature, with a job poring over insurance data, but she had never even spoken to the people who were about to move into her basement.

"I don't know if they even know we exist," she said.

At the hotel, Abdullah Mohammad's room phone rang, and an interpreter told him to go downstairs. His children's only belongings were in pink plastic bags, and the family's documents lay in a white paper bag printed with a Canadian flag. His sponsors had come, he was told. He had no idea what that meant.

Across Canada, ordinary citizens, distressed by news reports of drowning children and the shunning of desperate migrants, are intervening in one of the world's most pressing problems. Their country allows them a rare power and responsibility: They can band together in small groups and personally resettle — essentially adopt — a refugee family. In Toronto alone, hockey moms, dog-walking friends, book club members, poker buddies, and lawyers have formed circles to take in Syrian families. The Canadian government says sponsors officially number in the thousands, but the groups have many more extended members.

When Ms. McLorg walked into the hotel lobby to meet Mr. Mohammad and his wife, Eman, she had a letter to explain how sponsorship worked: For one year, Ms. McLorg and her group would provide financial and practical support, from subsidizing food and rent to supplying clothes to helping them learn English and find work. She and her partners had already raised more than 40,000 Canadian dollars (about $30,700), selected an apartment, talked to the local school, and found a nearby mosque.

Ms. McLorg, the mother of two teenagers, made her way through the crowded lobby, a kind of purgatory for newly arrived Syrians. Another member of the group clutched a welcome sign she had written in Arabic but then realized she could not tell if the words faced up or down. When the Mohammads appeared, Ms. McLorg asked their permission to shake hands and took in the people standing before her, no longer just names on a form. Mr. Mohammad looked older than his thirty-five years. His wife was unreadable, wearing a flowing niqab that obscured her face except for a narrow slot for her eyes. Their four children, all under ten, wore donated parkas with the tags still on.

For the Mohammads, who had been in Canada less than forty-eight hours, the signals were even harder to read. In Syria, Abdullah had worked in his family's grocery stores and Eman had been a nurse, but after three years of barely hanging on in Jordan, they were not used to being wanted or welcomed. "You mean we're leaving the hotel?" Abdullah asked. To himself, he was wondering, *What do these people want in return?*

Much of the world is reacting to the refugee crisis—21 million displaced from their countries, nearly 5 million of them Syrian —with hesitation or hostility. Greece shipped desperate migrants back to Turkey; Denmark confiscated their valuables; and even Germany, which has accepted more than half a million refugees, is struggling with growing resistance to them. Broader anxiety about immigration and borders helped motivate Britons to take the extraordinary step last week of voting to leave the European Union.

In the United States, even before the Orlando massacre spawned new dread about "lone wolf" terrorism, a majority of American governors said they wanted to block Syrian refugees because some could be dangerous. Donald J. Trump, the presumptive Republican presidential nominee, has called for temporary bans on all Muslims from entering the country and recently warned that Syrian refugees would cause "big problems in the future." The Obama administration promised to take in 10,000 Syrians by September 30 but has so far admitted about half that many.

Just across the border, however, the Canadian government can barely keep up with the demand to welcome them. Many volun-

teers felt called to action by the photograph of Alan Kurdi, the Syrian toddler whose body washed up last fall on a Turkish beach. He
had only a slight connection to Canada—his aunt lived near Van-
couver—but his death caused recrimination so strong it helped
elect an idealistic, refugee-friendly prime minister, Justin Trudeau.

"Angry Mob of Do-Gooders"

The *Toronto Star* greeted the first planeload by splashing "Welcome
to Canada" in English and Arabic across its front page. Eager sponsors toured local Middle Eastern supermarkets to learn what to
buy and cook and used a toll-free hotline for instant Arabic translation. Impatient would-be sponsors—"an angry mob of do-good-
ers," the *Star* called them—have been seeking more families. The
new government committed to taking in 25,000 Syrian refugees
and then raised the total by tens of thousands.

"I can't provide refugees fast enough for all the Canadians who
want to sponsor them," John McCallum, the country's immigration minister, said in an interview.

In the ideal version of private sponsorship, the groups become
concierges and surrogate family members who help integrate the
outsiders, called "New Canadians." The hope is that the Syrians
will form bonds with those unlike them, from openly gay sponsors to business owners who will help them find jobs to lifelong
residents who will take them skating and canoeing. Ms. McLorg's
group of neighbors and friends includes doctors, economists, a
lawyer, an artist, teachers, and a bookkeeper.

Advocates for sponsorship believe that private citizens can
achieve more than the government alone, raising the number of
refugees admitted, guiding newcomers more effectively, and potentially helping solve the puzzle of how best to resettle Muslims
in Western countries. Some advocates even talk about extending
the Canadian system across the globe. (Slightly fewer than half
of the Syrian refugees who recently arrived in Canada have private sponsors, including some deemed particularly vulnerable who
get additional public funds. The rest are resettled by the government.)

The fear is that all of this effort could end badly, with the Canadians looking naive in more ways than one.

The Syrians are screened, and many sponsors and refugees take offense at the notion that they could be dangerous, saying they are often victims of terrorism themselves. But American officials point out that it is very difficult to track activity in the chaotic, multifaceted Syrian war. Several Islamic State members involved in the 2015 Paris attacks arrived on Europe's shores from Syria posing as refugees.

Some of the refugees in Canada have middle- and upper-class backgrounds, including a businessman who started a Canadian version of his medical marketing company within a month after arriving. But many more face steep paths to integration, with no money of their own, uncertain employment prospects, and huge cultural gaps. Some had never heard of Canada until shortly before coming here, and a significant number are illiterate in Arabic, which makes learning English—or reading a street sign or sending an email in any language—a titanic task. No one knows how refugees will navigate the currents of longing, trauma, dependence, or resentment they may feel.

And volunteers cannot fully anticipate what they may confront —clashing expectations of whether Syrian women should work, tensions over how money is spent, families that are still dependent when the year is up, disagreements within sponsor groups.

Still, by mid-April, only eight weeks after their first encounter with Ms. McLorg, the Mohammads had a downtown apartment with a pristine kitchen, bikes for the children to zip around the courtyard, and a Canadian flag taped to their window. The sponsors knew the children's shoe sizes; Abdullah and Eman still had keys to Ms. McLorg's house. He studied the neighborhood's supermarkets, and his wife took a counseling course so she could help others who had experienced dislocation and loss. When the male sponsors visited, she sat at the dining room table with them instead of eating in the kitchen—as she would have done back home—as long as her husband was around too.

Mr. Mohammad searched for the right words to describe what the sponsors had done for him. "It's like I've been on fire, and now I'm safe in the water," he said.

But he and other new arrivals were beginning to confront fresh questions: How were they supposed to work with these enthusiastic strangers? What would it mean to reinvent their lives under their watch?

Being Ready for Anything

As sponsors sign the paperwork that commits them, no one really explains the potential range of their unofficial duties: showing a newcomer to spit in a dentist's sink by miming the motions, rushing over late at night to calm a war-rattled family terrified by a garage door blown open by the wind, or using Google Translate to tell children who lived through war and exile that they are supposed to wear pink at school for anti-bullying day.

One April morning, Liz Stark, the grandmother in chief of another sponsor group, could not find Mouhamad Ahmed, the father in the family. She tried his phone and waited in vain outside their new apartment. This was a problem: Wissam, his wife, was in labor with their fifth child.

The pregnancy had been anxious because the couple had lost even more than their old life in Syria, where Mr. Ahmed used to farm wheat, cotton, and cumin. They had spent years in a refugee camp in Lebanon, their three children never attending school because tuition was too expensive. Ms. Ahmed became pregnant there with their fourth child, but labor was troubled and the girl lived only six hours. They named her Amira, which means princess.

"I was thinking maybe the same thing will happen to me here as well," Ms. Ahmed said.

As Ms. Stark hunted for Mr. Ahmed, Peggy Karas, another sponsor, stayed at the hospital massaging Ms. Ahmed's hand during contractions. Like other such pairs, the two women had come together through opaque, bureaucratic machinery. A United Nations agency referred Ms. Ahmed and her family to Canadian officials who interviewed and screened them, then passed their file to a new nonprofit dedicated to matching Syrians with private sponsors, who had twenty-four hours to say yes or no based on the barest of details.

Ms. Stark and many of her cosponsors were retired teachers, bossy and doting, and they had become hell-bent on bringing this new child into the world safely. They had introduced Ms. Ahmed to the vitamins she would take, the machines that would monitor her, the hospital ward where she would deliver. The older women had repeated the doctors' reassurances that all would go smoothly this time. They had helped her pick out tiny outfits and baby gear, but she was too superstitious to take them home, so they formed a small mountain in a sponsor's living room.

Ms. Stark had recruited another newly arrived Syrian refugee to serve as an interpreter during labor. When she finally found Mr. Ahmed, who had been playing soccer, unaware of what was happening, she ushered him to the hospital room, where he took over holding his wife's hand.

Suddenly a medical team rushed her away, saying the umbilical cord was in a dangerous position and she needed an emergency cesarean section. Ms. Ahmed, terrified, asked her husband to take care of their children if she did not survive. As Mr. Ahmed collapsed, sobbing, the sponsors asked his permission to pray.

When a nurse finally appeared to say the newborn was healthy, whisked off to intensive care for observation, Ms. Ahmed said she would not believe it until she held the baby, but Mr. Ahmed was jubilant. He called his father in Syria and let him choose a name: Julia, the family's first Canadian citizen.

Once the infant was home, she went from being the Ahmed family member the sponsors worried about most to the one they fretted about least. She would grow up hearing English, going to Canadian preschool and beyond. For her siblings—ten-year-old twins, a boy and a girl, and an eight-year-old brother—the sponsors found a program for children who had never been to school. Their father, who had gone through only second grade, worked on learning enough English to find a job.

Everyone was on a deadline: After one year, the sponsors' obligation ends, and the families are expected to become self-sufficient. Toronto rents are high, and the Ahmeds may not be able to stay in the relatively inexpensive apartment the sponsors found for them—the monthly rent is 1,400 Canadian dollars, or about $1,100—even if Mr. Ahmed finds a job.

Ms. Stark was optimistic because she had lived through other versions of this story. Almost four decades ago, as a young geography teacher, she joined in the first mass wave of Canadian private sponsorship, in which citizens resettled tens of thousands of Vietnamese, Cambodians, and Hmong. She helped sponsor three Vietnamese brothers and a Cambodian family, later attending their weddings, celebrating the births of their children, and watching them find their places in Toronto, a city so diverse that half the population is foreign-born. Now some former Southeast Asian refugees are completing the cycle by sponsoring Syrians.

Why Canada Makes Sense

Like many sponsors, Ms. Stark believes that her country is especially suited to resettling refugees, with its vast size, strong social welfare system, and a government that emphasizes multiculturalism. Canada has not endured acts of terrorism like the September 11 hijackings or the Paris attacks, or even an assault on the scale of the Orlando nightclub killings. And with only one land border, little illegal immigration, and a tenth of the population of the United States, Canada is hungry for migrants. Officials around the country have clamored to bring Syrian refugees to their provinces.

"We are an accident of geography and history," said Ratna Omidvar, who cofounded Lifeline Syria, a group that matches Syrians with sponsors.

Opposition to the influx has been relatively muted. The Conservative Party argues that the country is taking in more refugees than it can provide for, but supports accepting Syrians. Some Canadians complain that the country should take care of its own first, and new chapters of the Soldiers of Odin, a European anti-immigrant group, have cropped up in recent months. A few incidents targeting Syrians—graffiti reading SYRIANS GO HOME AND DIE at a Calgary school, a pepper spray attack at an event welcoming refugees—drew widespread condemnation.

One May evening, three weeks after Julia's birth, Ms. Stark stopped by the Ahmeds' apartment with a plastic table for the balcony and cradled the baby. She had a new grandchild, but she had spent more time with Julia. The cookie-baking retirees were planning a party to welcome her the Syrian way, by feasting on a newly slaughtered lamb on her fortieth day. Meanwhile, Mr. Ahmed had adopted a new custom: He sometimes brought his wife breakfast in bed and got the children ready. "When I came here, I saw men just doing everything that women do in Syria," he said. "And I thought, yeah, of course, I will do the same."

That night, Ms. Ahmed handed Ms. Stark a form from the twins' school, unsure what it was about. "What? You're going to the Blue Jays game?" she crowed to the boy, Majed, who grinned back under his dark curls. Then she turned to his parents. "This costs money, but your sponsors will pay for it because this is important."

The Ahmeds were so frugal that their benefactors sometimes worried whether they were buying enough to eat. Ms. Ahmed said they wanted to purchase no more than the family needed.

Before leaving, Ms. Stark explained the proper Tylenol dosage for the couple's daughter, Zahiya, who had a fever. She and her twin now spent their school bus rides exchanging language lessons with a pair of Chinese brothers, pointing to objects and naming them. One day when their parents tried to bring them home after a dentist appointment, the Syrian children refused, insisting on returning to school for the time remaining.

English words were starting to emerge from the older children's mouths, but the sponsors and the adult refugees could barely understand one another without help, often relying on mimed gestures or balky translation apps. Even when the groups use interpreters, they often get stuck in roundelays of Canadian and Syrian courtesy, so reluctant to impose that they do not say what they mean. Ms. Ahmed, who had a first-grade education and was not attending English classes because she was home with a newborn, said that not being able to communicate was painful.

"Sometimes I feel like I am losing my mind," she said, because she felt so close to the sponsors but could not even tell them little things about the baby.

Still, some groups faced greater challenges. Some Syrians have backed out before traveling to Canada, intimidated by the geographic and cultural leap. Sam Nammoura, a refugee advocate in Calgary, said he was tracking dozens of cases in which Syrian-Canadians sponsored friends and relatives and then left them destitute. Other pairings have turned out to be mismatches of expectations; one formerly well-off Syrian family expressed disappointment that its apartment was a second-floor walk-up and lacked a washing machine. Others were shocked to discover that their sponsors were posting Facebook messages and blog entries about them that strangers could read.

Even when sponsors and refugees become enmeshed in one another's lives, they do not fully know one another. Not every family is open about its history, and many sponsors would like to know the worst but do not want to ask. (The Ahmeds and the Mohammads asked not to be identified by their full surnames, and were reluctant to publicly share details of their experiences in Syria because they feared reprisals against relatives still there. Most of the refugees in this article left Syria around 2013, during fighting between the Assad regime and rebels.)

The sponsors do not share everything about themselves either. Emma Waverman, the leader of another cluster, was telling her cosponsors about the stirring bar mitzvah speech her son had written about the Syrians they were aiding when another woman stopped her.

"Do they know we're Jewish?" she asked.

Nurturing Without Nagging

Few issues are as delicate as how hard the sponsors should push and when the refugees can say no. Should the Syrians live close to downtown sponsors or in outer-ring neighborhoods with more Middle Easterners—and is it right for sponsors to decide without consulting them? The Canadians raise tens of thousands of dollars for each newcomer family; who controls how it is spent?

Some worry that sponsors are overpowering the refugees with the force of their enthusiasm. Kamal Al-Solaylee, a journalism professor at Ryerson University who is originally from Yemen, said he had noticed a patronizing tone, as when some sponsors highlighted their volunteering on social media. "The white savior narrative comes into play," he said.

When Muaz and Sawsan Ballani and their two-year-old son arrived here in February, they seemed so disoriented and alone that their sponsors became especially eager to nurture them. Mr. Ballani, twenty-six, had once worked in his father's clothing store, which was run out of their home. Now he introduced himself to his sponsors by showing them a picture of his oldest brother: not a smiling snapshot, but an image of the young man lying dead back home, blood streaming from his body. (Mr. Ballani believed that his brother had been caught in fighting between the regime and the opposition, but in the chaos of the conflict, he said, he could not learn more.)

Sawsan wed Muaz when she was sixteen in an arranged marriage, rushed because of bombings and failing electricity; a month later, they fled. Now twenty, she had not seen her family since.

The couple had been languishing in Jordan, sleeping in a house crammed with too many people, not enough beds or blankets, and ants that crawled over their son, named Abdulrahman, after Mr. Ballani's dead brother, and nicknamed Aboudi. One of Mr. Ballani's brothers was still stuck in the house in Jordan, he said, and his brother's widow was living in a park in Syria with her three children, foraging for food.

"If we hadn't come here, we would have died," he said.

The family's sponsors started as mostly strangers to one another —a few former colleagues, a friend of a friend. Helga Breier, a market research consultant and one of the organizers, was drawn into sponsorship last summer, when she felt haunted during her Mediterranean vacation by the suffering across the water.

The Ballanis became their galvanizing cause. Together they found a bright apartment near their homes and countered the bareness—the family had few belongings—with cheery posters and tags labeling everything in English: lamp, cupboard, wall, door. The couple spoke almost no English, so to teach Mr. Ballani to get where he needed to go, the sponsors helped him photograph the route. When Aboudi threw tantrums in day care, they sat with him so his mother could stay in language class. The couple cooked elaborate Middle Eastern thank-you meals for the sponsors and mostly welcomed their interventions. Mr. Ballani donned a Toronto Maple Leafs hat that he wore day after day, and his wife gamely hopped on a toboggan.

Sometimes the sponsors barely hid their views of how the Ballanis should adjust. At a spring potluck dinner, Ms. Ballani described how she had recently traveled by subway on her own, a trip she could not have imagined taking just a few weeks before. The sponsors around the table, firm feminists, asked what else she might like to do herself.

She turned to her husband. "I'm going to ask you an honest question," she said. "Would you let me work here?" As they waited for the answer, the Canadian women held their breath.

"Yes, but I wouldn't have let you work back" in Jordan, he said, adding that even women who behaved traditionally there were often harassed and that those who appeared too independent faced worse. Ms. Ballani pressed forward: She wanted to attend university and have a career of her own, she said, a daunting set of goals for a woman with only a seventh-grade education. The Canadians beamed; two high-fived each other.

At the same time, the sponsors worried that they were becoming helicopter parents, as Ms. Breier put it. When the Syrians skipped English lessons (Aboudi sometimes kept them awake at night) or missed an appointment for donated dental services (a misunderstanding), the sponsors agonized over what to say, debating on the messaging app Slack. Should they show up every morning at the Ballanis' apartment to make sure they got to class? Aboudi did not nap regularly and seemed to consume a lot of sugar—he drank soda, sometimes for breakfast—so should they offer advice?

Mr. Nammoura, the refugee advocate in Calgary, said he saw a pattern among the cases. The Canadians, who feel responsible for the refugees' success, want to give them as much help and direction as possible. But many Syrians, finally safe after years of war and flight, want to exhale before launching into language regimens and job searches, and sometimes feel that sponsors are meddling.

When the Ballani sponsors sought advice from an Arab community center caseworker and an older Syrian mother, they were told to be harsher—to threaten fines or loss of sponsorship if the couple did not accept their guidance. Instead, the sponsors tried to strike a balance, being insistent on issues like health and education but easing off in other areas.

A few weeks before Ramadan, the Ballanis raised the prospect of missing school during the month of long fasts. "It's really hard because we have to fast sixteen or eighteen hours," Muaz Ballani told the sponsors.

Ms. Breier and her partners dismissed the idea, saying they feared that the couple would lose their slots if they missed too many classes. The Ballanis quickly relented. It was not clear how much freedom they felt to express disagreement to outsiders; they seemed reluctant to acknowledge anything but gratitude.

That morning, Ms. Ballani said she and her husband never had different opinions from the sponsors. "We've never felt like they were telling us what to do," she added.

Another weekend, the extended group gathered for a picnic, the first birthday party anyone had thrown for Mr. Ballani. He was deeply moved by the gesture. "A human life has value here," he had said in an interview. "You can feel it everywhere."

But the conversation at the party turned to his relatives in Syria, and he seemed distant as the Canadians presented his cake. Like many of the newcomers, he regularly receives calls and texts from family members, some in harrowing straits, as news reports describe starvation back home and mass drownings in the Mediterranean.

"I am really thankful to them; I don't want them to misunderstand," he said later about the sponsors. "It's like I'm two people at the same time, one happy and one unhappy," because of his family's continued suffering.

The sponsors had been working on that too, helping match Mr. Ballani's brother in Jordan with another Toronto sponsor group and laboring over the paperwork. By late spring they had news: his relatives could arrive by year's end.

Mr. Ballani, overjoyed, started planning what he would show his relatives in the city that had taken him in. This time, he would be the guide.

"Now it's my turn to help," he said.

Navigating Their Own Way

Three months after the Mohammads' awkward first meeting with Kerry McLorg and the other sponsors at the airport hotel, they had clicked into a productive rhythm, settling into Canada faster than anyone had expected.

They went on a picnic to Niagara Falls and danced around a maypole at a spring festival. The girls won student-of-the-month honors. Bayan, the eldest, who had whipped past the boys she raced on Jordanian streets, was now beating runners from schools across the city. When the sponsors came to give informal language lessons, Ahmad, the four-year-old, liked to try new phrases in English, such as "Good job!"

Still, there was some culture shock. When Abdullah Mohammad took the children to a community pool, he encountered a woman in a string bikini. "I ran away," he said later. "I've never seen that before in my life."

Ms. McLorg, measured and methodical, had organized the

sponsor group, but the most energetic member was an artist named Susan Stewart, with a seemingly endless list of activities for the family and long email exchanges with the children's teachers. During her turn to give English lessons, she brought flash cards down to the courtyard, telling the children to alternate between loops on their bicycles and new words. She was sweetly relentless, which was partly why the family had made so much progress, the other sponsors said.

When Mr. Mohammad voiced interest in working, Ms. Stewart became consumed with helping him find a job. Of all the tests for the family—and, by extension, the sponsors—this was perhaps the most crucial. So Ms. Stewart found an Arabic-speaking settlement counselor to advise Mr. Mohammad and drove him to a job fair for refugees, where they struck up a conversation with a Syrian supermarket owner. After he invited Mr. Mohammad for an interview, Ms. Stewart fashioned a résumé from a questionnaire she had helped him fill out.

"I am keen to learn all aspects of the trade from stocking and organizing shelves to marketing strategies and Canadian shopping habits," she wrote. Describing his work experience—doing odd jobs during his three years in Jordan—she wrote, "As a refugee I had to be resourceful and find work wherever I could." Even though the interview would be in Arabic, she drilled him in English phrases like "I can stock shelves."

"Ten more times!" she told him as they drove to the interview.

When he was offered the part-time position, the sponsors were thrilled. But a few days later, he called the Canadians to say he would turn it down. He struggled with taking money from the sponsors—back home, others had come to his family for help, and it was "really hard to be on the receiving end," he said. But he wanted to consider options, such as becoming a mechanic. In Syria or Jordan, he had never had the freedom to choose his work. "It's always what you have to do to earn a living rather than what you really want to do," he said later.

And he did not want to take a job until he improved his English, he said, because he did not want any more favors or charity. At the supermarket, unable to answer basic questions from customers, "I would be a burden to my employer," he added. He had been annoyed at Ms. Stewart for pressing so hard, he said later, but mostly he was embarrassed to pass on the job after she had done so much.

But Ms. McLorg saw a plus side: Mr. Mohammad was starting to navigate his own path in Canada, and the relationship between the sponsors and the family, so lopsided at the start, was beginning to balance out. "Our job was to help them come into Canada and show them the options that are here," she said.

In mid-May, at the end of a routine meeting with the sponsors and the Mohammads, she shared news of her own: She had breast cancer. Now that she was facing surgery, she was the one who was vulnerable, and the Syrians were the ones who were checking on her.

They brought flowers and chocolates; the other sponsors, now practiced in the logistics of caring, offered meal deliveries and other assistance. "I had no intention of building my own support group, but I have one now," Ms. McLorg said.

Bayan and Batoul, the two oldest Mohammad children, made get-well cards using the same set of watercolors the sponsors had used to make greeting signs that first day at the airport hotel. The morning after Ms. McLorg's operation, when she made her way down to her living room, the cards were the first things she saw.

Finding the Forgotten

FROM *Garden & Gun*

FOR SOME ODD REASON, I keep thinking of William Faulkner's *Intruder in the Dust*. The classic novel is best remembered for the scene in which a black man and a white man dig up a body in order to clear another man jailed for murder. And though race, the dead, the South, and crime are all involved in the story of Richmond's historic Evergreen Cemetery, the scene this morning is in many ways the complete opposite of Faulkner's whodunit. Now the dead remain underground, and black and white folk are collaborating in the sunshine to clear and honor their resting places. A century ago Evergreen was the premier burial place for African Americans in Richmond. But the sixty-acre site has been severely neglected for decades. Attempts to reclaim it from the forest have started and stopped for more than thirty years. Today is the first concerted effort in three years, and it is remarkable to see how swiftly a forest can retake a graveyard.

It's Saturday, bright and early. A line of cars lead the way, and at the entrance to Evergreen, a silver-haired woman stands behind a folding table, taking names. Three men hang up a long banner—MAGGIE L. WALKER HIGH SCHOOL CLASS OF 1967 (an all-black school at the time)—and smile for pictures. Marvin Harris, a member of that class and the lead Volunteer Cleanup Coordinator for this formidable project, greets me. He is a powerfully built man with hands as strong as wire cables. In the distance: chain saws, lawn mowers, the sounds of chopping, cutting. People calling out to one another. About forty people have gathered, and all are at work.

A Richmond native, Harris is the owner and CEO of Harris Group Promotions and Supply, an industrial supply company in the city. Eight years ago he read an article in the local paper about Evergreen and other African American cemeteries in Richmond. He called a friend who had a relative buried here, and scheduled twelve people to come help. Only four showed up. "It was quite a situation," Harris says. This initial effort led to more and more investment of time, and sweat, and outreach for help. "Somebody had to step up to the plate," he continues. "If we handle this as a community, we can get it back to the glory days."

The forest is dense and thick and reminds me of the woods I roamed as a boy. But this density was once a place for families to come honor their dead in pastoral reverence and green splendor. In the late nineteenth and early twentieth centuries, having picnics in cemeteries was not uncommon for most Americans. Save for the marble markers now poking up periodically—choked by weeds, surrounded by tall grass, or swallowed by ivy—one might never realize we're in the midst of a graveyard.

II.

This part of the city east of I-95 is distinctly suburban, the towers of Richmond receding in the distance. A multitude of cemeteries dot the landscape, decorously. Most are well manicured and unassuming. Hollywood—near the center of town, on the banks of the James River—is where the high and mighty ultimately come to rest. Presidents Monroe and Tyler and Confederate president Jefferson Davis are buried there. Following Reconstruction, four African American cemeteries were established in this eastern section of town, in light of Jim Crow segregation: East End, Colored Pauper's Cemetery, Woodland Cemetery, and the largest, Evergreen. Established in 1891, Evergreen was meant to be the dark mirror of Hollywood.

Of all the bustling cities of the American South during the Jim Crow era, Richmond laid claim to one of the nation's largest black middle classes. As a result they had the means to memorialize their dead grandly.

The most commanding grave marker stands in the central section of Evergreen, a marble cross about ten feet tall. It rests over

Maggie L. Walker, the first woman (of any color) to establish and become president of a bank in the United States. In 1903, she successfully chartered the St. Luke Penny Savings Bank. This led to a merger with two other banks to form the Consolidated Bank and Trust Company, which became a significant institution for African Americans in Richmond. Walker was also a teacher and a leader in education and women's rights. Many organizations throughout Richmond and the rest of Virginia have been named after her, and her home has become a National Historic Site. Until this morning her grave and monument had been engulfed in impassable brush, hard to find, even harder to reach. But already volunteers have cleared the immediate area surrounding it, the grave and marker now free and clear, along with dozens of others.

Not too far from Walker are the graves of John Mitchell Jr. and his mother. Mitchell was a bank president, and the editor and publisher of the *Richmond Planet,* a leading voice against lynching at the turn of the twentieth century. He unsuccessfully ran for governor of Virginia in 1921.

For more than thirty years African Americans were interred here, the prominent—eminent ministers, doctors, lawyers, successful businessmen, and their families—and the not-so-prominent. But something went sadly wrong. Neglect set in sometime after the Crash of 1929 and the onset of the Great Depression. Burials continued for a while, but the graveyard slowly disappeared into the forest. Nobody knows exactly how many people are buried here. Some estimates run as high as 60,000 graves in Evergreen alone.

III.

John Shuck is originally from Iowa. A farm boy, he has lived in Virginia since 2001 and over the years has taken the lead in many ways in reclaiming much of the smaller, neighboring East End Cemetery. (He estimates East End, at sixteen acres, is now approximately 25 percent cleared.) Now he coordinates volunteer work for the reclamation of both Evergreen and East End, and most Saturday mornings you can find him cutting brush, raking, pointing out resting places of note.

Shuck is tall and professorial, with the mien of a museum docent, and a touch of Indiana Jones with his wide-brimmed floppy

explorer's hat. No cemetery records for Evergreen exist prior
to 1929, he tells me. "So there are no existing records of who is
buried here, or where." He had been a graveyard hobbyist, photographing tombstones and researching genealogies, when he
first heard about the cemeteries and came out to photograph in
June 2008. He had never seen a cemetery that looked like this. "I
thought it might be interesting to clear a plot or two, and that was
eight years ago," he says. "Investigating the history of these people
helped me learn the history of Richmond." Shuck and his team of
volunteers recently uncovered their two thousandth grave marker
at East End. He posts photos of the markers online so that family
members can find them.

Shuck leads me to a particularly heartbreaking monument in
Evergreen. It lies away from the central area the workers have
been clearing this morning. Trees and overgrown ivy surround
the monument, and it's difficult to negotiate. We climb over felled
trunks and limbs; the final step includes a big jump down over a
ledge. Not much is known of the Braxton family, though some of
their descendants still live in Richmond. The narrow mausoleum
was probably erected in the mid-1920s. Five coffins rest within. At
some point, probably in the 1950s, the steel door was ripped off,
and the caskets removed and desecrated. Someone ran an illegal
still inside the mausoleum, Shuck tells me. You can still see smoke
stains on the ceiling.

The graveyard has a tendency to attract paranormal seekers.
Shuck remembers finding odd string structures hung above and
among the graves, telltale signs of hoodoo rituals. Vandals in-
truded for decades. Marijuana was grown on the property. It became, perversely, a destination for prostitution. Condom wrappers
were a common find.

IV.

The volunteers are mighty busy. Within hours, an area at the center of the graveyard, radiating out from the Walker marker, looks
as if it has always been well kept.

"God called us to help fix it," Marvin Harris tells me. "If the
owners allow us to help fix it, it will get fixed." The land is privately

owned, and work came to a halt three years ago because of a dispute about using volunteers on private land. But that conflict was
recently resolved. "For the average person with any type of heart,"
Harris says, "I can't see how they could not get involved."

I speak with some of the volunteers. Bud Funk is a seventy-one-
year-old trial attorney. He joined in after hearing Harris speak to
a local group. "Marvin gets inside your heart," Funk says. The first
time Funk saw the site years ago it was "daunting." Now he not
only volunteers his back and limbs, but also does legal work in
partnership with Enrichmond, a nonprofit that supports the effort. Other members of the Maggie L. Walker High School class
of 1967 here this day include civil servants, an executive chef, and
family members of those buried here. "My grandfather," one man
tells me. "I would come by here before, looking, and all I could
see was trash."

"No cemetery should fall into this type of landscape," says John
Baliles, a Richmond city councilman representing the First District. When I first spot him, he is doing battle with a long vine
snaking its way about a large tombstone. "This will take a strong
volunteer effort. But it is easier to preserve if you maintain it."

There's a stark contrast between the acreage cleared this morning and the work yet to be done. Just within a copse of trees a
dozen or more gravestones poke up from the grass and under-
growth. Clearing the area will require heavier equipment and skill.
Shuck and Harris have been discussing bringing in a herd of goats
to help, and inviting a different corporate sponsor each month to
pay for them.

V.

A Virginia historian and business owner, Veronica Davis literally
wrote the book about Richmond's African American cemeteries,
Here I Lay My Burdens Down, in 2003. Davis says the reclamation
efforts began with a former National Park Service superintendent,
Dwight Storke. Heartsick at these languishing sites of African
American history, he spearheaded an attempt in the 1980s to have
them cleared and restored. One part elbow grease, another part
education, it started with a gathering of volunteers in celebration

of Maggie Walker's birthday. The initial volunteers removed fifteen truckloads of debris.

Over the decades, a series of Parks officials and local organizations arranged cleanups, and in the late nineties Davis herself
created a group, Virginia Roots, to continue the efforts, but it has
been slow going. Family members and volunteers move away or
die off, and the cemeteries have gone through a number of private
owners through the years. Without a system of perpetual care or
funding, the work is difficult to maintain. Nor is the situation at
Evergreen unique. Migration of families to the North during Jim
Crow, scanty records, and a lack of public and private funds for up-
keep have all led to the neglect of other historic African American
cemeteries across the region.

"I thank God for this work every day," Davis says. "We have to
show our ancestors respect for what they have done. We're talking
about choices here, and we need to remember that one of the
choices that the dead made was to fight for our freedom. Now we
have another choice to make."

VI.

Midday: the Tony Award–winning actress L. Scott Caldwell arrives,
dressed to work. Caldwell plays a formerly enslaved woman named
Belinda on the PBS historical drama *Mercy Street,* which is shot on
location in Richmond and nearby Petersburg. The actress is known
for taking her research seriously, and visits not only the local museums and historical societies, but also places and sites central to
African American history. She had heard about the project on the
morning news. "It was a question of doing what I can to become a
part of the community," she says. "Where we are, there I am." She
was haunted by the story of Julia Hoggett, who was born into slav-
ery. Hoggett's gravestone is tucked under a mighty oak, and kudzu
threatens to overgrow it. Caldwell had read about this marker during her research, and was keen to see it in person. It reads:

> In Memory of my Mammy, Julia Hoggett 1849–1930
> She was born a slave and a slave she chose to remain.
> Slave to duty, a slave to love.
> Few people of any race or condition of life have lived so unselfishly,
> which is the same as saying so nobly.—LaMotte Blakely

Who was LaMotte Blakely? Was he a white child Julia Hoggett raised? "This spoke to me in a literal way," Caldwell says. She is referring partly to her character, who in her freedom chooses to be the good and faithful servant of a well-to-do white family. But it's more than that—there is a humanity here, a complexity, a dignity. She's less interested in the big names and monuments, she tells me, than in those workers with unsung lives whose secrets are interred with their bones. "I'm more intrigued by the unknown than the known," she says. "This is history."

SAKI KNAFO

Waiting on a Whale at the End of the World

FROM *Men's Journal*

ABOVE THE ARCTIC CIRCLE in Alaska, a half-day's journey by snowmobile from the nearest paved road or tree, a village called Kivalina sits on a slip of permanently frozen earth bracketed by water—a lagoon on one side and the Chukchi Sea on the other. Every spring, when daylight returns to the village after months of darkness, people stand in the snow outside their storm-battered cabins and look out at the sea, hoping this will be the year.

Some Alaskan villages catch a whale every year. Kivalina was never that lucky, partly because it occupies a spot on the coast that's farther from the migratory path of the bowhead whale. Still, there was a time when villagers could reasonably expect to land a whale every three or four years. Those days are gone.

Last March, as the bowheads were beginning to head north on their spring migration, I flew to the village to accompany a group of villagers on a quest to catch a whale. It had been twenty-one years since the last successful whale hunt, twenty-one years of futility and disappointment, and yet, for reasons I didn't fully understand, the villagers hadn't given up. When I asked Reppi Swan why they still did it—why they still risked their lives and spent so much of their time and money pursuing a goal that always eluded them—he was succinct. "It's who we are," he said.

Reppi is one of the village's nine whaling captains. He's forty-two. He has a copper tan shaded black on the cheekbones from frostbite, and the kind of ropy physique you get from chopping wood and shoveling snow. His jaw starts just below his ears and narrows sharply, giving him a wolfishly handsome look despite the fact that he has lost all his teeth. If you're a whaling captain in an Eskimo whaling village, you're a big deal, something like the coach of a small-town Texas football team. But Reppi doesn't carry himself like anything special. He never brags. He doesn't say much more than he has to. When I first spoke to him on the phone from New York, I nervously pressed him for advice on what to wear. What kind of boots? How many layers? "Bring your warm stuff," he said.

A different sort of man might have a hard time coping with life in Kivalina. Outsiders who spend time in the village sometimes feel as though they've traveled in time to some not-too-distant future in which the government has finally imploded after years of dysfunction, leaving the people to fend for themselves, like *Mad Max* but with snowmobiles. In most of the houses, the toilet is a bucket. Kivalina's 468 residents have no running water, so Reppi drives his Polaris 550 snowmobile to the town pump twice a week to fill a pair of 55-gallon garbage bins for the family. The people of Kivalina have become as reliant as the rest of us on certain perks of modernity—smartphones, stupid TV—even as they lack many of the things we take for granted. There are no restaurants or coffee shops in the village, no libraries or fitness centers, no police officers. The homes are as crowded as the tenement apartments of the Lower East Side at the turn of the last century. In the village store, the Pepsi boxes are stacked halfway to the ceiling, but there is no dentist or doctor within a hundred miles. There are no roads connecting Kivalina to anywhere else.

If you don't have a snowmobile or an ATV, the only way to get to and from Kivalina is by boat or on one of the nine-seat planes that touch down on the airstrip most days. The closest neighboring village, Noatak, lies fifty miles inland. To travel there for basketball tournaments, young people from Kivalina ride their snowmobiles or ATVs over the tundra and through the mountains. The island once served only as a staging area for the whale hunt that took place, as it still does today, each spring. In the early 1900s, the Bureau of Indian Affairs came and built a school and told people they would get thrown in jail unless they sent their kids there year-round to learn English. So the people gave up the nomadic ways that had sustained them for generations and moved into a permanent settlement on the island. Punished, sometimes physically, for speaking their native Inupiat in school, children who grew up in that era became parents who hesitated to speak Inupiat to their children. But one Inupiat word everyone still uses is *tammaq,* to lose or to get lost. People in Kivalina have lost many things, big and small—boats, gloves, much of the Inupiat language itself.

Someday soon the villagers may lose their homes. Over the last decade, as the oceans have grown warmer, storms have been hurling powerful waves onto the island, causing the land to gradually wash away. The villagers have been trying to relocate for years, but none of the relevant government agencies have agreed to foot the estimated $400 million it would require. The U.S. Army Corps of Engineers predicts that Kivalina has about ten years before it disappears.

Many of the villagers seem to think it's too late to save Kivalina or, for that matter, the world. Spend enough time on the island and you'll hear about the *inugaqalligauraq,* a primitive race of superstrong little people said to be hiding in the Alaskan bush, armed with bows and arrows, their bodies and minds uncorrupted by exposure to gasoline, Pepsi, and reality TV. "The elders say when the world ends, when Jesus comes, these little people will come back," one middle-aged woman told me. "And people have been seeing them around, here and there."

Whatever's coming to Kivalina—whatever's coming to all of us—the villagers may be better equipped to deal with it than most. The values Eskimo culture advocates and teaches—cooperation, vigilance, an ability to improvise under duress—have allowed its people to withstand some of the harshest conditions on earth. In the old days, a stranded hunter could build a makeshift sled out of only caribou skins, fish, and water, rolling the fish tight in wet skins so that the rolls would freeze solid and could then be used as sled runners. Reppi, for one, seems to long for those days. "I think I would have loved to live back then," he told me one evening, "but we're too used to modern conveniences." As if to illustrate his point, three of his kids were huddled over a phone, ignoring the reality show playing on the TV. "They discovered the movies on my phone," he said, shaking his head. "Now I never see it."

To catch a whale, Eskimo hunters hitch their sleds and a small boat to their snowmobiles. Then they travel over the ice that stretches across the sea for miles. They head out in the spring, when the plates of ice begin to break apart, and drive until they come to a crack or a channel—an *uiniq.* There they set up a big canvas tent and wait—for days, sometimes weeks—ready to jump into the boat, harpoon gun loaded, at the first glimpse of a whale coming up for air.

There are countless ways to get killed doing this. You could drive over thin ice and fall in. Your harpoon gun could jam and explode in your face. You could get too close to a walrus, a whale, a polar bear. One teenager told me a story about ambushing a sleeping walrus from a boat. As the gun went off, the boat's motor died, leaving him and his uncles to watch helplessly as the wounded walrus streaked toward them through the water and rammed a hole in the bow, snapping off a tusk. They managed to restart the engine in the nick of time and quickly piled into the stern, driving home with the damaged bow raised just above the waves.

A whaling captain is responsible for the safety of the men and women in his crew. This calls for the equivalent of an advanced degree in the ancient Eskimo art of survival. Reppi began whaling with his father, a captain, when he was five and inherited the position only five years ago. Before he could prove himself worthy of the job, he had to learn all about the seven types of ice and how the combinations of wind and current affect them. He had to learn that if the crew got stranded on the ice pack, they should always walk east, using the stars as their guide, and that if they encountered a sleeping walrus, they could talk as loud as they wanted but never whisper because it would wake it up. He had to learn how to draw on his knowledge as danger closed in, weighing the pros and cons of each possible course of action before making a last-second decision that could save people's lives.

Judging when it's safe to be on the ice is one of the most difficult decisions a captain has to make. Over the last two decades, the same forces that have been eating away at the island have been causing the sea ice to melt away earlier and earlier in the season, shrinking the window of opportunity for whaling from about two months to a couple of weeks. Last year, Reppi's crew stayed out too long and had to race back to land at full speed as a powerful wind began to tear the sheet of ice where they'd been camping from the shore. If they hadn't made it off in time, they might have ended up in Siberia.

This year, at the start of the season, climate change seemed to be working in Reppi's favor for once. When I called him in early March, he said a channel had opened in the ice right outside of town, something he couldn't remember happening so early before. His voice rose with excitement as he told me that someone flying overhead had actually seen a whale. His crew just had to get the gear ready, and then they'd head out on the hunt.

I made plans to arrive in Kivalina in late March and stay for a little less than a month. I assumed I would spend most of that time out on the ice with the hunters as they tried to land their first whale in more than twenty years. But in Kivalina, as I would soon learn, it is pointless, perhaps even foolish, to make many assumptions about the future. As Reppi put it, "Something always comes up."

The first delay came up before I even arrived. Days before my departure, Reppi told me that there had been a death in the village. We'd have to stick around at least until the funeral, he said. Reppi, the whaling captain, is also the village gravedigger.

Five days after, I watched mourners stream into the church, past the young man lying in an open casket. Friends and family stood before the congregation and spoke of the boy's passion for traditional Eskimo dancing, his caring nature. No one said anything of how he died until one of his uncles, staring out at the crowd, confessed that he, too, once tried to take his own life. "And for what?" he shouted hoarsely, his raw voice ricocheting against the bare walls of the church. There was a heavy silence as the mourners waited for him to go on. When he spoke again, all he said was, "You have to live."

When Eskimos talk about "the whale," they mean only one kind: the bowhead. Every spring the bowhead's northward migration heralds the return of life to the Arctic after months of some of the most inhospitable weather on Earth. When hunters kill one, the whole village drags it onto the ice and butchers it. Then everyone feasts and parties for three days straight. The meat, skin, and blubber of a single whale, divided among the hunters and friends and family in accordance with a set of age-old guidelines, can feed a village for more than two months. Almost every part of the sixty-ton animal is used. (The head is returned to the sea so that the animal's spirit can live on.)

According to the traditions of some Eskimo groups (Inupiat is a more historically accurate term, but people in Kivalina usually refer to themselves as Eskimo), the whale operates on a higher plane of intelligence and spirituality than most human beings.

When you see pictures of the powerful animal, with its deep frown and small, sad-looking eyes, it's hard not to feel that this is true on some level. Not long ago, biologists examining a dead bowhead found old harpoon fragments buried in its flesh. Research revealed that the harpoon was of a kind last manufactured in New Bedford, Massachusetts, in the nineteenth century. The scientists conjectured that bowheads can live for up to 200 years. In other words, some of the whales still undulating through the icy waters off Alaska may have already been fully grown by the time Herman Melville wrote *Moby-Dick*. Today, international law allows Eskimo whaling crews to catch a limited number of bowheads each year.

One night, three days after the funeral, Reppi and the other captains lugged their harpoon guns to the church so the preacher, Enoch Adams Jr., could bless them for the hunt. Adams surveyed the pews, many of them empty, and told the captains what they all already knew. "A lot of people out there are saying, 'What's the point?'" God had given the captains a choice, Adams said. If they surrendered to apathy and stayed home this year, no one would starve. At the village store, you could use cash or food stamps to stock up on Top Ramen and frozen burritos. But cash or food stamps wouldn't keep the community together, wouldn't give the people pride or joy or a reason to keep struggling through the long, dark winters to come. "Choose life!" Adams shouted, his voice booming through the chapel. "Choose life!"

One of the most successful captains in Reppi's father's day was a man named Oran Knox. I kept hearing stories about him while we waited to go whaling. People said he had been a postal worker for a time, delivering the mail by dogsled, and had raced in the first Iditarod, the thousand-mile dogsled race from Anchorage to Nome, in 1973. One day someone invited me to his home. I half expected to find some intimidating figure, an Eskimo Ahab, flames of vitality dancing in his eyes. But a recent bout of pneumonia had taken a toll on him. Now in his late seventies, he was slumped back on an overstuffed couch, struggling to breathe as he watched North Carolina pummel Syracuse in the Final Four.

As he watched the game, he launched into an unprompted reminiscence about the leader of his old dog team. "Tough, smart," he recalled between heavy breaths. "Find his way home in a storm." Later I asked one of his eight children, Oran Knox Jr., what hap-

pened to the dogs. A sad smile came over his face. "I killed them,"
he said. It was the late '70s, and his father had found work on
a construction site farther north and moved his family there. No
one could take care of the team, so the father asked his son to do
the deed. "The dogs knew," the son said. "They looked at me, then
down at the ground."

By that point in Alaskan history, some enterprising salesman
had introduced Eskimos to snowmobiles, or snow machines, as
they're called in Alaska. They could cruise three or four times as
fast as a dog team, shortening a hunter's journey over the ice or
tundra by hours and days. "Snowgos" had other advantages too.
They didn't fight over food. You didn't have to train them or feed
them sacks of trout. But there was also a new class of disadvan-
tages. The machines ran on fuel and oil, which is to say they ran
on money, something much harder to find in Kivalina than trout.
And they were always breaking down. In a way, the machine was
like Western civilization: people came to rely on it but could never
depend on it.

It was two days after the funeral when I realized Reppi's snow
machine would be an issue. We were sitting at Reppi's kitchen
table, drinking coffee. Earlier that morning, he had gone out in
search of a polar bear that someone had seen on the ice outside
of town. Instead of the bear, he'd encountered a problem with his
snow machine. He didn't think it would be able to pull a boat very
far. But when I asked how he planned to get out on the ice, he just
shrugged. "Gotta take it day by day," he said. Then he spread some
shredded caribou and mayo on a Nabisco cracker and leaned back
in his chair to eat it, like a man who had never known a moment's
anxiety.

There had been several setbacks already, and I was beginning
to worry that he would miss his chance to go whaling, never mind
catch a whale. I asked if there was any way he could fix the engine.
Or if he could borrow someone else's snow machine. For every
question he had an answer, and the answer was always "No," and
the "No" was always followed by a persuasive explanation. Tiring
of my questions, he eventually said he could see only one solution:
buying a whole new engine for $800. I wondered how he would
afford that.

People in Kivalina who earn any income at all tend to work
in one of two places: the store or a sprawling zinc mine about

fifty miles northeast of town. Reppi works at both, but not very often. The store employs him on an as-needed basis, paying him just enough to keep him from qualifying for food stamps and cash assistance, and the mine, which pays better, typically needs him for only a few weeks in the warmer months, during shipping season. Like other native people in northwest Alaska, Reppi and his wife, Dolly, receive an annual check from something called NANA, one of the thirteen economic development corporations entrusted with managing the money and lands "given" to native people as part of the 1971 Alaska Native Claims Settlement Act, the federal law that saw native Alaskans relinquish their claims to vast swaths of Alaskan territory coveted by the oil and mining industries. In good years, Reppi got a check worth about $1,000. But in the last few years, NANA has struggled and people throughout the region were feeling the effects.

It takes a lot of money to fund a whaling expedition. Last year Reppi and the crew spent $10,000 on food and fuel, with some of the crew members chipping in what they could and Reppi and several relatives covering the rest. This year Reppi and Dolly were having a tough time paying for things like diapers for their three-year-old. At one point I overheard Dolly quietly telling Reppi that they didn't have enough on hand to buy a cake for their daughter's birthday. Reppi cheerfully replied, "We'll make one out of snow."

If you haven't seen what the ocean looks like when it freezes, imagine a sparkling, ridged, lunar surface stretching as far as you can see. Off in the distance, near the horizon, you may spy a band of bluish gray—an *uiniq*. That's where the bowheads are, and the seals and belugas. If you're a hunter, that's where you want to be. The question is how to get there. The answer is very carefully or not at all.

The real hazard is the *sikuliaq*—the thin ice. Up until about twenty years ago, the ice was as thick as six feet in some places, and hunters could travel across it without falling in. This year the sea ice in the Arctic has been melting at an unprecedented rate, and by Kivalina it was just inches thick, if that. Camping on it would be risky, even for someone as experienced as Reppi.

Reppi eventually figured out a way to repair the snow machine himself. But it took a few days—enough time for the ice to get even thinner. So he decided to try driving about ten miles north, around a bend in the coast, to look for thicker ice and open water. This plan had some drawbacks. The section of the coast where he wanted to camp lay in the direct path of the fierce north wind, which could blow a plate of ice and whoever happened to be camping on it out to sea. Also, getting there would require more time on the snow machines, which would mean more fuel, more money, more problems.

I started worrying out loud that we'd never make it out on the ice to hunt. What if the trip didn't pan out? "Now's not the time to start thinking negative," Reppi said. I stopped asking questions, and we went to the store.

About half the food Reppi and his family eat comes from animals Reppi shoots. He keeps the caribou in the snow in front of his house, frozen with their hooves sticking up in the air. Whenever he and Dolly feel like eating one, Dolly flattens a cardboard box on the living room floor and butchers the animal on top of it. Then it's caribou all week—roast caribou with carrots and onions one night, boiled caribou with broth the next, shredded caribou on Nabisco crackers for lunch.

The family eats seal too, and *maktak,* a delicacy of navy-blue whale skin and pale-pink blubber sent to them by relatives in other villages. I tried it with Tabasco. The fat melts in your mouth, and the skin is tough and chewy. You need only a few small pieces to feel full. The rest of the food comes from the "Native Store," the only store in Kivalina apart from a candy shop that a family runs out of the front room of their house. I don't know why it's called the Native Store. It's owned by a company based in Seattle, and nearly all the products come from Kraft and PepsiCo. The prices are amazingly high. A tourist trap in Midtown Manhattan would seem reasonable by comparison. We loaded a cart with OvenJoy white bread, Foster Farms Variety Pack sandwich meats, and a $10.45 box of Entenmann's glazed doughnuts. At the last minute, Reppi threw in two cases of Pepsi. Reppi drinks about one six-pack of Pepsi a day. He says he wants to quit, but his hands start shaking when he goes too long without one.

We set out from the village the next afternoon, driving four miles north along the coast before veering west onto the ice. A distant sliver of open water came into view, an encouraging sight. Reppi's twelve-year-old son, Sakkan, sat proudly on the back of his father's snow machine, a rifle strapped across his back. I rode in a sled behind him. Riding a sled across the frozen ocean is like bouncing down a rutted dirt road in a junker with no shocks. It wasn't comfortable, but I was thrilled to get out of the village, to see the water gleaming like the blade of a knife. I was staying positive, like Reppi had told me to. Suddenly the sled rattled to a stop. Reppi climbed off his snow machine. "The crack," he said, pointing to something behind us.

At first I didn't understand. Then I saw it: a narrow depression snaking through the ice just behind the sled. To me, it didn't look much different than the ice we'd been driving on, but it wasn't ice at all. It was a strip of water concealed under a treacherously thin layer of snow.

Reppi unhitched the sled from the snow machine, turned the vehicle around, opened the throttle all the way, and practically flew back over the channel. Then he repurposed the sled as a little footbridge, which I wobbled over to safety. We drove back toward shore until Reppi deemed the ice thick enough to sit and have lunch. He opened a Pepsi. From where we sat, we could still see the shining band of water way out beyond the snow-covered crack. "Wa-ter," he said, like someone dying of thirst in the desert. A smile creased his face, but I could tell he was disappointed. If we had tried to camp beside the open water, on the other side of the crack, the crack might have opened wider and stranded us at sea. I asked what he would have done if we had fallen in. "Sakkan and I would have got pinned down by the sled," he said. "Maybe you would have survived."

Back in the village, the waiting continued. Reppi seemed to think that if the wind started blowing in the right direction, it would clear away the thin, weak ice, leaving only the quality stuff. But the wind refused to cooperate, as wind does, I guess, and soon the last of the food was gone.

We went back to the store. More cold cuts, more Pepsi. To save money, I moved from the floor of a guidance counselor's office at the village school, where there was Internet and a shower, to a one-room shack that used to serve as the jail.

About a week before I was scheduled to go home, I was picking up a few things at the store when the cashier told me that Reppi and the crew had been trying to find me, but they'd left town. They were headed north with the boat and sleds. They'd gone hunting, finally. And there I was at the store.

I had been in the village for about three weeks by that point. As I marched back to the jailhouse, muttering to myself, my thinking, I have to admit, was not at all positive. It seemed likely that I would soon return to New York without having seen anyone even look for a whale. As I approached the cabin, I ran into one of Reppi's crew members, JoeJoe, a friendly, soft-spoken guy who, at twenty-four, had taken up hunting only recently and was still basking in the glow of his nascent romance with the lifestyle. JoeJoe and two of his friends, Jake and Kenneth, were standing around JoeJoe's snow machine and staring down at the exposed engine. I asked JoeJoe if he could drive me north to join the rest of the crew. "If I can get this working," he said. Fifteen minutes later, JoeJoe knocked on the door of the jailhouse: we were good to go.

I climbed onto the back of the vehicle, and we headed north, past the cabins, past the airstrip, past the ravens drifting over the dump. We were about a mile outside of town when the machine puttered out. JoeJoe opened the hood and performed some mysterious procedure on the engine, and it rumbled back to life. We drove maybe another fifty yards before it died again. "Motherfuck," he said.

He fiddled with the engine again. Nothing happened. "Motherfuck!" he repeated, more emphatically this time. He looked back at the town, a smudge of black in a world of white. "At least we're not as far as I was the last time," he said.

"The last time?"

In the casual, plainspoken tone of someone recounting, say, the ordeal of getting off at the wrong exit of the New Jersey Turnpike, he related the story of a recent misadventure that, from the sound of it, had nearly cost him his life. A few weeks ago, the same snow machine had broken down twenty miles outside of town. Unable to fix it, and lacking any means of contacting anyone back home, he had been forced to trek back to town through a windstorm, the snow gusting up from the ground in such thick swirls that he could barely see more than a few feet ahead. Eleven hours after abandoning his vehicle, he reached the edge of the lagoon that abuts the village. By then, however, he was so exhausted that he could not keep going without resting after every fifteen steps. He would collapse in the snow, count to fifteen, then stagger back to his feet and take another fifteen steps.

Somehow, while relating this story, JoeJoe had managed to restore the engine to a fragile state of functionality, and so we got back on and returned to the village. His two pals were standing exactly where we had left them. They didn't seem surprised to see us. For days one of them had been telling me about the virtues of Alaskan weed. He said it grew in greenhouses on the Kenai Peninsula. He said Snoop Dogg was a fan. "Wanna take out your depression on a toke?" he asked now. I told him I admired his persistence. "Never give up," he said, grinning.

They got the engine working again, and then JoeJoe and I got back on and headed north, past the houses, past the airstrip, past the dump, past the spot where the engine died. I tried to think positive. I said a prayer under my breath. I told the snow machine I believed in it. Maybe, just maybe, we would get out on the ice. Maybe I would even get to see them catch a whale.

We spotted a group of riders heading our way. No, I thought, it couldn't be. But it was. Reppi and his crew pulled up alongside us. "It's too windy up there," he said. "Too dangerous." We followed him back to town.

Over the next few days, the weather got warmer and the snow began to melt in the village. Soon the ice would melt too, and then whaling season would be over. Scrolling through Facebook on his phone one night, Reppi learned that a village to the north had seen a whale. I think the idea of another village catching a whale while he stayed home was more than he could take. "Soon I'm gonna start taking chances," he said.

We drove north again the next day. This time we spent three nights on the ice, the cold wind pummeling the walls of the tent. We were just a short walk from the water, but we barely spent any time outside. The weather was just too harsh, even for Reppi, who has hunted wolves at sixty below.

People came and went throughout the week. There were between five and ten of us on any given night. We spent most of our time just sitting in the tent, waiting for the wind to subside. We drank Pepsi. We ate bowls of caribou stew that Dolly heated up on the rusty camp stove. We joked around. A lot of the joking was about me. Probably most of it. One of the jokes was that I was always forgetting where I'd put things—my sunglasses, my socks, the coffee thermos, the Tabasco. Dolly, laughing affectionately, gave me an Eskimo name: Tammaq, "Lost." I certainly felt out of place. Once we were walking across a sketchy stretch of ice when I stepped in a crack, submerging my leg nearly to the knee before yanking it out in a panic. "Always carry a knife on your belt," Reppi's brother Dennis called out. "You fall in, you can stick it in the ice and pull yourself out."

A wood-burning stove in the tent was pretty much the only thing that kept us from freezing at night, so keeping it hot was a critical task. Normally this would have been a job for the youngest boys on the crew (the "boyers"), but since I was basically an infant in Eskimo terms, it fell to me. One night as the others slept, I pulled on my boots and parka and went out into the night to replenish the dwindling woodpile. I must have hacked away at a single log for more than an hour, sweating and freezing in turns. I swung the ax until my back screamed at me to stop, then swung some more. Now and then I looked around for polar bears. The men had left a rifle by the door, not that I would have known what to do with it. After what felt like an eternity, I found myself staring down at the last hunk of log. I brought the ax down until the wood surrendered with a satisfying snap. I threw back my head and let out a triumphant roar. A ghostly green mist was swirling through the sky—the aurora borealis.

Reppi and his crew did not get a whale. Neither did anyone else in Kivalina. Still, Reppi had not lost faith in the tradition. Next year, he said, he would try to get out on the ice at the very beginning of the season. With luck, the crew would not run into too many "situations." After three weeks in Kivalina, I did not have to ask what he meant by that.

By the time I left the Arctic, after nearly a month, I had seen only one animal get killed. Oddly enough, I was the one who'd killed it. It was the day after JoeJoe's snowmobile broke down outside of town, a Saturday. He knocked on the door of my cabin to see if I wanted to go fishing with him and some friends. We spent an hour crouching on a frozen river, holding rods made of willow-bush branches over holes that JoeJoe had hacked in the ice with a metal pole. The fish weren't biting, so we got on our snow machines and rode off through the tundra in search of larger prey.

We drove around for hours without seeing any animals apart from ptarmigans and the occasional fox. (Foxes, too small and foul-tasting to excite the passions of the local hunters, might be the luckiest animals in this part of the Arctic.) JoeJoe's friends took off, but he wasn't done trying. He smashed two more holes into the ice and we sat and dangled our rods over them. Still nothing. Around nine, the light began to fade, and it got very cold.

We headed downriver, our eyes on the banks, watching for flickers of movement in the willow bushes, until we came to the place where the river empties out into the lagoon. On the opposite shore, the lights of the village were glittering invitingly. The time had come to accept that the day—like all the days I'd been in Kivalina—had been a failure, in hunting terms anyway. Just then, JoeJoe shouted something unintelligible and the snow machine lurched forward and then we were tearing across the tundra, the snow machine bucking over every bump, so that I had to squeeze the seat between my thighs and wrap my arms around JoeJoe to keep from falling off. And then I saw them, in what was left of the light: three small caribou racing away from us across the lagoon. Joe-Joe handed me his rifle. There was no scope, and the back half of the sight had broken off. The stock and barrel were held together with electrical tape. I had fired a rifle only once in my life, and that was almost ten years ago, at a can. I pulled off a glove and squeezed the trigger. The wind grabbed the glove from under my arm and tossed it away. Soon my hand was so cold that I couldn't feel my fingers. I was firing wildly, and the shots were missing. Then a splotch of blood appeared on the left hindquarter of the caribou, and I shot again, and some fur came flying off. And then I shot again, and she fell.

JoeJoe made a whooping sound and we ran over to where the doe collapsed in the snow. She was struggling to get up on her forelegs, looking me right in the eyes. JoeJoe told me to shoot her in the back of the head, so I did. Then he slit her belly with his knife, and her steaming guts spilled out onto the snow. We strapped the carcass to the back of the snow machine and headed back for the village in the dark. My heart was beating hard and fast. My knees trembled. I was stunned and exhilarated and, if I'm being honest, a little proud of having done something that just about everyone there regarded as a basic requirement of manhood.

As the glittery blur of Kivalina resolved into a jumble of individual homes, JoeJoe shouted over the roar of the engine that we were passing the spot where he had begun to collapse on his epic walk across the tundra through a windstorm. A few days earlier, when he'd first told me that story, I hadn't managed much more than a dumbfounded "wow." Now, as I rode with him back to the village, I asked if he thought he would die that night. "I thought about ending it myself," he said. "But I never gave up."

GWENDOLYN KNAPP

Plum Crazy

FROM *Oxford American*

I ARRIVE AT THE SeaShell Motel in Naples around midnight. After an unexpected credit-shaming at the Budget rental car counter in the Fort Lauderdale airport, I've hauled ass through the Big Cypress Swamp in a downpour, enduring a static-ridden NPR station and the onset of McDonald's farts, to find my late check-in instructions aggressively taped to the office door, as if by somebody familiar with Saran-wrapping frat boys to pine trees. I push open the door to my room, recalling one Travelocity commenter's description of the place: *scary at first.* But it's not scary at all; the room is spacious and clean. It's just that a security light shines in the window like the angel of death all night, making it impossible to sleep without suffocating your face with pillows that another Travelocity commenter accurately described as *flat.*

In the morning, the receptionist asks, "Did you get your envelope okay? I was so scared it would fall off." Rather, she yells this to me over an Eastern European couple who are fighting about a botched room reservation, a situation that turns out to be of the husband's own doing, much like his unbuttoned floral shirt and plaid swim trunks combo. They may be the type of people who go on a beach vacation but never leave the motel pool. Not like myself—I've come on a beach vacation to hang out with plant nerds at the International Plumeria Conference.

Plumeria, also known as frangipani, is a tropical flowering tree most people associate with Hawaiian leis. The fragrant flowers usually have five petals, and, in the wild, most species of plumeria have white blooms with a yellow center. In nurseries and backyards, though, flowers of the species *Plumeria rubra* vary in color, size, and scent, with growers giving them fanciful names such as Fruit Salad and Vera Cruz Rose. A catalog of blooms—the industry leader is Jungle Jack's out of San Diego County—might sound like a strip club roster if heard out of context: Essence, Temptation, Fantasia, Xquisite, Mystique. The plants are native to Mexico, South America, and the Caribbean, and weren't brought to Hawaii until the 1860s, about 200 years after they were first classified by the French botanist Charles Plumier, the original plumeria addict.

The Plumeria Society of America was founded in Houston in 1979 by three women who aimed to spread interest in the plant, then familiar only to those who'd vacationed in Hawaii. One of the women was a famous singer named Nancy Ames, but it was another, Elizabeth Thornton, the Queen of Plumeria, who was known for her breathtaking hybrids like Texas Aggie and Thornton's Lemon Drop.

Plumeria rubra alone now consists of close to 4,000 cultivars. (When PSA registration began in 1989 there were just 51.) Celadine is commonplace in many cemeteries, hence its nickname: Graveyard Yellow. There is no such thing as a blue plumeria, or a green or a black, though people keep buying color frauds on Amazon and eBay. Depending on whom you ask, there are now legit purples: the Metallica, the Purple Jack. There are reds that turn almost black in intense, scorching heat: Black Widow, Black Tiger. There is a bloom called Plum Crazy, a deep purple and red with upturned edges and slithery, eel-like veins, devastatingly beautiful. In the mid-aughts famed grower Jim Little released a vibrant orange-gold plumeria in honor of Don Ho. It is said that Thornton, a University of Texas grad, spent her lifetime hoping to cultivate a burnt-orange bloom from seed, but she never did.

While researching her bestseller *The Orchid Thief,* Susan Orlean came upon plumerias in South Florida but didn't know them by name: "Along the path there were enormous tropical trees with pimply bark and flowers the color of bubble gum, the kind of trees you would draw in a tropical cartoon." Trees for perpetual adolescence. Trees for people like me.

The International Plumeria Conference takes place every ten years. The last time it was held—the inaugural convention, in Galveston—I was twenty-five and my experience with houseplants ran toward half-dead crotons and dank nightstand weed. My dad got me into plumeria. He's an old surfer with a dozen trees in Satellite Beach, Florida, including a light pink bloom that he keeps calling Surfqueeny after my first AOL screen name. The Plumeria Society of America would identify it as a NOID—pronounced like the Domino's mascot of yore and simply meaning "no ID," origin unknown. Dad gave me a Kauka Wilder variety when I left grad school in North Carolina for New Orleans nine years ago. I did just about everything to kill it. The plant didn't bloom until it was ten feet tall—the flower like a pop star's fake nails, with long, narrow petals in hues of bright yellow and fuchsia—an umbrella with a clunky nine-foot handle. These days I have eight plumerias and I consider myself fairly obsessed, which is why I'm here in South Florida this May weekend: to convene with the especially obsessed.

Outside the motel, the morning sun encroaches on the putty-colored downtown drag. It's 8:00 a.m. sharp and already so muggy that sweat dampens my suggested hat and suggested comfortable shoes as I walk toward the mob waiting for a bus at the Naples Botanical Garden to take us down to Florida Colors Nursery in Homestead, home to more than 1,000 plumerias.

I check in at a folding table, where a tall, handsome woman in a plumeria-print aloha shirt and starched khakis greets me. "Hetty," she says, by way of introduction. She has the side-parted, straight blond hairdo of a *Gleaming the Cube*–era Tony Hawk. Tucked behind her ear is a large red plumeria, worn to the left to show that she's married. "Where are you from?" Hetty asks, sounding less curious than suspicious. She curates the botanical garden's 500-deep plumeria collection and helped put together this year's conference.

"New Orleans," I tell her. "But originally from Florida."

"Nobody is really from Florida."

"I'm a sixth-generation Floridian."

At this impasse, Hetty walks away to greet the others. Lots of retirees are here, and more middle-aged people than I expected, all of them strapped into fanny packs and backpacks and bulky camera bags. Some sport raccoon-eyed sunburns; others have the type of doughy white skin that yearns to be pretreated with calamine for the various rashes it will soon acquire.

On the bus, I take a seat behind a Thornton disciple named Emerson Willis, an old guy rocking a straw hat and an enormous gold plumeria on a chain of Mr. T–level proportions. His wife, Nancy, wears a perfect black bouffant. Emerson has a flower named after him called the Mr. Ambassador; he's pretty much the Johnny Appleseed of frangipani. The Willises are from LaPorte, Texas, but they travel around America in a twenty-nine-foot RV with a painting of a plumeria on the side, spreading seeds and cuttings. Emerson has planted trees from California to the very southern end of A1A in Key West, at a KFC/Taco Bell. He goes down there every spring to check on it. "They keep planting gumbo limbo next to it," he complains. "You don't want gumbo limbo growing around anything."

Another Texan, a retiree named Virginia, takes the seat next to mine. She's into Grove Farm, a Hawaiian bloom known for its intense smell of rose and nutmeg. I tell her I have a San Germain, also known for its smell, that of honeysuckle. She pulls up some photos of her house in the country, her plumerias, her vegetable garden.

You can't turn up at a conference like this and start showing off pictures of your Celadine without provoking some serious eye rolls from the elders, but that's what I do.

"They call that Common Yellow," Virginia says.

"Yeah," I say. I also show her my Candy Stripe and a hot pink NOID that first bloomed for me last year, but she's not sure what it is, just common pink, or hot pink, or maybe something better, maybe a registered plant. She taps Emerson on the shoulder.

"What do you think this is?"

"I'm not sure," Mr. Ambassador says after examining it for a minute. "You always want to get registered plants. That way you'll know."

Out the window, Royal Poinciana trees and gators fly on past, but most everybody is on a phone, flaunting their tropical plants to seatmates bedecked in all manner of apposite flair: plumeria shirts, plumeria pins and barrettes, plumeria tattoos. From the front of the bus, Hetty announces over a microphone that it's time for a raffle. She has a number of items to give away, but in the world of plumeria freaks there is only one prize—a good cutting. The easiest way to add a new plumeria to your collection is by chopping a limb off an existing one and rooting it. It's also the reason there is so much theft involved with these plants; people will just roll up in front of houses and get to hacking. In his book

Growing Plumerias in Hawaii and Around the World, Jim Little writes that Hawaiian farm producers suffered $11.4 million in agricultural theft back in 2004. Hundreds of cultivars and thousands of plumeria enthusiasts have emerged in the years since.

Hetty gives out a few mystery cuttings and some seeds. Virginia's raffle ticket number is called, and she wins a bottle of Bath & Body Works plumeria-scented lotion. She squirts a little into her palm and sniffs. Everyone gets a swag bag: canvas IPC totes filled with mixed seeds, a schedule and lanyard, a water bottle and clip-on mini-fan, the new volume of the Jungle Jack's catalog—"a fourteen dollar value," she informs us—and, for some, an IPC shirt.

"Now who didn't get a shirt in their bag?" she asks over the mic. I raise my hand. Apparently I'm the only one.

"Did you sign up for the shirt online?"

"I don't know," I say. "No."

"Well, that's why you didn't get a shirt."

I don't bring up the fact that under the registration web page, the conference fee is said to include, bullet point: *IPC polo shirt (purchase additional shirts for $20, add $2.50 for XXL).*

Later, in line for our barbecue lunch on the nursery grounds, a hand reaches out and grabs me. It's an older woman with a cane I haven't met yet. She doesn't introduce herself. She just says, "You should get your shirt." She tells me it is, in fact, included in registration and "if you don't want it, I'll take it."

The Naples Botanical Garden is 170 acres, every one gorgeous. The entry opens up into a lush jungle of plants that would make an ideal set for a velociraptor scene in *Jurassic Park.* Toward the conference room there's an entire courtyard of shaded orchids and fountains that's flooded with selfie-takers on the regular. There are succulents and ferns that look like intricate Alexander McQueen gowns, and there are the Plumeria Hills off in the scorching sun, where plumerias like to be.

The second morning of the conference, we're supposed to tour the grounds for three hours, but even though nobody has checked Weather In Motion courtesy of the conference room's free Wi-Fi, it's evident the sky is turning root-rot black to the west of us. A handful of attendees, be they obese or just plagued with bad hips, set off toward the dense foliage on people-movers with speeds topping out at three miles an hour. It's all very foreboding.

Virginia mounts a people-mover because she just had knee surgery four months ago and the trip to Florida Colors yesterday really took it out of her. We get through the Asian Garden and past some prehistorically huge birds-of-paradise, arriving at the Hills as a band of rain finally hits us, coming down hard enough to skin a cat. I'm safe in the trusty raincoat that gets me through every Jazz Fest, but Virginia has brought no rain protection at all. Her dress is soaked, her hair and camera soaked, even her hiking boots look like they're turning into soggy paper bags. A golf cart bearing other ill-prepared evacuees comes racing up. "Hop on," the driver tells Virginia, who asks me, very kindly, if I'll man her machine back to the conference room. "Sure," I say, staring at the drenched seat. I putter along the path but get lost on the way. There's nothing more unsexy than being thirty-five, single, and driving a people-mover through a thunderstorm with water creeping under your raincoat, inundating your underwear. Eventually I roll up to the Caribbean Gardens, where several people have taken shelter in a little open-air house. They look at me like I'm insane.

A Hawaiian DNA expert is soaked to the bone and silently seething by a tree covered in more spikes than Rob Halford. A French woman is playing steel drums while her partner takes in several plumeria species native to the Caribbean just beyond the little house. When the rain lets up, we all make a run for it, and I abandon the people-mover at the hut.

"We'd like to thank the Fogg Café for supplying these dish towels for all of us to dry off with," says our emcee, Mike, as we reconvene a half-hour later.

When a slide show of recently deceased members of the PSA starts up, I kind of shiver—maybe from soggy-bottomed hypothermia after the people-mover experience, or just the general feeling of being a total outsider in a room of openly weeping people. Turns out plumeria enthusiasts are a close-knit group. They take trips together, to Bali and Hawaii; chat daily via online forums; and many of them have plumeria collections with multiple hundreds of cultivars. If I'm able to successfully root my new cuttings when I get back home, I will have twelve plumerias—but there is a good chance they'll perish. My murder rate is about 50 percent. My preferred method: overwatering.

*

Virginia introduces me to Terry on day three. Clad in snakeskin boots and a ten-gallon hat, he says that back home women call him the Plumeria Cowboy. With glasses on, he looks intensely pensive, but in conversation he keeps telling people, "You can't use them big words with me now, boy, I'm from Texas." The sun is back today so we resume our tour of the Botanical Garden. Despite the getup, Terry seems comfortably free of perspiration, whereas I can only be described by his spot-on commentary: "Boy. You sure know how to sweat."

I never catch what Terry does for an actual profession, but he likes to weld horseshoes into folk art. He shows us his horseshoe boot racks, horseshoe crosses, horseshoe crosses that spell out AMAZING GRACE. He's really into God. He tells us he didn't think he was going to make it to the IPC and it is by the grace of God that he's here. "I was in church, and I asked God to give me the money to get to the conference," he tells me. "Not an hour later, a lady at church handed me one thousand dollars."

Terry says he does a lot of the PSA plant sales around Houston. He has the good ones—Mardi Gras, Aztec Gold, Raspberry Sundae, the Penang Peach.

The hills are alive with the sound of plumeria freaks saying *I have five of these, and let me tell you, they're the gift that keeps on giving,* or *I tried to root this one and it rotted on me.* Irish Spring soap is strung from the trees, which Hetty tells us is to prevent deer from eating the flowers. Apparently plumeria are very tasty to certain animals, the American bulldog, for instance. "Mine used to eat the whole dang plant," Terry says. Plumeria's many known enemies include wild hogs, fungi, spider mites, and borer beetles. In Australia, there's an endangered turkey that's known to dig up and shred the plants to make its enormous sexing heaps.

Dennis, an Aussie grower who pronounces flowers *flarers,* has brought us all twirlers, a contraption he's invented consisting of fishing line glued to a tiny toothpick-size stick, which various people on the hill are now using to feel up the insides of the flowers, thereby encouraging the anthers to drop their pollen and produce a seedpod. This is called hand-pollination, and it can create new types of plumeria, since seeds aren't always true to the mother plant. Cross-pollination is the surest bet for a new type of bloom, but it requires a scalpel and a surgical method first discovered in the 1950s by hybridization pioneer Bill Moragne, who named dozens of cultivars in honor of his family: the Cyndi Moragne, the Edi Moragne, and the crowd-pleasing Jeannie Moragne.

There are trees out here with seedpods already on them, which is something to behold—they resemble giant glossy beans or over-ripe bananas or anorexic eggplants conjoined at the tip. In the end, though, they all dry out and turn the same crispy brown like a giant dead roach that splits open to reveal a bunch of smaller roachlike seeds inside. It's kind of gross, but seedlings are the only way to get a new, undiscovered bloom.

"Let's talk about seeds," Mike, the emcee, says when we reconvene after lunch. "What's the best way to store them?"

"Prescription bottle!" the audience answers.

"Yes, we have a lot of those around, don't we?"

I notice a few other attendees like me—people not in the PSA, interlopers, curious neophytes who have never grown from seed, who have no business even dreaming about discovering new cultivars. On Saturday, one woman interrupts a discussion about propagation methods and says, "Hey, sorry, newbie here. What do you mean by inflo?" The audience collectively gasps.

"It's short for inflorescence," Mike clarifies. "It's the flowering part of the plant. Where you get the flower clusters."

The IPC is divided into five or six lectures a day covering topics such as industry trends (dwarf hybrids and grafted plants are hot), plumeria DNA and biology, and how to register a new cultivar with the PSA. There are lei-making workshops and grafting demos—in which rootstock and scions are stitched together with sewing pins, rubber bands, and tape, like some sort of voodoo doll.

It's all a bit exhausting, and some topics verge on the depressing: One lecturer admits to having killed hundreds of cuttings in his quest to grow tropical plants in Kansas. An owner of Jungle Jack's, regarded as the most successful commercial nursery in America, recounts the time the USDA destroyed 17,000 cuttings he'd shipped in from Thailand. Turns out this beautiful, buoyant flower can hit the lows too. In the essay "Letter from Paradise, 21° 19' N., 157° 52' W.," Joan Didion writes of a visit to the National Memorial Cemetery of the Pacific: "One afternoon a couple came and left three plumeria leis on the grave of a California boy who had been killed, at nineteen, in 1945. The leis were already wilting by the time the woman finally placed them on the grave, because for a long time she only stood there and twisted them in her hands."

The IPC luau on the final evening perks me up. We are all adorned in our finest flip-flops and aloha shirts. We wear our Celadine leis. We eat from a buffet and drink from an overpriced cash bar. There is pineapple upside-down cake, another raffle, and an auction. A blackish red flower from Thailand pulls in $250. A new rainbow bloom, Hypnotic, goes for $275. A table over, I hear the Jungle Jack's guy declare, "Orchids are over. Orchids are done." He says plumeria could be the next bromeliad, which had a moment in the 1980s, much like Wham! enjoyed. Plumeria is already big in Japan, and the Dutch are catching on.

When it's dark out, we're ushered outside onto the lawn for a performance, but the hula dancers have trouble with the PA. The women are invited to hula, then the men. "You can't dance in cowboy boots," Terry grumbles, though I think he's actually excited. He heads toward the back and makes a big giggly ordeal of learning the dance. I have Virginia sign my IPC schedule like it's a yearbook. Terry gives me a cutting of Miami Rose, a leathery pink bloom that smells remarkably similar to suntan lotion. I can't promise that I will or won't kill it, but I take it with me and resolve to do my best.

There are some things a plumeria conference can't cover. The scent of San Germain wafting from your front porch on a summer night. The gunk of a rotted cutting between your fingers, that black mushy death. The heartache when a small plant comes crashing off your stoop in a heavy rain. The terror of a landlord with a hose. The joy of an inflo bursting up like a solid fist. The pleasure in learning that the plumeria, like the plumeria addict, should be left to her own devices.

DAVID KUSHNER

Land of the Lost

FROM *Outside*

BEFORE NOEL SANTILLAN became famous for getting lost, he was just another guy from New Jersey looking for adventure. It was last February, and the then-twenty-eight-year-old Sam's Club marketing manager was heading from Iceland's Keflavík International Airport to the capital city of Reykjavík with the modern traveler's two essentials: a dream and, most important, a GPS unit. What could go wrong?

The dream had been with him since April 14, 2010, when he watched TV news coverage of the Eyjafjallajökull volcano eruption. Dark-haired, clean-cut, with a youthful face and thick eyebrows, he had never traveled beyond the United States and his native Mexico. But something about the fiery gray clouds of tephra and ash captured his imagination. *I want to see this through my own eyes,* he thought as he sat on his couch watching the ash spread.

It took a brutal week in October 2015 to finally get him to go for it—Tuesday a taxi hit his Mazda; Wednesday a tree nearly fell on the car; Thursday, when he went to his girlfriend for comfort, she dumped him. "I was heartbroken and just wanted to get away," he recalls feeling at the time. Scrolling through his Facebook news feed, he came across a friend's photo of Iceland's famous Blue Lagoon spa. "So Iceland comes back into my head," he says.

Four months later, on a frigid, pitch-black winter morning, he was driving away from Keflavík airport in a rented Nissan Versa hatchback toward a hotel in Reykjavík, excited that his one-week journey was beginning but groggy from the five-hour red-eye flight. As a pink sun rose over the ocean and illuminated the snow-covered lava rocks along the shore, Santillan dutifully followed the commands of the GPS that came with the car, a calm female voice directing him to an address on Laugarvegur Road—a left here, a right there.

But after stopping on a desolate gravel road next to a sign for a gas station, Santillan got the feeling that the voice might be steering him wrong. He'd already been driving for nearly an hour, yet the ETA on the GPS put his arrival time at around 5:20 p.m., eight hours later. He reentered his destination and got the same result. Though he sensed that something was off, he made a conscious choice to trust the machine. He had come here for an adventure, after all, and maybe it knew where he was really supposed to go.

The farther he drove, the fewer cars he saw. The roads became icier. Sleeplessness fogged his brain, and his empty stomach churned. The only stations he could find on the radio were airing strange talk shows in Icelandic. He hadn't set up his phone for international use, so that was no help. At around 2:00 p.m., as his tires skidded along a narrow mountain road that skirted a steep cliff, he knew that the device had failed him.

He was lost.

Getting lost is a fading phenomenon of a distant past—like pay phones or being unable to call up the lyrics of the *Welcome Back, Kotter* theme song in a heartbeat ("... *your dreams were your ticket out*"). Today, more than fifty years since the Navy built the first suborbital navigation system, our cars, phones, and watches can track our every move using signals from the seventy-plus satellites circling the earth twice a day.

Most people would agree that this is a good thing. It's comforting to know where you are, to see yourself distilled into a steady blue icon gliding smoothly along a screen. With a finger tap or a short request to Siri or Google Now—which, like other smartphone tools, rely heavily on data from cell towers and Wi-Fi hot spots as well as satellites—a wonderful little trail appears on your device, beckoning you to follow. Tap the icon of a house and you're guided home from wherever you are. By knowing the most direct route—even one that changes on the fly with traffic conditions—we save time and fuel and avoid hours of frustration. The mass adoption of GPS technology among wilderness users has, it seems, helped make backcountry travel safer. According to the National Park Service, search-and-rescue missions have been dropping, from 3,216 in 2004 to 2,568 in 2014.

The convenience comes at a price, however. There's the creepy Orwellian fact of Them always knowing where We are (or We always knowing where They are). More concerning are the navigation-fail horror stories that have become legend. Last March, a sixty-four-year-old man is believed to have followed his GPS off a demolished bridge in East Chicago, Indiana, killing his wife. After Nicaraguan troops mistakenly crossed the Costa Rican border in 2010, to stake their nation's flag on rebel turf they thought was in their country, they blamed the snafu on Google Maps. Enough people have been led astray by their GPS in Death Valley that the area's former wilderness coordinator called the phenomenon "death by GPS." The source of the problem there, as in most places, is that apps don't always have accurate data on closed or hazardous roads. What looks like a bright and shiny path on your phone can in fact be a highway to hell.

Then there's the bigger question that's raised when we hear about people like Santillan who, in their total dependence on technology to find their way, venture absurdly off course. What, we wonder, is our now habitual use of navigation tools doing to our minds? An emerging body of research suggests some unsettling possibilities. By allowing devices to take total control of navigation while we ignore the real-world cues that humans have always used to deduce their place in the world, we are letting our natural wayfinding abilities languish. Compulsive use of mapping technology may even put us at greater risk for memory loss and Alzheimer's disease. By turning on a GPS every time we head somewhere new, we're also cutting something fundamental out of the experience of traveling: the adventures and surprises that come with finding —and losing—our way.

By the time Santillan white-knuckled down the mountain in northern Iceland, he figured that despite the insistence of his GPS, he wasn't anywhere near his hotel. There was no one else on the road, but at that point there wasn't much else to do but follow the line on the screen to its mysterious end. "I knew I was going to get *somewhere*," he says. "I didn't know where else to go."

The directions ended at a small blue house in a tiny town. He parked his car out front and slipped his hotel-reservation printout into his jacket as he headed toward the door. A pretty blue-eyed blond woman answered after the second ring. She smiled as he stammered about his hotel and handed her his reservation.

No, she told him in accented English with a laugh, this wasn't his hotel, and he wasn't in Reykjavík. That city was 380 kilometers south. He was in Siglufjördhur, a fishing village of 1,300 people on the northern coast. The woman, whose name happened to be Sirry, pronounced just like the Apple bot, offered to phone the hotel for him. She quickly figured out what had happened: the address on Expedia (and his reservation printout) was wrong. The hotel was on Laugavegur Road, but Expedia had accidentally spelled it with an extra *r*—Laugarvegur.

Santillan checked into a local hotel to get a good night's sleep, with the plan of driving to Reykjavík the next day. When he told his story to the woman at the front desk, she chuckled. "I'm sorry, I shouldn't laugh at this," she said, "but it's funny."

"It's funny to me also," Santillan replied.

And when she told him that her name was also Sirry, Santillan felt like he was part of some grand cosmic joke. The next morning, when he went to check out, the joke became even grander. "Some reporters want to talk with you," said Sirry.

The first Sirry had posted his absurd story on her Facebook page the previous day, Santillan soon learned, and it had quickly been shared around. Something about the tale struck a nerve. Here was a sympathetic character who personified a defining aspect of the modern human condition—and hilariously so. A Facebook friend of Sirry's who's the editor of an Icelandic travel site wrote a blog post on the "extraordinary and funny incident." Soon the misadventure attracted the interest of TV and radio journalists.

They weren't the only ones who wanted to talk with him. "Everybody in the town knew about me," he says. Some of the locals of Siglufjördhur came to the hotel to welcome him and take pictures. One offered him a tour of their local pride and joy, the Icelandic Herring Era Museum, a small red building devoted to the town's biggest industry that plays films on the salting process and has an exhibit of a *brakki,* a dorm for the so-called herring girls who worked the docks. The chef at Santillan's hotel prepared the local beef stew for him, on the house.

Enjoying all the hospitality, Santillan decided to spend an extra night. The following day he went on TV, explaining to a reporter that he'd always found GPS to be so reliable in the past. By the time he made it to Reykjavík that evening, he had become a full-blown sensation in the national media, which dubbed him the Lost Tourist. *DV,* an Icelandic tabloid, marveled that despite all the warning signs, the American had "decided to trust the [GPS]." Santillan sat down for a radio interview on a popular show. "World famous here man!" one Icelandic fan posted on Santillan's Facebook page soon after. "Like your style. Enjoy our beautyful country." Before long, his experience made international news, with reports in the *Daily Mail,* on the BBC, and in the *New York Times,* which headlined its story "GPS Mix-Up Brings Wrong Turn, and Celebrity, to an American in Iceland."

The manager of the hotel in Reykjavík had seen reports on Santillan's odyssey and, to make up for the traveler's hard time, offered him a free stay and a meal at the fish restaurant next door. Out in the streets, which were full of revelers celebrating the annual Winter Lights Festival, Icelanders corralled the Lost Tourist for selfies and plied him with shots of the local poison, Brennivin, an unsweetened schnapps. As a band played a rock song outside, Santillan kept hearing people shouting his name. Some guys dragged him up a stairway to a strip club, where one of the dancers also knew his name. The whole thing seemed surreal. "I just felt like, *This isn't happening to me,*" he says.

Still, he was going to ride it out as long as he could. After the marketing manager of the country's most famous getaway, the Blue Lagoon geothermal spa, wrote him offering a free visit, Santillan headed out the next day. The address came preloaded in his rental car's GPS, since it was the one place everyone wanted to go.

As Santillan drove out under the winter sky, he marveled at how far he had come. Not long ago, he'd been just another working stiff on his couch in New Jersey. Now he was a rock star. He pictured himself resting in the cobalt blue waters, breathing in the steam. But half an hour later, when his GPS told him he had arrived, he got a sinking feeling. Looking out the window, he saw no signs of a geothermal spa, just a small lone building in what seemed like the middle of nowhere. The Lost Tourist was lost again.

Scientists have long sought to understand how we navigate our physical environment. A key early moment came in the 1940s, when psychologist Edward C. Tolman was studying how rats learned their way around a maze. He concluded that they were building representations of the layout in their nervous systems, "which function like cognitive maps."

Some thirty years later, neuroscientist John O'Keefe located cognitive maps in mammalian brains when he identified "place cells" in the hippocampus region which became active when lab rats were in specific locations. In 2005, Norwegian neuroscientists Edvard and May-Britt Moser expanded on O'Keefe's findings, discovering that the brain also contains what they called grid cells, which, in coordination with the place cells, enable sophisticated navigation. The trio was awarded the 2014 Nobel Prize in Physiology or Medicine for uncovering what the committee called our inner GPS. Their work has profound implications—not only for our understanding of how we orient ourselves but for how our increasing reliance on technology might be undercutting the system we carry around in our heads.

Individuals who frequently navigate complex environments the old-fashioned way, by identifying landmarks, literally grow their brains. University College London neuroscientist Eleanor Maguire has used magnetic resonance imaging to study the brains of London taxi drivers, finding that their hippocampi increased in volume and developed more neuron-dense gray matter as they memorized the layout of the city. Navigate purely by GPS and you're unlikely to receive any such benefits. In 2007, Veronique Bohbot, a neuroscientist at McGill University and the Douglas Mental Health University Institute, completed a study comparing the brains of spatial navigators, who develop an understanding of the relationships between landmarks, with stimulus-response navigators, who go into a kind of autopilot mode and follow habitual routes or mechanical directions, like those coming from a GPS. Only the spatial navigators showed significant activity in their hippocampi during a navigation exercise that allowed for different orientation strategies. They also had more gray matter in their hippocampi than the stimulus-response navigators, who don't build cognitive maps. "If we follow our GPS blindly," she says, "it could have a very detrimental effect on cognition."

There's no direct link between habitual use of navigational technology and memory loss, but the implications are certainly there. Bohbot cites studies showing that a smaller and weaker hippocampus makes you more vulnerable to brain diseases like Alzheimer's, since it's one of the first regions to be affected. "It may be the case that if you don't use the hippocampus, it shrinks and you're at greater risk," she says.

Other researchers suggest similarly foreboding possibilities. Julia Frankenstein, a psychologist at the Center for Cognitive Science at the University of Freiburg, has found that people are capable of orienting themselves within a city based on memories of traditional maps, which help us develop a larger perspective of an area. When you navigate by GPS, focusing only on a route without a broader spatial context, you never gain that perspective. "It is likely that the more we rely on technology, the less we build up our cognitive maps," she says.

New research is adding to our understanding of exactly how we create those maps. Maguire recently worked with programmers to create Fog World, a shadowy virtual-reality environment studded with alien landmarks. By scanning test subjects' brains as they made their way around the scape, she could observe the spatial-learning process in action. In a series of tests last summer, she found that the retrosplenial cortex, located in the middle of the brain, played a key role in logging landmarks that were useful for navigation. Once enough landmarks were logged, the hippocampus would engage. These two sections of the brain, it appears, work together to form a cognitive map. Maguire's data also suggests that some of us just have a stronger sense of direction than others. "What we found was that poor navigators had a harder time learning the landmarks," she says. "They never did as well as the good navigators."

Maguire is planning experiments to see if it's possible to intervene with the learning process to improve navigation. As for what we can do to retain our skills, she and other researchers offer the same strong suggestion: as often as you can, turn off the GPS.

One of the most passionate and informed champions of that advice is Harvard professor John Huth. A highly respected experimental physicist who was part of the team that discovered the Higgs boson (the so-called God particle, because it endows other particles with mass), he became obsessed with our disappearing ability to find our way in the world after a tragic event near his home on Cape Cod.

On a Sunday in October 2003, two young kayakers set off onto

Nantucket Sound from the southern coast of the Cape. Mary Jagoda, a twenty-year-old from Huntington, New York, and her nineteen-year-old friend Sarah Aronoff, from Bethesda, Maryland, paddled into the choppy, sixty-degree waters without a compass, map, or GPS. A dense fog soon rolled in. When they were reported missing an hour or so later, a frantic search ensued. The following day, their kayaks were spotted tied together but empty. Coast Guard cutters, helicopters, and local police canvassed the area through the night to no avail. Jagoda was recovered on Tuesday, having died from drowning. Aronoff was never found.

Huth was kayaking just a half-mile from the women when they went missing. He, too, had become disoriented in the fog, but he'd been sure to take note of the wind and wave direction before leaving the shore, a habit he'd picked up after a scary experience several months earlier in Maine. He paddled back to shore blindly but with a strong sense of where he was headed.

The deaths of the women left him with a serious case of survivor's guilt. His response was to embark on what he now calls a year of self-imposed penance by learning everything he could about navigation. He used flash cards to memorize constellations, studied the routes of 1600 BC Pacific Islanders and medieval Arab traders, and learned to orient himself using shadows. Eventually, he says, "I realized I was looking at the world very differently than I had beforehand."

He dug in deeper, compelled by a sense of duty to fight back against automation bias, the human tendency to trust machines more than ourselves. In 2009, he began teaching a new undergraduate class at Harvard on primitive navigation techniques. The course led to his 2013 book, *The Lost Art of Finding Our Way,* which makes a powerful case for learning how to get where you need to go simply by paying attention to the environment around you.

Last summer, I visited Huth on Cape Cod to get a primer on what he teaches his Harvard students. One morning, he suggested we try a method for tracking distance used by the Roman legionnaires. Huth, an athletic, bearded fifty-eight-year-old, was wearing cargo shorts and a white T-shirt as we walked silently along a rocky beach near his home, counting paces, with every 1,000 paces equaling *mille passus,* the Latin phrase at the root of the word "mile." We passed lobster-red tourists, stopping every so often so he could compare our paces, which he penciled into a small notebook for later calculation. After a little while, he led us up a series of sand dunes.

"It was right here," he said, pointing to an overgrown patch of beach grass where, he explained, there used to be a handmade wooden sign with a picture of one of the kayakers. There had been one phrase on it, he recalled: "No one is lost to God."

Over Huth's years of research on traditional navigation, one of the places that turned out to be an especially rich source of techniques was Iceland, an isolated island frequently shrouded in fog and surrounded by tempestuous seas. Europeans discovered it by accident, just like they had North America. As Huth recounted to me, a Norse sailor named Naddodd arrived there after drifting off course on his way to the Faeroe Islands. Others found means of reaching it purposefully. When the Norse colonized the country in the ninth century, they found it populated by Irish monks who had arrived, Huth speculated, by following the paths of migrating ducks. (Subsequent Norse explorers employed ravens.) As the Norse learned, Iceland's weather was so unruly that summer offered the only reliable winds to get there. Sailing fifty-foot wooden boats with tar-soaked moss sealing the hulls, they would hug the coast of Norway as they traversed between known landmarks.

Huth was particularly fascinated by how "for the Norse," as he writes in his book, "time reckoning and direction were intertwined." They divided days into eight pieces that reflected the eight divisions of the horizon—north, northeast, east, southeast, south, southwest, west, and northwest—and created clocks by reading the sun's relative position to markers, like a farmhouse or large rock. "The time of day," he writes, "is then associated with a place."

Huth hopes that modern humans will rediscover that deep sense of place. In the meantime, he rails against our choice to "outsource so many of our cognitive functions to automation." There are, he told me, "tons of examples of people substituting automation for actual reasoning." None better, of course, than Noel Santillan.

As it happens, Huth could have found himself in his own lost-tourist predicament a couple of summers ago, when he took a vacation to Iceland with his wife and daughter. As usual, he relied on a map instead of a GPS to get around. But as he drove into Reykjavík from the airport, he got mixed up on the city's winding roads. At that point, he did what the Norse did centuries before:

he sought out markers that he had already identified and coordinated them with the cognitive map he'd created in his head—the water shouldn't be over here, it should be over there.

"I just stopped, looked around, and tried to identify landmarks," he told me as we completed another *mille passus*. Fairly soon he was back on the right path.

This, he said, is what Santillan should have done. "If I've gotten to the point where the roads start looking impassible, I would say, 'Okay, this is fucked.' Then I'd basically try to retrace my steps."

Santillan had no idea how he'd become lost again. For whatever reason, the GPS had led him not to the Blue Lagoon but to some convention center off an empty road. All he wanted to do was submerge himself in those wondrous warm waters, but instead he was trudging through the snow to see if anyone inside could help him find his way.

As he stepped into the building, a funny thing happened. He was recognized—again. The people inside were workers from the Blue Lagoon who had assembled there for a meeting, and they had seen the news reports about him. The fact that Santillan was lost again made him all the more credible. After patiently posing for a bunch of pictures, he succumbed to an old-fashioned way of getting to where he was going: following the directions given to him by another human being.

And so, with the GPS turned off, he drove on—a right here, a left there—looking for landmarks along the way. His hippocampus, activated by the incoming data, stitched together the beginnings of a cognitive map. Before long he was soaking in a steamy bath, white volcanic mud smeared on his face—though not enough to mask his identity from some fawning spa employees. By then he'd already vowed to return to Iceland. *Maybe,* he thought, *I'll even live here at some point.* Until he returns, he has something to remember his misadventure: an Icelandic GPS. The rental agency presented it to him when he returned his Nissan. Santillan tried hooking it up to his car when he got back to New Jersey, but alas, the foreign model didn't work. So now it sits in a box in his bedroom, a reminder of his time as the Lost Tourist, a nickname he considers a badge of honor. "I like it," he says, "because that's how you find interesting things. If you don't lose yourself, you're never going to find yourself."

On the Road

FROM *The New York Times Magazine*

THERE IS A vast gulf between how people tend to think of "tourism," an agreeable pursuit for themselves and a great benefit to their local economy, and how people tend to think of other tourists, as interlopers, beholden to oafish appetites for packaged experience. Those of us who travel professionally, with a view to record for those at home our encounters on the road, try to bridge that perceptual divide. This can be uncomfortable. Tourists in bad faith, we are paid to elevate our naive consumption (of city, museum, vista, ruin, breakfast) to the level of a vocation. The internal anxiety that this contradiction inspires in us often gets displaced, in an amusing way, onto others on the same circuit. Professional travelers like nothing better than the opportunity to point out the crumminess of other professional travelers.

The classic formulation is the opening salvo of the anthropologist Claude Lévi-Strauss's 1955 "Tristes Tropiques": "Travel and travellers are two things I loathe—and yet here I am, all set to tell the story of my expeditions." It has been fifteen years, he continues, since he left the remote interior of Brazil, but the prospect of this book has been a source of shame. All he wants to offer is a humble contribution to the anthropological record, "an unpublished myth, a new marriage rule, or a complete list of names of clans." But those delicacies of knowledge are so rare, the tribulations of their collection so great, that it has proved almost impossible to separate the wheat of anthropology from the chaff of adventure: "insipid details, incidents of no significance." It is with great hesitation, then, that he takes up his pen "in order to rake over memory's trash-cans." He parodies a typical travel-book sentence of his day: "And yet that sort of book enjoys a great, and, to me, inexplicable popularity. Amazonia, Africa, and Tibet have invaded all our bookstalls."

Mark Twain pioneered this aggressive self-defense in the 1860s, the early years of democratized and commodified guidebook travel. By the time Lévi-Strauss took up the cudgel, photography was beginning to catch up with tourism, and since then travel writing and travel photography have come to seem, to the skeptical, like two sides of the same counterfeit token. Lévi-Strauss continued: "Travel-books, expeditionary records, and photograph-albums abound . . . Mere mileage is the thing; and anyone who has been far enough, and collected the right number of pictures (still or moving, but for preference in colour), will be able to lecture to packed houses for several days running."

The travel writer, at least, had to sit down and actually bash it all out, which gave him or her some measure of self-respect. The travel photographer had it worse. The right to call itself art rather than mere mechanism had been photography's struggle since the medium was invented, but now practitioners had to differentiate their efforts from the unstudied shutter-clicks of rank amateurs. The problem grew even more dire as travel photography transitioned from a hobby to perhaps the ultimate signifier of the inauthentic and the conformist. In his 1954 essay "The Loss of the Creature," Walker Percy imagines a sightseer upon his first approach to the Grand Canyon: "Instead of looking at it, he photographs it. There is no confrontation at all. At the end of forty years of preformulation and with the Grand Canyon yawning at his feet, what does he do? He waives his right of seeing and knowing and records symbols for the next forty years." In this case, the travel photographer has committed the original sin: His job is to create the ideal image against which the multitudes will inevitably find their own experiences wanting. The travel photographer is thereby caught in a bind. Either he is no better than the desultory tourist, or he is responsible for the fact that our experiences rarely resemble the advertisements or postcards.

By now, Percy's contempt for this cliché—the traveler so busy with documentation that he misses out on some phantom called the "experience itself"—has itself become a cliché. But we are not much closer to resolving the fundamental paradox of travel, which is just one version of the fundamental paradox of late-capitalist life. On the one hand, we have been encouraged to believe that we are no longer the sum of our products (as we were when we were still an industrial economy) but the sum of our experiences. On the other, we lack the ritual structures that once served to organize, integrate, and preserve the stream of these experiences, so they inevitably feel both scattershot and evanescent. We worry that photographs or journal entries keep us at a remove from life, but we also worry that without an inventory of these documents —a collection of snow globes for the mantel—we'll disintegrate. Furthermore, that inventory has to fulfill two slightly different functions: it must define us as at once part of a tribe ("people who go to Paris") and independent of it ("people who go to Paris and don't photograph the Eiffel Tower").

Now that social media has given us a public forum, both theatrical stage and deposit institution, for this inventory, we have brought to this paradox increasingly elaborate methods of documentary performance. But the underlying strategies are nothing new. The most elementary strategy is the avoidance of the Grand Canyon/ Eiffel Tower conundrum entirely, but this works only if you're confident that you've identified a satisfying alternative. (As Paul Fussell put it in his 1979 book *Abroad,* "Avoiding Waikiki brings up the whole question of why one's gone to Hawaii at all, but that's exactly the problem.") Another is to forefront our own inauthenticity as a disclaimer. In his 1987 book *The Songlines,* Bruce Chatwin described his lifelong attempt to write a book about nomads as a repudiation of his earlier involvement with art: "I quit my job in the 'art world' and went back to the dry places: alone, travelling light. The names of the tribes I travelled among are unimportant: Rguibat, Quashgai, Taimanni, Turkomen, Bororo, Tuareg—people whose journeys, unlike my own, had neither beginning nor end." People, that is, who had a motive for travel that went well beyond the vanity of documentation.

Even if you understand and sympathize with obsessive documentary travel, summer can make anyone feel as uncharitable as Percy felt toward that poor sightseer at the lip of the Grand Canyon. More than one friend told me that their main vacation in August was a vacation from Instagram, because they'd endured more than enough ostentatious displays of wealth and leisure for one season.

I know other people who deliberately switched to Snapchat, but then sent out reminders to that effect; they wanted a contemporaneous audience but felt uncomfortable going on the permanent record. For some reason, the real-time digital exhibitionism of excessive summer holidaying makes me feel generous; the more desperate a bid to be liked, the more enthusiastically I go ahead and like it. I have an acquaintance—someone I like but barely know —who spent what seemed to me to be an exorbitant amount of time doing absolutely nothing at all on the remote Italian island Pantelleria, photographing that nothing at all as though he were on sabbatical inside a Fellini film. I assiduously liked every single post. (I'm not perfect. I still categorically withhold my likes from some classes of image: photos of chefs in Copenhagen; photos of food in Copenhagen; photos of people who have recently eaten in Copenhagen.)

My favorite social-media vacation of the summer, however, belonged to my friend David, who intermittently recorded a long cross-country road trip. It was a solo undertaking, and the loneliness of much of the imagery made me feel as though it deserved special attention.

A week before David left, in mid-August, he posted a brief prelude in the form of a diptych: an uneventful video of a street scene taken from his stoop in Brooklyn followed by a black-and-white shot, taken between Chelsea and Hell's Kitchen, of a horseless buggy covered with a clear tarp; one of the new skyscrapers of the Hudson Yards development rises in the background. The two images in succession—the sentimentality of home, the gently self-mocking irony of the black-and-white wagon—felt like a personal send-off in a minor key, an understated announcement that he was on his way.

His first road picture was geotagged "Chicago Downtown" but could have been anywhere: the battered steel door between the faux fluted pilasters of a down-at-heel industrial building, its cinder-block facade unevenly repaired; above the door, someone had stenciled a simple, charming scene of white snowcapped mountains and a floating white moon. The image was lovely but nothing special, but it seemed to me instantly legible: *I'm mooning around alone on this random block in Chicago, if anyone wants to hang out.* If he'd posted a photo of the Sears Tower, say, it wouldn't have played as invitation. The next series of images were taken from art museums, one from a permanent collection and the other from a show on view for only a short time. There was something reassuring about these posts, which seemed to me to advertise both the actual artworks depicted and the fact that he was doing a salutary job keeping himself company.

Over the course of the next week, there were some images I found inscrutable (audio CDs, stamped in red as RESTRICTED, of Bruce Dern doing a *Henry V* monologue at the Actors Studio), some readily intelligible as artifactual Americana (Smith & Wessons in the case of a Badlands pawnshop), and others that attempted sidelong glances at tourist landmarks (not Mount Rushmore itself but a shot of a family selfie in front of it; a photo of the Rocket Motel's neon next to its own identical postcard). There were a few pretty sunsets—one in Minnesota, one in Wyoming—that spoke of a late-day solitary melancholy.

The best image of his trip was of a nighttime gas station. "What is it," his caption asked, "about #gasstationsatdusk?" The picture got a lot of likes—more than his others tended to—and occasioned a number of passing remarks in the comments, especially from other artists and art critics. One contributor said something about Ed Ruscha and Matthew Barney. But the unmistakable reference, one art historian pointed out in the comments, was to Edward Hopper. Hopper was a painter, of course, but as Geoff Dyer points out in his book *The Ongoing Moment,* Hopper "could, with some justification, claim to be the most influential American photographer of the twentieth century—even though he didn't take any photographs." Dyer wrote that in 2005, long before Instagram existed, but the platform's retro filters only deepen the likeness.

Hopper might remind Dyer of a photographer like Walker Evans, but the first thing a gas station at dusk recalls, for many travelers and travel writers who feel the need to justify their restlessness, is Elizabeth Bishop's "Questions of Travel" and its "grease-stained filling-station floor." Earlier in the poem, Bishop asks us to think of travel's arduous return, and asks rhetorically if we might have been better off staying put. The answer is familiar. We were right to go, but not because we got anywhere or achieved anything. It's because of the small moments of incidental grace, the insipid bits Lévi-Strauss disparaged (and subsequently indulged): "But surely it would have been a pity/not to have seen the trees along this road."

It's hard not to suspect that we've seen Bishop's gas station before; it's the same Hopper we recognize from David's Instagram feed. At this point, given the layers of quotation and allusion, it seems silly to treat David's image as if it were, as Percy might have had it, some flimsy representation standing between himself and an unmediated world, or a private snow-globe reminder of that stretch of interstate. It wasn't an act of representation at all, and it certainly wasn't private. It was the expression of affect he wanted to communicate in that moment—something a little smart, and a little sad, and a little funny, and all in all very *David*. The image, an Internet square of labyrinthine self-referentiality—a photograph that recalled a painting that was at home in a poem—recalled for me a different line of Geoff Dyer's, where he quotes John Berger on Paul Strand's portraits: They arrested a moment "whose duration is measured not by seconds, but by its relation to a lifetime."

One difference between a quest and a "road trip"—in the broadest sense of the term—is the degree to which the traveler knows what he or she wants. This is how we know to differentiate between the necessary and the incidental. Lévi-Strauss set out for Brazil's interior with a point, so it was obvious to him what was relevant (an unpublished myth, a new marriage rule) and what was dross (the logistics of transport). The appeal of the road trip, or the long through-hike, or the pilgrimage, is that the "point" is so deliberately minimal—to arrive at, you know, the end—and the decisions involved so banal (*stop for gas now, or in a bit?*) that the distinction between signal and noise is blurred. When the question of significance is deferred, all moments are rendered equally significant.

The tourist caricature is in a funny position. The "point" of his or her vacation is not something discrete, like Lévi-Strauss's registration of a new marriage rule, but simply the accumulation of rarefied experience for its own sake, which means that every single moment must be optimally memorable—that is, photographable. Unlike the tourist, the traveler accepts that the point isn't the intensity of the peak experiences but the way the journey itself sacralizes any given moment as a metonym for the whole. Feel free to photograph the gas station.

There's a parallel in photography. The first time I looked at David's gas station, I was at the San Francisco Museum of Modern Art, where I'd just seen galleries of large-format photographers, including Andreas Gursky and Thomas Struth. They document all the shipping containers in a southern Italian port, the controlled chaos of the Hong Kong Stock Exchange. Their painterly intensity and formal composition derive from Henri Cartier-Bresson's definition of photography as "the decisive moment," the juncture of maximal effect and maximal information. In *Diana and Nikon*, her 1980 book on photography, Janet Malcolm expanded on the idea, remarking that "the arresting of time is photography's unique capacity, and the decision of when to click the shutter is the photographer's chief responsibility." She contrasts the pictorialism of such photographers as Cartier-Bresson, Steichen, and Atget with the apparent vulgarity of subsequent generations of street photographers.

For Dyer, the road trip plays a crucial role in this midcentury photographic turn to the vernacular. It was Robert Frank, Dyer writes, who gave us the "ongoing" moment instead of the "decisive" one. He invented America as "a place to be seen from a car, a country that could be seen without stopping. If we do choose to linger it is often to try to work out why Frank took a particular picture (what's so special about this?)." Garry Winogrand "pushed things a stage further, combining Frank's ad hoc aesthetic with a pictorial appetite so voracious it bordered on the indiscriminate." The point of a photograph of a trail, or some billboard half-seen out the window of a bus, is that it could easily be exchanged for the image taken immediately before or immediately afterward. The random sample communicates in one unpremeditated frame all the significance that particular person's drive down that particular road could possibly contain.

This is the aspiration common to road-trip literature and road-trip photography: the moment at the gas station is held, insistently, to express as much about the total experience as the shot of the Eiffel Tower. But there remains, at least for me, a tension between the stories we tell about the road and the photographs we take along the way. When I've returned to things I've written about extended overland travel—whether a book, or travel articles, or just emails to friends—I feel settled, almost subdued, by my own accounts, by the way a succession of random gas-station incidents has been given a form. Though in each case I tried to capture the miscellaneous experience of that particular interlude, the mood of each has inevitably been coerced into coherence. *Yes*, I think, *this is how it happened, and this is what it meant, and what it will now continue to mean in retrospective perpetuity.* These texts, over time, overwrote the memories from which they were drawn.

Revisiting my photographs from those same trips is dislocating in a different way. The difference may, of course, be a question of my own orientation: I'm habituated to the way a given experience is encoded in language. Writers love to repeat the truism that they need to see what they write to know what they think; seeing what you shot betrays the extent to which what you think is produced, and thereby constrained, by its method of thought. Always I find my photographs replete with remainders, pedestrian details that contradict and undermine the equally pedestrian account I committed to words. The colors are different. Drops of scarlet blood on a hard tarmac black as obsidian. An overturned brass samovar in a dingy brown train compartment. A bright alarum of pink cherry blossoms against a glass-flat cobalt sea. There is something about those moments, fugitively apprehended as they might have been, that seem to me now odd and decisive. They don't at all seem like random samples of the ongoing. I never think, *What was so special about this?* I think instead, *Yes, I remember now exactly what was so special about this.* They mutely twitch with escaped significance. When we see what we saw, we are reminded of what was apprehended—and let go.

ROBERT MACFARLANE

The Secrets of the Wood Wide Web

FROM *The New Yorker*

EPPING FOREST IS a heavily regulated place. First designated as a royal hunting ground by Henry II in the twelfth century, with severe penalties imposed on commoners for poaching, it has since 1878 been managed by the City of London Corporation, which governs behavior within its bounds using forty-eight bylaws. The forest is today almost completely contained within the M25, the notorious orbital motorway that encircles outer London. Minor roads crisscross it, and it is rarely more than four kilometers wide. Several of its hundred or so lakes and ponds are former blast holes of the V1 "doodlebug" rockets flung at London in 1944. Yet the miraculous fact of Epping's existence remains: almost 6,000 acres of trees, heath, pasture, and waterways, just outside the city limits, its grassland still grazed by the cattle of local commoners, and adders still basking in its glades. Despite its mixed-amenity use— from golf to mountain biking—it retains a greenwood magic.

Earlier this summer I spent two days there, wandering and talking with a young plant scientist named Merlin Sheldrake. Sheldrake is an expert in mycorrhizal fungi, and as such he is part of a research revolution that is changing the way we think about forests. For centuries, fungi were widely held to be harmful to plants, parasites that cause disease and dysfunction. More recently, it has become understood that certain kinds of common fungi exist in subtle symbiosis with plants, bringing about not infection but connection. These fungi send out gossamer-fine fungal tubes called hyphae, which infiltrate the soil and weave into the tips of plant roots at a cellular level. Roots and fungi combine to form what is called a mycorrhiza: itself a growing-together of the Greek words for fungus (*mykós*) and root (*riza*). In this way, individual plants are joined to one another by an underground hyphal network: a dazzlingly complex and collaborative structure that has become known as the Wood Wide Web.

The relationship between these mycorrhizal fungi and the plants they connect is now known to be ancient (around 450 million years old) and largely one of mutualism—a subset of symbiosis in which both organisms benefit from their association. In the case of the mycorrhizae, the fungi siphon off food from the trees, taking some of the carbon-rich sugar that they produce during photosynthesis. The plants, in turn, obtain nutrients such as phosphorus and nitrogen that the fungi have acquired from the soil, by means of enzymes that the trees do not possess.

The implications of the Wood Wide Web far exceed this basic exchange of goods between plant and fungi, however. The fungal network also allows plants to distribute resources—sugar, nitrogen, and phosphorus—between one another. A dying tree might divest itself of its resources to the benefit of the community, for example, or a young seedling in a heavily shaded understory might be supported with extra resources by its stronger neighbors. Even more remarkably, the network also allows plants to send one another warnings. A plant under attack from aphids can indicate to a nearby plant that it should raise its defensive response before the aphids reach it. It has been known for some time that plants communicate aboveground in comparable ways, by means of airborne hormones. But such warnings are more precise in terms of source and recipient when sent by means of the myco-net.

The revelation of the Wood Wide Web's existence, and the increased understanding of its functions, raises big questions—about where species begin and end; about whether a forest might be better imagined as a single superorganism, rather than a grouping of independent individualistic ones; and about what trading, sharing, or even friendship might mean among plants. "Whenever I need to explain my research to someone quickly, I just tell them I work on the social networks of plants," Sheldrake told me.

Sheldrake is twenty-eight years old and tall, with a tight head of dark curls. When we met, he was wearing a blue paisley-pattern neckerchief, a collarless woolen jacket, and a khaki canvas rucksack with gleaming brass buckles. He resembled a Victorian plant hunter, ready for the jungle. In addition to his academic pursuits, Sheldrake plays accordion in a band called the Gentle Mystics, whose tracks include a trance epic called "Mushroom 30,000," and whose musical style might best be described as myco-klezmer-hip-hop-electro-burlesque. Once heard, bewildered. Twice heard, hooked.

As an undergraduate studying natural sciences at Cambridge, in the late aughts, Sheldrake read the 1988 paper "Mycorrhizal Links Between Plants: Their Functioning and Ecological Significance," by the plant scientist E. I. Newman, in which Newman argued boldly for the existence of a "mycelial network" linking plants. "If this phenomenon is widespread," Newman wrote, "it could have profound implications for the functioning of ecosystems."

Those implications fascinated Sheldrake. He had long loved fungi, which seemed to him possessed of superpowers. He knew that they could turn rocks to rubble, move with eerie swiftness both above ground and under it, reproduce horizontally, and digest food outside their bodies via excreted enzymes. He was aware that their toxins could kill people, and that their psychoactive chemicals could induce hallucinogenic states. After reading Newman's paper, he understood that fungi could also allow plants to communicate with one another.

"All of these trees will have mycorrhizal fungi growing into their roots," Sheldrake said, gesturing at the beech and hornbeam through which we were walking. "You could imagine the fungi themselves as forming a massive underground tree, or as a cobweb of fine filaments, acting as a sort of prosthesis to the trees, a further root system, extending outwards into the soil, acquiring nutrients and floating them back to the plants, as the plants fix carbon in their leaves and send sugar to their roots, and out into the fungi. And this is all happening right under our feet."

We reached a broad clearing in which hundreds of bright-green beech seedlings were flourishing, each a few centimeters high, drawn by the ready light. Sheldrake knelt down and brushed away leaves to reveal a patch of soil the size of a dinner plate. He pinched up some of the earth and rubbed it between his fingers: rich, dark humus. "Soil is fantastically difficult stuff to work with experimentally, and the hyphae are on the whole too thin to see," he said. "You can put rhizotrons into the ground to look at root growth—but those don't really give you the fungi because they are too fine. You can do below-ground laser scanning, but again that is too crude for the fungal networks."

Gleaming yellow-brown spiders and bronze beetles battled over the leaves. "Hyphae will be growing around in the decomposing matter of this half-rotting leaf, those rotting logs, and those rotting twigs, and then you'll have the mycorrhizal fungi whose hyphae grow into hot spots," Sheldrake said, pointing around the glade. In addition to penetrating the tree roots, the hyphae also interpenetrate each other—mycorrhizal fungi on the whole don't have divisions between their cells. "This interpenetration permits the wildly promiscuous horizontal transfer of genetic material: fungi don't have to have sex to pass things on," Sheldrake explained. I tried to imagine the soil as transparent, such that I could peer down into this subterranean infrastructure, those spectral fungal skeins suspended between the tapering tree roots, creating a network at least as intricate as the cables and optical fibers beneath our cities. I once heard the writer China Miéville use a particular phrase for the realm of fungi: "The kingdom of the gray." It captured their otherness: the challenges fungi issued to our usual models of time, space, scale, and species. "You look at the network," Sheldrake said. "And then it starts to look back at you."

After two hours we ran out of forest, rebounded off the M25, hopped a barbed-wire fence, and came to rest in a field that looked as if it belonged to a private landowner. We weren't lost, exactly, but we did need to know where the forest widened again. I pulled up the hybrid map of Epping on my phone, and a blue dot pulsed our location. The forest flared green to the southwest, so that was where we headed, crossing a busy road and then pushing deeper into the trees until we could hardly hear car noise.

When Sheldrake began his PhD, in 2011, there was no single figure at Cambridge with an expertise in symbiosis and mycorrhizae, so he contacted researchers he admired at other institutions, until he had established what he calls a "network of subject godparents—some in Sweden, in Germany, in Panama, in America, in England, where I was beholden to none, but part of their extended families." In the second year of his doctorate, Sheldrake went to the Central American jungle for fieldwork: to Barro Colorado Island, located in the man-made Gatun Lake, in the Panama

Canal. There he joined a community of field scientists, overseen by a grizzled American evolutionary biologist named Egbert Giles Leigh Jr.

Some of the science undertaken on the island was what might be called methodologically high-risk. One young American scientist, researching what Sheldrake called the "drunken-monkey hypothesis," was attempting to collect monkey urine, after the monkeys had feasted on fermenting fruit, and assess it for intoxication levels. Sheldrake faced his own research frustrations. Much of his early work involved him taking spore samples back to the lab for scrutiny, and he became uncomfortable with how so much of what he dealt with in the lab was "absolutely dead, boiled, fixed, embalmed." He longed for more direct contact with the fungi he was studying. One afternoon, he was examining mycorrhizal spores under a microscope, when it occurred to him that they looked just like caviar. After hours of cleaning and sifting, he had enough to pile, with a pair of tweezers, onto a tiny fragment of biscuit, which he then ate. "They're really good for you, spores, full of all these lipids," he said. On occasion he has cut them into lines and snorted them.

During his second season on the island, Sheldrake became interested in a type of plants called mycoheterotrophs, or "mycohets" for short. Mycohets are plants that lack chlorophyll, and thus are unable to photosynthesize, making them entirely reliant on the fungal network for their provision of carbon. "These little greenless plants plug into the network, and somehow derive everything from it without paying anything back, at least in the usual coin," Sheldrake said. "They don't play by the normal rules of symbiosis, but we can't prove they're parasites." Sheldrake focused on a genus of mycohets called *Voyria*, part of the gentian family, the flowers of which studded the jungle floor on Barro Colorado Island like pale purple stars.

A central debate over the Wood Wide Web concerns the language used to describe the transactions it enables, which suggest two competing visions of the network: the socialist forest, in which trees act as caregivers to one another, with the well-off supporting the needy, and the capitalist forest, in which all entities are acting out of self-interest within a competitive system. Sheldrake was especially exasperated by what he called the "super-neoliberal capitalist" discourse of the biological free market. One of the reasons Sheldrake loved the *Voyria*, he explained, is that they were harder to understand, mysterious: "They are the hackers of the Wood Wide Web."

Working with local field assistants on the island—"the best botanists ever"—Sheldrake carried out a painstaking census of the soil in a series of plots, sequencing the DNA of hundreds of root samples taken both from green plants and the *Voyria*. This allowed him to determine which species of fungi were connecting which plants, and thereby to make an unprecedentedly detailed map of the jungle's social network. Sheldrake got out his phone and pulled up an image of the map on his screen. The intricacy of relation it represented reminded me of attempts I had seen to map the global Internet: a firework display of meshing lines and colors.

We stopped to eat in a dry part of the forest, on rising ground amid old pines. Sheldrake had brought two mangoes and a spinach tart. He drank beer, I drank water, and the pine roots snaked and interlaced around us. He told me about the home laboratory he runs on his kitchen table, and the microbrewery he runs in his garden shed. He has brewed mead from honey, as well as cider from the apples of Newton's apple tree, at Trinity College, Cambridge (batch name: Gravity), and from the apples of Darwin's orchard at Down House (batch name: Evolution).

Later in the day we came to a lake, where a hard-packed mud bank sloped down into shallow water. Carp burped in the shadows. Moorhen bickered. The lake bed belched gas bubbles. Sheldrake and I sat facing the setting sun, and he explained how, for each formal scientific paper he published about mycorrhizae, he planned also to publish the paper's "dark twin," in which he would describe the "messy network of crazy things that underlies every piece of cool, clean science, but that you aren't usually allowed to see—the fortunate accidents of fieldwork, the tangential serendipitous observation that sets off a thought train, the boredom, the chance encounters." Two dog-walkers interrupted our conversation, looking hopeful. "Do you know where the visitors' center is?" one asked. "We're lost." "No, we're lost too," I said, happily. We traded best guesses, exchanging what little information we had, and they wandered off.

ANN MAH

Volunteering for the Harvest

FROM *The New York Times*

AS A WINE LOVER with an active imagination, I'd always pictured the French wine harvest as a cross between *Sideways* and *I
Love Lucy,* a sun-drenched bacchanal featuring boozy lunches en
plein air, rosy-cheeked peasants crushing fruit with their bare feet,
and a bit of insouciant grape picking.

But on my first morning of a week spent working in a Champagne vineyard, the clouds hung low and leaden, an ominous dark
mass biding its time. I wore rubber boots, bought not thirty minutes earlier, the smallest pair at the garden supply center, and still
three sizes too big.

I wielded a pair of secateurs (one-handed pruning clippers),
their orange handles flashing through dew-drenched vine leaves
as I hunted for the correct stem to cut. The foliage rustled, crisp
as newspaper, and my sweater cuffs, peeping from beneath the
sleeves of a borrowed rain slicker, became itchy shackles of sodden
wool.

Finally, my shears snipped the right stem, and a bunch of grapes
tumbled into my outstretched hand. As I reached for the next cluster, a gentle patter began to echo through the vineyard; it turned
into an urgent beat before I realized what it was: rain. Ahead of me
were rows of vines stretched as far as I could see, lushly verdant,
laden with fruit.

I had come to the rolling slopes of Champagne to participate
in the age-old tradition of *les vendanges,* the annual wine harvest
that takes place at summer's end. From grape picking, to pressing,

to juice fermentation, the harvest—which lasts from two to three weeks—generates myriad extra tasks, and most wineries rely heavily on temporary labor, both paid and unpaid.

In exchange for long days of toil, they often offer meals, wine, and lodging, making this an ideal vacation for the budget traveler. And, as I found when I volunteered last September with AR Lenoble—a family-owned Champagne house in Damery, about five miles northwest of Epernay—the camaraderie, breathtaking vineyard views, and rare glimpse of French culture can almost make the backaches disappear. The free-flowing Champagne doesn't hurt either.

Before the quaffs of Champagne, though, I had to do some legwork. In recent years, more French wineries have begun harvesting by machine, which is cheaper and faster, though it offers inconsistent quality. Winemakers that still harvest by hand—predominantly in the premier regions like Champagne, Burgundy, Bordeaux, and Châteauneuf-du-Pape—are regulated by rigid French labor laws, particularly during the harvest season, with fines levied to discourage black market employment. Volunteers fall into a gray area, but some wineries are reluctant to take the risk.

On the other hand, there exists a timeless tradition of volunteer grape harvesting—as ancient, perhaps, as wine itself—necessitated by the sheer volume of urgent activity required to collect ripe cultivated grapes and initiate supervised fermentation. Many properties, especially the small and family-owned, still welcome volunteers in exchange for food and lodging, but they follow a key principle: discretion.

"Volunteer help is clearly the way it's always been done in France," said Caroline Jones, the winemaker at Domaine Rouge-Bleu, a small Côtes du Rhône winery that she owns with her husband, Thomas Bertrand. "For us, it's a question of quality. We always want to hand-harvest our grapes, but the cost of a team of pickers is prohibitive for us. By using volunteers, we get a group of people who are excited to be here, and they become personally involved."

Several months ago, I had emailed three small French wineries, offering my (free) services. To my surprise, all of them responded with an invitation—one winery for a day, the other two for the entire harvest.

In the end, I chose the type of wine I like the best. And that is how I found myself picking pinot meunier grapes amid a minor tempest in Champagne.

Earlier that morning, around eight o'clock, I had hitched a ride from the winery to this patch of vines above Damery. As I clambered down from the farm van, Hervé Blondel, one of the vineyard managers, handed me a bucket and a pair of garden shears and set me to work picking fruit without much further advice. The art to harvesting grapes, I soon realized, is to know exactly where to clip so that the bunch falls free.

I spent a lot of time hunting for those elusive key stems, which hide camouflaged in thick clusters of grape leaves, kneeling, stooping, and bending my body into regrettable contortions, snipping aimlessly until a cluster dropped into my free hand (or, just as often, onto the ground). The grapes went into a bucket that grew heavy as I crept down the row.

Around me, the other *vendangeurs* (a family of eight from Nord-Pas-de-Calais) worked in pairs, facing each other from opposite sides of the vine, a vantage point that allowed them to seize every cluster with efficiency. They descended upon the fruit like locusts, the sound of their secateurs as sharp as snapping jaws.

There are, I discovered, many small kindnesses in the vineyard. Like the plastic cup of coffee offered to me by the team, a rejuvenating sugary boost against the damp. Or the way a heavy bucket of grapes gets passed over the vines, moving from hand to hand, to save you from lugging it to the wheelbarrow at the end of the row.

Or the thoughtfulness of Mr. Blondel, who, when he saw me struggling to tackle an unwieldy thicket of vines, picked up a pair of secateurs and faced me on the other side. "It's sad to pick grapes alone," he said. For a few moments we clipped companionably while chatting about viticulture and the general indolence of French youth (the latter, I suspected, a topic as eternal as the vendange).

Lenoble's vineyards are scattered throughout the region in small parcels—a patch of chardonnay here, a swath of pinot noir there, each terroir adding a distinct note to the wine's character.

The heart of the operation remains the winery, which is tucked into the village of Damery, beside the church and the school. The sprawling eighteenth-century building—once the family home of

Lenoble's current owners, siblings Anne and Antoine Malassagne
—includes offices, a sleek and modern *cuverie,* which holds the fermentation vats, and a web of clammy cellars where the temperature never rises above fifty-five degrees.

Upstairs, the rambling, empty rooms became, during the harvest, a dormitory. One section housed four burly young Polish
men who had driven from Gdansk to operate the antediluvian
grape presses (both they and the family from Nord-Pas-de-Calais
were paid for their labor); another, separate area was for me, the
only woman.

I had been warned that the lodgings would be spartan. At the
end of that first day in the vines, however, even my room's simple
furnishings seemed enticing, the narrow bed and coat rack draped
in pools of late-afternoon sunshine. At the opposite end of the
empty apartment, a bathroom sported pink tiles dating to about
1963, but I noticed only the hot water in the shower.

Late that night, however, entombed in a deep rural silence,
my imagination began to cartwheel. Could my bed, which bore
the hallmarks of midcentury hospital furniture, have come from
an insane asylum? Had I brushed the key in my door, or did its
chain start swinging by itself? Did I have enough courage to walk
through the endless dark rooms, with their creaking floorboards
and peeling wallpaper, to reach the bathroom?

Outside, the clanging church bells announced every quarter-
hour until midnight. I decided to sleep with the lights on.

Mornings came early, heralded first by the neighboring church's
bells at six and then by the insistent *thwack* of the *pressoirs,* or grape
presses. Their deafening rhythm formed the background noise of
my stay, with the old-fashioned machinery operating from dawn to
dusk, and a current of precious grape juice coursing like a spring-
time creek.

The Polish team muscled loads of grapes into the three wooden
presses and used pitchforks to fluff the crushed fruit between each
cycle, a task called the *retrousse,* which requires brute strength and
helps extract as much juice as possible.

One afternoon, José Hernandez, the pressoir manager, showed
me how to operate the machines. I ran between them increasing
or decreasing the pressure at the appropriate moment, all while
hosing, mopping, and sweeping the floors. I discovered that work-

ing inside the winery had certain advantages: less kneeling and stooping, less annoyance from rain—and unlimited glasses of fresh grape juice, crisp and bright.

Harvest days were long, but they included an extended break for that venerable French institution: lunch. Every afternoon, we gathered around the long kitchen table, a motley crew of Polish men who spoke no French, Frenchmen who spoke no Polish, and me.

I had dreamed of the slow-simmered dishes I read about in cookbooks like *Recipes from the French Wine Harvest,* but as its author, Rosi Hanson, later told me, "More families, especially wives and daughters, work outside the home now, and they're not available to do the cooking." Still, our meals, provided by a local caterer, offered four hearty courses with dishes like grated carrot salad and veal stew, followed by cheese and dessert.

Given the table's language barrier, conversation was often hesitant. But some things need no translation—like the day I heated a tray of couscous in the oven and everything burst into flames. Smoke billowed and everyone ran to the kitchen, panicked. I quickly doused the fire with a glass of water, and Antoine, the winery owner, couldn't have been kinder about my mistake.

One evening, the Polish guys and I sat after dinner and drank the house Champagne, glass after glass poured from the wine refrigerator in the corner of the kitchen. In halting English, they told me about their children and, as they warmed to the language, waxed enthusiastic about the foods they missed from home.

"Winemaking seems a lot like cooking," I said to Franck Michaud, the head *vigneron,* or winemaker, the day I assisted him in the cuverie. We had just finished preparing a fermentation solution, adding warm water, yeast, plus a good shot of juice, and allowing the mixture to proof, or foam—just like breadmaking.

Under Mr. Michaud's tutelage, I stirred up a batch of malolactic bacteria, tenderly allowing the frozen sachets to defrost, before mixing them with tepid water and packets of powdered nutrients. I learned how to measure the juice's density using a thermometer and bobbing hydrometer to determine the amount of sugar needed for chaptalization (a process that increases the wine's final alcohol content).

I cleaned towering steel *cuves* (vats), inserting my upper body inside the reception vat, aiming a high-powered hose, and spraying the interior (and myself) with fierce jets of water. I climbed a ladder to the top of a fermentation tank and agitated the young red wine within, pushing the floating grape skins back beneath the surface; it smelled warm and festive, faintly reminiscent of mulling spices, and left me splashed in crimson droplets.

Mr. Michaud's work as a winemaker, I realized, relied on hoses and industrial pumps. There was always some kind of liquid on the flow, from the press to a cuve, or the removal of residue to the waste tank. He bustled about the cuverie, moving hoses from one receptacle to another, chatting with me over one shoulder (we talked a lot about the pigs that he butchers annually) while always fretting about where he would store the vast quantities of fresh juice that continued to arrive from the pressoir.

In the midst of his flurried activity, I often feared I was underfoot: a hindrance who needed instruction, rather than a helping hand. But awkward moments are part of the volunteer experience. Patience, good humor, and resourcefulness are helpful traits to have on hand.

Before I arrived in Champagne, I had wondered: could long days of physical labor feel at all relaxing?

The answer, I think, came on my last afternoon of grape harvesting, when the clouds lightened and the sun finally appeared, creating a sudden hothouse warmth. The other vendangeurs and I peeled off our outer layers, draping raincoats and sweaters on trellis posts, lifting our faces to the streaky rays of light that had nourished the very plants surrounding us, and encouraged them to bud, flower, and fruit. My cheeks turned pink, and my hands —which were constantly touching the red grapes—grew black, stained with sticky tannins that would prove impossible to scrub from my fingernails.

As I worked, I fell into an almost meditative state, admiring the bright flash of a ladybug moving across a green leaf, the soft violet of clustered pinot meunier grapes, the faint striated pattern of vineyard rows running toward the village below, the crumble underfoot of the region's cherished chalky soil. Picking grapes requires no particular skills or training, only a measure of agility. This work was the inverse of my daily deskbound grind: it taxed my body and left my mind free.

"Do you mind if I join you?" It was an older woman, the one the team addressed as "Ma mère." As we harvested together, we talked about her grandchildren, and, this being France, her favorite things to cook. "Layer a baking dish with sliced potatoes, onions, crème fraîche, some mussels and scallops," she said. "Put in the oven and bake for thirty minutes. I make it at Christmas. It goes well with Champagne." We clipped together in silence for a few minutes. "Maybe you will cook it and think of me," she said.

I never learned her name. But she gave me the best kind of souvenir.

The Away Team

FROM *The New Yorker*

AROUND ELEVEN O'CLOCK on the night of October 10, 2015, Samson Arefaine learned that he had been selected to play on the national soccer team of Eritrea, a sliver of a nation in the Horn of Africa. For two months, he had been in a training camp in the capital, Asmara, with thirty-three other men, vying for ten open spots on the Red Sea Camels. Now the team was due to fly to Botswana in less than two hours, to play in a World Cup qualifying match. Arefaine needed to pack quickly, so he ran to his room, in a house that team officials had arranged for players to use during the camp. The house had no electricity, and he struggled to see in the dark, but he managed to throw some shirts, shorts, and sandals into a bag. On the way to the airport, he called his parents and told them the exciting news.

At twenty-six, Arefaine is lean and wiry, with bright-copper skin, tight-cropped curls, and a narrow face with a faint beard. On the team, he was known for being outspoken and funny, a reliable source of jokes and stories, and also as sensitive and watchful. "He knows how to read faces," one teammate said. Though he played on the defensive line, at right back, he was the fastest member of the team, and he often rushed forward to score unexpected goals. His teammates described him as one of Eritrea's best players.

When Arefaine boarded the plane, he had never been outside the country. For Eritreans, this is not unusual: Eritrea is one of the few nations that require an exit visa. An isolated, secretive state of some 4 million people, it has been under emergency rule since 1998. The United Nations has accused its military and its government—including the president, a former rebel leader named Isaias Afewerki—of crimes against humanity toward their own people, including indefinite conscription, arbitrary arrests and torture, and mass surveillance. "There are no civil liberties, there is no freedom of speech, there is no freedom to organize," Adane Ghebremeskel Tekie, an activist with the Eritrean Movement for Democracy and Human Rights, said. "The regime can do anything it wants." According to the UN, as many as 5,000 people flee the country every month, making it one of the world's largest sources of refugees. Last year, 3,800 people drowned while trying to cross the Mediterranean Sea; many of them were Eritreans.

Despite its self-imposed isolation, Eritrea wants to be seen as a normal country, and international sporting competitions are a way to present a good face to the world. Eritrean athletes—runners, cyclists, and soccer players—are sometimes permitted to compete in other countries. The Red Sea Camels are a particular source of pride; Eritrea is no less soccer-mad than Italy or Brazil. But, embarrassingly for the government, members of the national soccer team have repeatedly defected after games abroad: Angola in 2007, Kenya in 2009, Uganda in 2012.

After the last defection, the government disbanded the team. Then, in the fall of 2015, it came up with a solution. It would form a team mostly of Eritrean athletes who lived abroad and held dual nationality, and therefore had no incentive to defect. The remaining positions could be filled with loyal athletes living in Eritrea. "They have to trust you," Yohannes Sium, one of the chosen local players, said. "Trust was the main thing, not skill."

When Arefaine and his teammates landed in Nairobi for a layover, the foreign-based players wandered through the terminal, shopping and eating. The local athletes sat at their gate in hard blue plastic seats, uncomfortably eyeing one another, while their coaches and the president of the Eritrean National Football Federation sat behind them, holding their passports. The players felt like hostages. "The others can do anything they want, but you just sit and wait," Henok Semere, a striker, said. Then a representative from the Eritrean embassy in Kenya arrived at the gate and began talking with the officials. While they were distracted, Arefaine turned to Alex Russom, a baby-faced left back, sitting next to him, and told him that he wanted to escape. "He asked if I want to join him," Russom recalled. "I said, 'How did you know I was also thinking that?'"

Arefaine had been contemplating escape for years. He had kept in touch with several players who defected in Uganda, and after they resettled, in Holland, he had asked them for advice on how to get asylum. The most important thing, they told him, was to persuade the entire team to go with him. Any one of his teammates who refused to go could betray him.

It was hard to know whom to trust. Some of his teammates later confessed that Eritrean security officials had asked them to inform on the others in case of an escape plot. "There was no closeness among the ten of us—we were not friends," Arefaine said. "I just took the risk." It turned out that many of his teammates were interested. But Nairobi wasn't a good place to defect: there was nowhere to run at the airport, and they had only two hours before their next flight. Besides, his friends in Holland had given him a second piece of advice: don't escape until after the game. "If you escape without playing, no one will notice you, because you are not on the media," they explained. "You need radio, television."

After landing in Francistown, the sleepy city in Botswana where the match was being held, the team members took a nap, had practice, and went to dinner. Then Arefaine gathered the local players in a hotel room, to determine who wanted to join the escape. Everyone enthusiastically agreed, except Semere, the striker. He had another way out: as the only college graduate and the only one fluent in English, he could apply for graduate programs abroad. The idea of leaving his family and friends made him nervous, and he knew that his father, a successful farmer, would not approve. "Henok was scared at first," Arefaine said. But he was also afraid of going back. What if he didn't get accepted at a foreign university, or the government didn't allow him to go? The other option— crossing through the desert to Sudan, Libya, or Ethiopia—was too dangerous. Finally, he agreed to join. In the hotel lobby, Arefaine helped the others purchase SIM cards and exchange their money for pula, the local currency. He asked the manager to arrange for a taxi to pick them up at 4:00 a.m., explaining that they wanted to go on vacation after the match.

They lost the game that evening. "Our minds were elsewhere," Arefaine said. Back in their rooms, the team's captain, a Swedish-

Eritrean, turned on some music to help everyone relax, but the mood remained tense. Eventually, one of the dual-nationality players asked what was wrong, and Arefaine revealed the escape plan. The player gave Arefaine 200 pounds, and some of the other foreign-based teammates contributed dollars and euros.

At 4:00 a.m., Arefaine and the others assembled in the hall and packed their belongings into a single bag. They moved quietly; a Botswana policeman who was escorting the team was asleep in an adjacent room. Arefaine was in a fog. He had brought T-shirts, shorts, sandals, and track pants but had forgotten his phone. "We left the hotel in a rush—we didn't want to waste time," he said.

When they got to the lobby, there was no taxi on the street. They paused, wondering if they should wait for one. A few of the players went to the reception desk and asked where they could find the U.S. embassy or the Red Cross. The hotel staff wasn't sure, but told them that they could catch a minibus into the center of town. The players decided to try to find the offices on foot. As they walked out of the lobby, security guards watched with surprise. "We told them we were just going on a walk, relaxing," Arefaine said. "When we went out, there was nothing. It was dark, dark. We didn't know where to go."

Eritreans think of their sovereignty as hard-won, and with good reason. The country's modern borders were set in the late nineteenth century, when Italy invaded a funnel-shaped area of highlands and arid plains on Africa's northeastern coast and named it Eritrea, from the Latin phrase Erythraeum Mare, or Red Sea. The colonists could not have picked a more inhospitable environment: erratic rainfall, a desertlike coast, dry riverbeds, mangrove swamps, and valleys sunk below sea level. Their policies segregated Eritreans from Italians, in a precursor to South African apartheid, and forbade them to attend secondary school, even as they were drafted to fight Italy's wars. When Italy lost the colony to Britain, in 1941, the new administrators stripped Eritrea of much of its naval, rail, and industrial infrastructure, and then, with little use left for the colony, turned it over to the United Nations.

At the time, Eritreans had high hopes that they would finally be able to govern themselves. Instead, their neighbor Ethiopia intervened. The two countries share common ethnic groups, languages, customs, and historical origins, in the ancient Christian empires of the Horn of Africa. They also share a border, and, for centuries, Ethiopians looking across the frontier have coveted the territory, which offers both fertile farmland and a pathway to the sea. Emperor Haile Selassie, who believed that the land was his by right, lobbied the UN, and Eritrea was designated an autonomous territory under the Ethiopian crown. In the coming years, Selassie replaced Eritrea's flag with Ethiopia's, supplanted the national languages of Tigrinya and Arabic with Amharic, and finally abolished the federation, erasing the Eritrean state.

"Eritreans who were living under the Ethiopian occupation never felt at ease," Abraham Zere, an Eritrean journalist who lives in exile in the United States, told me. "It has always been 'us' and 'them.'" When resistance movements formed, in the north of Eritrea, the crown's Army punished their supporters, killing villagers, burning homes, and slaughtering livestock. By 1961, Eritrean fighters had gathered in the mountains near the Ethiopian border, in a maze of underground bunkers that contained hospitals, a school, and living quarters. It was an uneven fight: Ethiopia's population was more than ten times that of Eritrea. Ethiopia had arms and equipment from the Soviet Union and the United States, while the Eritreans were forced to capture munitions from their enemies. The war affected everyone, Zere said. "My family was often hiding from the continuous bombings."

In 1991, the Eritreans, with the help of a rebel group in Ethiopia, finally defeated the occupiers. After thirty years of fighting, Eritrea had lost as many as 65,000 people in combat, and 200,000 more to famine and the effects of war. But, with almost no support or recognition from abroad, the Eritreans had won, and they emerged proud and defiant. When I visited Asmara recently, a national festival was celebrating twenty-five years of independence. On the sprawling Expo Grounds, among food vendors and historical displays, the government has preserved the fuselage of an airliner, which an Ethiopian fighter pilot had strafed on the runway. Across town, in a vast place called the Tank Graveyard, the rusting remains of Ethiopian tanks stand as a monument to the war.

After the victory, Isaias Afewerki, a hero of the struggle, became Eritrea's leader, and his party, the People's Front for Democracy and Justice, or PFDJ, promised to lead the country toward a constitution and democratic elections. Two years later, though, another dispute erupted between Ethiopia and Eritrea, over a border town called Badme. Both sides quickly escalated the conflict; Ethiopia cut off trade, and Eritrea's economy stagnated. When Afewerki decided to go into battle, Eritreans, accustomed to war to preserve their homeland, enlisted to fight. One of Arefaine's older brothers went, and was killed—one of an estimated 19,000 Eritreans who died in two years.

In 2002, a commission in The Hague ruled that Eritrea had legal rights to the disputed territory, but Ethiopia has continued its occupation. As the war dragged on, people around Afewerki began describing him as severe and brutish, given to autocratic tendencies. "The PFDJ is Eritrea, and I am the PFDJ," he proclaimed. After members of the Party's central council questioned his handling of the war—had there been no diplomatic alternative to the huge loss of life and the economic devastation?—Afewerki had eleven of them thrown in prison. He also shut down independent media, jailing editors. In 2010, after an *Al Jazeera* interviewer challenged him, he called her questions "a pack of lies." Then, according to Zere's reporting, he returned to his office and slapped Ali Abdu, the information minister, while his staff looked on. Two years later, Abdu defected while on a trip to Australia. Afterward, his fifteen-year-old daughter, his brother, and his elderly father were put in prison.

Afewerki has used the threat, real or imagined, of renewed war with Ethiopia to keep his citizens in a precarious state that they describe as "no war, no peace." Now, Eritreans say, they can be detained for crimes as slight as harboring ill will toward the government. There is usually no trial; detainees are often not told the offense, or for how long they will be held. Zerit Yohhanes, a midfielder on the national soccer team, told me that his father has been in prison for more than twenty-five years. The family has no idea why. Maybe he was detained by mistake.

Asmara, where Arefaine grew up, is a serene city of half a million people, set on a plateau at almost 8,000 feet. There are broad streets with peach-toned Art Deco buildings; on Harnet Avenue, lined with palm trees, people stroll past cafés, bars, bakeries, and cinemas. In the middle of the street stands a red brick cathedral, where, during my visit, teenagers sat flirting on the steps. The city is slow-paced, and crime is low. Western diplomats say, with evident relief, that Asmara is "not like an African city."

Because the government restricts permits for new construction, there is a housing shortage in the city, and people build homes in unregulated settlements on the edge of Asmara. Arefaine grew up in one of these quarters, named Godaif; a paved main street gives way to dirt roads into the neighborhood, where the homes range from pastel-painted brick houses to lean-tos with laundry hanging outside. His father, a judge, owned land there, and so he built an orange house with four bedrooms for the family—four boys and four girls. Arefaine's mother didn't go to school, dedicating herself to caring for their children. Arefaine still sometimes cries when he talks about her. "My mom is the sweetest person, because she devoted her life to us," he told me.

Arefaine's neighborhood was known for producing skilled, if rowdy, athletes. He described the local pastimes as playing soccer, fighting, and drinking *suwa*, a kind of beer made from sorghum. Arefaine wanted to be a professional soccer player from the time he could stretch his legs. His father, who was strict and controlling, pressured him to excel in school, and they argued. Arefaine wasn't serious enough, he said. He preferred the cinema and nightclubs to school, and he was always the first one on the dance floor at weddings. But his talent for soccer was evident. As early as high school, scouts began inquiring about him. He joined a club team called Tesfa, and sneaked out of the house to play matches.

School wasn't that interesting, anyway. In history classes, his teachers spent most of the time on the country's perpetual struggle against Ethiopia. In geography, Arefaine learned the names of the other countries in Africa, but that was about it. "Our knowledge about the outside world until we finish high school is very limited," he said.

Arefaine grew up surrounded by support for the Afewerki regime. During the liberation struggle, his father had spied on the Ethiopian occupiers, and then been caught and imprisoned for seven months; he never relinquished the revolutionary spirit. In Arefaine's classes, Afewerki was described as a modest, nearly omniscient man, focused on his people's well-being. On state-run media, he gives hours-long lectures, in which he spins connections among far-flung episodes in world history and politics; local channels feature him in multipart epics about the independence struggle.

At Santa Ana Secondary School, where Arefaine studied, Eritrea's national anthem is printed on a bulletin board at the entrance: "The pride of her oppressed people proved that truth prevails." But Arefaine began to see soldiers violently round up people who had been caught without identification papers. In his second year at Santa Ana, soldiers came to take the oldest students in each grade, saying that they were going to a vocational school. Instead, they were sent to military training camps.

Afewerki had instituted the camps in the mid-1990s, as part of a national program of mandatory military service. The term of service, beginning after the third year of high school, was originally eighteen months. It is now indefinite, and the program has become the country's dominant employer, shuttling recruits from camps into a wide range of occupations. A fortunate few, like children of government officials and generals, can get civil-service positions or white-collar jobs—though even they have to attend drills and guard government buildings. The rest are in a standing military of some 300,000, who work on government projects in construction, farming, and mining, or are deployed to the border with Ethiopia. Most are paid roughly 400 nakfa, or $30, a month. Everyone has a gun at home.

A trainee's experience is determined by his unit and location: generally, the more remote your station, the worse the conditions. "The one thing that is constant is the abuse," Yohannes Woldemariam, an Eritrean who taught international relations for a decade at Fort Lewis College, in Colorado, said. Arefaine's older siblings came home complaining about the camps; their parents told them to be patient, that everyone went through it. But Arefaine saw people he knew, students and teachers, fleeing Eritrea. Some walked to refugee camps in Ethiopia and Sudan, braving gunfire from border guards. Others paid smugglers thousands of dollars to lead them through the Sahara to Libya and then Europe. In 2012, Eritrean Air Force pilots flew a government plane to Saudi Arabia to seek asylum.

As people left the country, the regime began a more aggressive campaign of surveillance; in some cases, Eritreans told me, you could be detained for "thinking about escaping." In Arefaine's neighborhood, a woman named Saada reported evaders to the authorities, and boys avoided walking by her house. "I started being cautious whenever I talk about the government, about other

things, with friends, because someone could report me," Arefaine said. Zerit Yohhanes, the midfielder, told me that, when he
dropped out of school to avoid the camps, a friend's mother reported him. She even delivered the letter recalling him for duty.
Yohhanes was baffled; the woman's own son had fled to Sudan in
order to dodge service. "I told her, 'Your son is somewhere else.
Why are you doing this to me?'" he said. She replied, "I'm just the
messenger." Suspicion is so widespread that even long-acquainted
neighbors can be wary of one another. "The system has created an
atmosphere of mistrust among Eritreans," Ghebremeskel, of the
Eritrean Movement for Democracy and Human Rights, told me.
"You can't trust your own brother."

In 2004, Arefaine's older brother fled through the desert to Sudan, eventually making his way to England. "He was angry because
of the national service," Arefaine recalled. "That's why he left."
Still, their father encouraged the other children to volunteer for
service. It was their duty, he said. The government told them that
the service and the roundups were necessary, because of the threat
from Ethiopia, and they believed it.

As Arefaine finished his third year of high school, he wondered
which camp he would be sent to. Many of his classmates would
spend their last year of high school at Sawa, an enormous military
complex about 170 miles northwest of Asmara. Children of the
well connected were often allowed to attend Sawa because of its
proximity to Asmara. If you managed to find the time amid your
duties to study there, you could gain entrance to a college.

Arefaine's teammate Semere, the son of the prosperous farmer,
had lived in one of the hot, poorly ventilated hangars that function as dormitories for Sawa's thousands of trainees. In the mornings, he attended a school nearby, and then supervisors took him
and the other recruits to do hard labor at commercial farms, digging and plowing for no pay. "You think, I don't deserve this at this
age," he said. "You come just as a child. That's why they take you
at that age—you don't know anything, and you just follow them.
You are terrified."

Men and women trained together; during the independence
struggle, an idea had taken hold that women should be equally
involved in all national activities. But Asia Abdulkadir, an Eritrean-

German gender consultant for the UN, told me that the women were often abused. "The senior commander would always choose the best-looking girl and bring her to his unit to wash his clothes, cook his food, make sure his house is always clean," she said. "And there is a pressure for the girls to offer sexual services." At Sawa, Semere knew girls who had been impregnated by commanders.

The base was close to the border with Sudan, and thirty of Semere's hall mates eventually escaped. He stayed, and studied as much as he could, poring over math and physics textbooks in the hours before a 4:00 a.m. wake-up call. If trainees failed college-entrance exams, they would be immediately drafted back into service. "So you end up in the military for the rest of your life," Arefaine said. Eritrea has only seven colleges, and there is a shortage of qualified teachers, according to Tadesse Mehari, who heads the National Commission for Higher Education. The government spends $5 million a year to hire expatriate faculty, mostly Indians. It has sent students abroad for advanced degrees, in the hope that they would return to teach. But, Mehari said, "that's not faring very well, because many of the youngsters this time do not want to come back."

Those who graduate college have little assurance of working in the area that they studied; most seem to end up back in national service. One afternoon, at a breezy, secluded café in Asmara, I had tea with a young woman who had gone to Sawa and then completed a degree in engineering. The government assigned her to teach English at a school in Asmara for three years, with the understanding, she said, that "after that maybe they can put you in your field." She now worked part-time at a restaurant; other graduates she knew were working in kindergartens. "You try to be flexible," she said, laughing. "You have to, in order to live. You can even clean the streets." She went on, "Just waiting to be an engineer is losing time. I have to do my duty to my family."

Outside Asmara, I drove past a guard post manned by soldiers. There was a cluster of zinc shacks serving as a residence, but there was nothing to guard: no ammunitions depot, no intelligence post, nothing. "If you are not on a farming or a construction project, breaking stones, it's about keeping you in check," Ghebremeskel, the activist, said. In Asmara, a man who had worked for decades in the civil service told me that he was sometimes assigned to duty as a prison guard. "What's frustrating to the youth is that there is no end to national service," Woldemariam, the professor, said. "The suspense—you can't plan your life."

Because Arefaine was a gifted athlete, the Eritrean Sport and Culture Commission offered a deal: if he went to a remote camp in the east, called Wi'a, he would be allowed to leave after just six months and play for a club team in Asmara. He packed jam and peanut butter, a sorghum drink, a little money, a blanket, and a few changes of clothes. He felt ready to go.

To get to Wi'a, he and about 150 other recruits rode for three hours in the back of a giant truck, so crammed together that they could barely find room to stand. When they arrived, Arefaine was stunned. The camp is in a volcanic area on the Red Sea coast, a sun-blasted expanse of white sand. "There is just plain ground," he recalled. "There is no housing except for small shelters made out of sticks." Soldiers hustled the recruits out of the truck and told them to kneel, then divided them into groups. In a long shelter covered with branches and leaves, they dropped their things. A soldier was serving stale bread and watery lentil soup, ladled out from a cavernous pot. "You could barely see the lentils," Arefaine said. He ate some of the food he had brought from home, already regretting the decision to come.

That evening, the commander, a man named Jamal, laid out the rules: trainees had to obey whatever instructions their superiors gave them, and they would be shot if they tried to escape. "Immediately after the meeting, people started running," Arefaine said. Soldiers swarmed the remaining recruits, telling them to kneel. Arefaine could hear vehicles moving over the sand and guns firing into the air. No one knew if any of the runners were caught. If they were, they would be put in the camp prison, a hole in the ground that felt like a coffin.

At night, the recruits slept in the open, surrounded by a ring of sleeping soldiers. Arefaine poured water on the sandy ground to cool it, and then laid down his blanket. Each day, he and the other trainees had to wake up at 4:00 a.m., quickly stow their bedding and change clothes, and then jog to a clearing a mile away, where they could relieve themselves, under close watch by the guards. For the remainder of the day, they marched and had target practice, with a rest in the early afternoon to avoid the high sun. Every thirty minutes, a whistle shrieked, and everyone had to line up in formation. Their superiors were checking to make sure that no one had escaped.

The recruits were beaten for failing to show up on time, or for falling out of formation, or for stealing water. "You were treated like an animal," Arefaine said. At breakfast, they were given a cup of black tea, six rolls, and five liters of water to last the day. Lunch and dinner were more lentil soup. There were about 2,000 men in the camp, and every Wednesday afternoon they all went to the river to bathe. (The women went on Tuesdays.) People unfailingly tried to escape across the river, and Arefaine watched as they were shot down, their legs collapsing beneath them in the water. The ones who made it disappeared into the scrubland. Later, when soldiers dumped corpses on the ground in front of the recruits, Arefaine saw that many of them had been mauled by hyenas.

A man in the camp was tattooing recruits, using a thorn and kohl, and although religious practices were forbidden, Arefaine had a cross imprinted on his right forearm. "We were stressed and worried, and we wanted to think of our God," he said. When the tattoo became infected, he went to a medic to have it treated. The medic scolded him: "Why did you do this?" When Arefaine came for follow-up treatments, the medic beat him with a stick.

After six months, it was clear that Arefaine wasn't going to be allowed to leave early. Around that time, his parents were permitted to make a one-hour visit. His mother looked at the camp and at Arefaine, who was frighteningly thin, and sobbed uncontrollably. "I was telling her not to cry," he recalled. "From then on, whatever happened to me I kept to myself."

When his year of training was done, he was assigned to a military base in the village of Gelalo, in the south. He was often on the move, sent to man checkpoints or guard telecommunications infrastructure, or, worse, to carry out roundups. He and his platoon were dropped off in surrounding villages to look for evaders, grabbing boys who didn't have permits off the streets or from their homes. They searched under beds, in cupboards, and even took girls, herding them into a prison or a stadium for questioning. If someone resisted, Arefaine could end up having to shoot him. "I felt very bad," he said. "No one wanted to do it." He knew that, if he protested, his treatment would worsen.

Like many men in national service, Arefaine hoped that soccer would provide a way out. The club teams are owned by the military, the ruling party, and state companies, so coaches can recruit anyone they want. When he joined the service, he wrote on his entrance forms that he was a soccer player, but nothing had come of it. At last, three years into his service, he got a call telling him to come to the city of Assab to try out for a military-sponsored club team.

Arefaine wanted to play, but he was desperate to get home. If he tried out for the team and didn't make it, he knew, he'd have to go back into national service. Instead, he sought out a relative who lived in town and, with his help, bought a forged permit that said he was on medical leave. Early one morning, he heaved himself into the back of a transport truck, and, sitting on top of the cargo, rode north. When the truck reached its destination, several hours later, he got on another one, and then another, paying the drivers small bribes. At checkpoints, he showed the fake permit. When he got home, his family greeted him with happiness and surprise; he didn't tell them that his papers had been forged. He put his belongings down in his familiar bedroom, with posters of the Barcelona soccer team. He took a bath.

On Harnet Avenue, I visited an ornate, four-level theater called Cinema Impero, where people often gather to watch soccer games. In midafternoon, fans were scattered across the seats, engrossed in an English Premier League match that played on the giant screen. The fans sat in rapt silence, periodically bursting into shouts and cheers. Soccer is immensely popular in Eritrea, featured prominently on state media and dominating the discussion in public spaces. "It is a way of escape from the frustrating reality," Zere, the exiled journalist, said, "and a refuge to discuss safe issues that will not draw attention from state security."

In Asmara, there is much that critics can't comment on. The streets are filled with decades-old bicycles and cars, and the electricity goes out frequently. The state-run mobile-phone network is spotty, and people resort to pay phones. The ruling party's company, Red Sea Trading Corporation, is the country's primary legal importer, but most of what's for sale in Eritrea's small shops is smuggled into the country in giant suitcases—a practice that is tolerated, perhaps even sanctioned, by the government. On the outskirts of the city, police cars driving to Adi Abeto prison pass a thriving black market for diesel.

According to the UN Monitoring Group on Somalia and Eritrea, PFDJ officials skim millions of dollars a year from party-run companies, but the charges are difficult to investigate because the government never discloses its budget. Eritreans joke that Afewerki runs the country as if it were a small grocery store. Hagos Ghebrehiwet, the president's economic adviser, told me that the budget had to be kept secret, to protect against "economic sabotage" by Ethiopia and its supporters. A former treasury chief, quoted in Martin Plaut's book *Understanding Eritrea*, gave a simpler explanation: no budget has ever been committed to paper.

Eritrea has resources—gold, copper, zinc, and potash—but the majority of the population depends on subsistence farming. Ghebrehiwet told me that the problem was a limited workforce: "A small country with a lot of resources in agriculture, mining, and fisheries—I don't think we will have enough manpower to be able to exploit the potential here." Bronwyn Bruton, the deputy director of the Africa Center at the Atlantic Council, was more direct. "The government is broke," she said. "They can't pay people to do jobs that would normally be civil-service posts. So what they're doing is conscripting people." In 2016, the government increased the monthly pay to between 2,000 and 5,000 nakfa. But Eritreans are not allowed to withdraw more than 5,000 nakfa a month from a bank without approval. "You take it to the market and it's gone in five days," an Eritrean in Asmara told me.

Eritrean officials insist that the threat from Ethiopia forces them to divert resources to the military. Berhane G. Solomon, the chargé d'affaires at the Eritrean embassy in Washington, D.C., complained that the international community has done nothing to compel Ethiopia to withdraw its troops. "It has put the burden on us to protect our independence," he said. "Eritrea is only twenty-five years old. We are just crawling, trying to stand on our own feet."

Publicly, the U.S. has hesitated to criticize Ethiopia, a key ally in regional anti-terror efforts. Between 2006 and 2009, Ethiopia sent troops into Somalia to fight Islamists, including the terror group al-Shabaab. In 2009, the UN placed sanctions on Eritrea, for allegedly supporting al-Shabaab in order to undermine Ethiopia. But the UN's own Monitoring Group on Somalia and Eritrea has found no evidence to support that claim. (The group does say that

Eritrea has ties to Somali arms traffickers.) When a UN report alleged persistent human-rights abuses, the government called the claims "an unwarranted attack not only against Eritrea, but also Africa and developing nations." Amid the continuing dispute, Afewerki has barred the monitoring group from the country since 2013.

Eritrea and the United States are in a kind of standoff: a Western diplomat whom I spoke to acknowledged that Ethiopia is behaving thuggishly, but thought that the onus is on Eritrea to allow the monitoring group to inspect again. If the country were cleared of the allegations raised by the UN, the international community would be more amenable to helping resolve the border issue. Eritrean officials regard the U.S.'s reasoning as nearsighted. "Why should good relations with Ethiopia mean hostility toward Eritrea?" Yemane Gebreab, the PFDJ's head of political affairs, said.

In Asmara, Arefaine knew that he had to protect himself from informants, so he went to see Saada, the neighborhood spy, and told her that he was on medical leave and going to a military hospital in town for treatment. Without release papers from the military, he couldn't join a club team, so he got a job at a shop in the city. When he wasn't working, he stayed indoors to avoid the military's sweeps for evaders. After a few months, though, he reconnected with a high school friend, Mikal, and started going with her to Harnet Avenue at night, strolling from café to café or going to Cinema Hamsien, where they could watch Indian movies for a few nakfa.

Late one night, about a year later, he heard his father shouting for him to wake up. A contingent of soldiers had jumped the gate of their house and announced that they were looking for him. Arefaine recognized the men: three were platoon mates from Gelalo, and the fourth was the platoon leader. All were holding guns. They handcuffed him and led him out of the house, as his mother and sisters cried.

Arefaine spent the night in a local police station, and then was taken to a prison near his old base in Gelalo. He was confined, along with some sixty other men, to a cell where the only light came from small, high windows. The men weren't allowed out, so they had to relieve themselves in a corner. They all became infested with fleas. "I was about to lose my mind," Arefaine said. "You think about the way you've been taken from home. You think about your mom, your dad, how they feel."

After six months, prison authorities told Arefaine that he was being released: the military wanted him to play soccer again. It was true that he had briefly evaded service, but so did many other men. Evasion was normal, almost expected—and Arefaine was unusually talented. Arefaine immediately called his parents, who thought he had been killed, and told them that he was free. He cut his hair to get rid of the fleas.

Back in Asmara, he practiced with the team in the mornings, went to a mandatory political-education center in the afternoons, and worked as a guard at a national-service office on some nights. He made 450 nakfa, about $28, a month. "Once you go to the camp, you are the property of the government," a former journalist in Asmara told me. "Whether you work in a highly professional position or as a security guard, everybody gets 400 for life." On nights off, Arefaine bribed his commanders to let him broker houses and cars on the informal market, so that he could make ends meet.

Arefaine was sitting in a café when he got the news that he had been called to try out for the national team. He shouted so loudly that he startled the other customers. "It was a dream come true," he said. "One day, I would be able to leave the country." When he told his parents he wanted to escape, they were against it. The government has sometimes required families of national-team players to turn over the deeds to their houses as a guarantee in case their sons fled, and if Arefaine defected his family could lose their home. He assured them he wouldn't leave. But, he said, "I made up my mind—I would do it anyway."

The team members based abroad—in Sudan, Saudi Arabia, Sweden, and elsewhere—were flown in and put up in a five-star hotel. The local athletes moved into a guesthouse with no electricity and no running water, where they slept four to a room. While the foreign-based players were paid in dollars, the rest were told that they would receive nakfa—and then were given nothing. They trained for two months, and, as Arefaine and his teammates watched the coaches lavish praise on their foreign-based counterparts, they grew resentful. "There was a double standard," Minasie Solomon, the goalkeeper, said. Solomon, the oldest member of the team, had loved his country enough to volunteer for the war effort against Ethiopia, but now he was disillusioned. By the time the team got to the airport in Nairobi, nearly everyone was ready to join Arefaine's attempt to defect. "Samson is brave and smart," Yohhanes, the midfielder, said. "He knows what he's doing."

The night of their escape, after the players left the hotel, they walked for half an hour down a wide avenue called Marimavu Road. A police car drove up to them; a policewoman had recognized them from coverage of the match. "Are you okay, guys?" she asked. "What are you doing?" Semere spoke first. "We are refusing to go home because we don't have human rights," he said. All around him, his teammates began talking at once in Tigrinya, asking him to translate. "I told them, 'Keep quiet, please—give me time to think!'" he recalled. Semere asked the officer if it was safe for them to stay in Botswana. "Yes, it's safe—don't worry," she said, and then drove away.

Not long after, several police cars pulled up to the group, and officials from the team stepped out. The players backed up as if they were going to run. "Where are you going?" a coach said. "Please don't do this." The players shook their heads. "We said we are not going back—we have decided," Semere recalled. "We have been waiting for this time." As the police discussed the situation with the team officials in English, several of the players tried to convey their desperation without words. They mimed guns and made shooting sounds and grabbed the necks of their shirts.

Finally, the officers told everyone to go to the police station, a few minutes away. The Eritrean ambassador to Southern Africa, Saleh Omar, who had come to Francistown for the game, met them there. In a holding room, he pleaded with the players to return to Asmara, promising that he would protect them. "I'll take you home myself," he said. "Nothing will happen to you." When they didn't answer, he threatened that the Botswana police would arrest them if they stayed.

Filmon Berhe, another midfielder, had been quiet, listening as his teammates did the explaining. Bearded, with wary eyes, he was usually not much of a talker. But he was getting frustrated. The ambassador didn't understand what they were telling him. "Where are your children?" Berhe asked.

Omar paused. "They are living with me at the moment," he said.

"That is why you don't feel for us," Berhe said. "You don't understand what we are going through."

Omar angrily left the room and destroyed their passports. When he returned, he said, "I'm not responsible for you. You're on your own."

The mass defection was a humiliation for the government, and if the players were deported back to Asmara they could face severe punishment. (Refugees who have been forced to return speak of being tortured, and of being held for years in windowless shipping containers with little food and water.) Gebreab, the PFDJ official, suggested that the soccer team had been deliberately lured away. "How about our runners and our cyclists who compete and come back?" he said. "For me, this is cherry-picking. In Botswana, they were given cause—they said if they stay there they will be given green cards and they will be going to the United States, so most of them decided to stay. It shows that there are certain people in this country who will take any opportunity to leave."

At the police station, though, Arefaine became convinced that they had made the right decision. "It was like I was born again—I had been given a second chance," he recalled. As the teammates pleaded with the police chief, he softened, and admitted that they had the right to apply for asylum. After waiting a week in jail, they saw a Botswana lawyer, and were allowed to call their families. Arefaine told his that he was safe.

One Sunday afternoon in Asmara, I went to see Adulis, the Asmara municipal team, play Red Sea, owned by the Red Sea Trading Corporation. The players, wearing crisp uniforms in yellows and reds, warmed up on a wide green field, surrounded by a red-brown track. Old men in corduroy blazers sat on concrete bleachers, alongside boys in sweatshirts with headphones plugged into their ears. Everyone was talking and laughing with excitement.

The defection of so many good players in the past decade had left a dearth of talent. These were two of the best teams in the country, but the players' footwork was sloppy, and passes kept going out of bounds. "It's like the ball is moving on its own," one spectator said. Another, a bald man in a camel-colored blazer, looked on in disgust. "I'm not happy with this team," he said.

After halftime, Adulis scored a goal—but the ball trickled out through a hole in the side of the net. The stadium erupted. "How can that be a goal?" a bearded young man in a blue button-down shirt yelled in front of me. (The man asked not to be named, fearing retaliation from the government, so I refer to him as Freselam.) Freselam told me he had been a finalist for the national soccer team that had competed in Botswana but had narrowly missed the cut. Now he was playing for another club team. It was a decent life, he said: he practiced twice a week and got paid 1,600 nafka a month, along with room and board at the clubhouse.

As the game went on, the fans' frustration gave way to scuffles in the stands, and then to an all-out fracas. In the last minutes, a referee called a foul on Adulis, and Red Sea scored on a penalty kick, winning the match. Policemen wielding batons had to escort the referee out of the stadium amid fans shouting threats. "I'm going to kill you," Freselam shouted at a man who was hassling the referee. "People like you shouldn't even be here!"

After the match, Freselam headed to a pizzeria to celebrate with some of the winning athletes and fans. He had become friends with several national-team players who are now in Botswana, and had been saddened when he learned that they weren't coming back. "I was disappointed that I wouldn't see them again," he said. "But it was their choice."

When I asked about Arefaine, Freselam smiled broadly. "He was one of the strongest players, especially with his speed," he said. "He scored a lot of points."

"He's a nice guy," another player said. "We miss him a lot."

The two players said that they hadn't been surprised when Arefaine defected. It was just something that happened in Eritrea. But they were surprised to hear that he had been dissatisfied with his life there: he always seemed happy, they said. Later, Arefaine told me, "You don't want to seem to anyone that you are not happy in Asmara. Because if you do, they may arrest you."

A few months ago, Arefaine and Russom, the left back, took a minibus from the refugee camp where they have been staying to Galo Shopping Center, a fashionable mall in Francistown. An airy, light-flooded complex with an attached supermarket, it was filled with late-afternoon shoppers. The men were relieved to be away from the camp, an uncomfortable place with limited electricity and running water. "It's not what we expected," Russom said. Unaccustomed to the local food, the players had grown skinny. They had little money, scrounging what they could from sympathizers in the Eritrean diaspora and trading their food rations with local shops to buy pasta, as well as minutes for the phones they shared. They had nothing to do and nowhere to be.

"Most Eritreans—refugees and those inside the country alike —are living in extended limbo," Zere, the exiled journalist, said. "Home has turned into a source of deferred dreams and destitution, characterized by brutal dictatorship, while fleeing is becoming equally challenging." Refugees who flee the Horn of Africa face the risk of torture, rape, and murder by smugglers in the Sahara, and then a treacherous journey by sea. Yet those who make it fare much better than those who stay in Ethiopia and Sudan, who can get stuck in desolate camps. Some of the players who defected in 2008 have reconstituted their team in the Netherlands, and Arefaine and his teammates talked dreamily of their compatriots' new lives. At the camp, they ran and kicked around a ball when they could, but they were worried that they wouldn't get a chance to play professional soccer again. An official at the U.S. embassy in Gaborone, Botswana's capital, told me that the worldwide exodus of refugees, from Syria and elsewhere, had made the team a low priority for resettlement. The UN, which administers the camp, is turning it over to Botswana in a few weeks, and the government has expressed a desire to send refugees home.

A sister of one of the soccer players lives in the U.S., and she contacted John Stauffer, the president of an advocacy group called the America Team for Displaced Eritreans. Stauffer had been worried that the "astonishing" reach of the Eritrean government would thwart the team's asylum application. "The Eritrean regime strives to control the diaspora, including through agents operating out of the embassies, in order to punish refugees and defectors," he said. Refugees who wish to obtain an Eritrean passport are pressured to sign a "form of regret," admitting that they have committed an offense and agreeing to accept any punishment. They must also disclose the names of family members back home, who may become subject to fines and imprisonment. Sometimes Eritrean security forces seize refugees from camps and residences in Sudan and return them to Eritrea.

At the mall, the players tried to stay cheerful. In the parking lot, Russom gazed at the people walking toward the entrance. "I'm trying to find Samson a girlfriend," he said, laughing. But at times they still seemed disoriented by their situation. Arefaine mentioned that he had recently gone to Gaborone to meet with Eritreans living there, and they visited a huge, gleaming shopping mall called Game City. "I was confused. I thought, *Is this Europe?*" he said, half-jokingly.

The players missed eating *injera* and *fata* and hanging out at the cafés on Harnet Avenue. They missed their friends and families. Arefaine's older sister Helen told him on Facebook Messenger to be strong, and sent him photos and updates from home. "It makes me homesick, but it's better than not having any news at all," he said. Their families have yet to experience repercussions from their defections; the players hope that the team's high profile will prevent the government from retaliating, but they can't be certain. "My family was angry I left them, and they were afraid," Arefaine said. "The government is going to do something. I am still afraid."

Outside the supermarket, Arefaine surveyed the mall: a stretch of boutiques selling clothing, shoes, books, electronics. "There's nothing like this in Asmara," he observed. "It's nice." After a moment, he corrected himself. "The cafés in Asmara are better. There's nothing nicer than the streets of Asmara." At last, though, he had managed to leave Eritrea. When I asked how it felt, he said, "We are one step ahead from where we were."

A Palpable History

FROM *T: The New York Times Style Magazine*

"IN THE NAME of God and of the Virgin Mary and all the Saints of Paradise," the story begins, "this book belongs to Matteo di Nicholò Chorsini, and in it I, the said Matteo, will write down every thing of mine and other facts about me and my land and houses and other goods of mine."

The year was 1362. A trader in woolen cloth, Matteo Corsini had just returned from years abroad with enough money to buy property around San Casciano, eleven miles south of Florence. From then on and for 600 years his descendants followed his example, writing down everything about themselves and preserving everything they wrote. Again and again, huge old books of accounts begin with an invocation to God the Father, Son, and Holy Spirit, then proceed to list endless incomings and outgoings, profits and losses. But mainly profits. By the seventeenth century the Corsinis would be among the richest families in Florence.

"At what point," I ask Duccio Corsini, present head of the family, "did they start to think of their papers as an archive?" We are standing at the window in the grand villa that was eventually built on the land his ancestor bought and where all these papers have recently been gathered.

"From the very beginning," he replies proudly. "It was a Florentine thing."

In fact, all the Florentine merchant bankers of the Renaissance could be recognized, it was said, by their "ink-stained fingers." Partly it was a matter of careful accounting, but also of passing on family identity and attitudes from one generation to the next.

Up to the seventeenth century the papers in the Corsini archive were written by men who all bore the same half-dozen "Corsini names"—Filippo, Tommaso, Duccio, Neri, Bartolomeo, Andrea—as if they were hardly individuals but temporary representatives of an ongoing family project.

Built in the fourteenth century but massively enlarged in the sixteenth, Villa le Corti is a half hour from Florence by winding road. The sweep of vineyards and olive groves is breathtaking, as is the view of the villa, a white stuccoed pile topped with two towers set in geometric lawns. Do not, however, expect comfort inside. When Duccio and his wife, Clotilde, moved here in 1992, the house had not been lived in for almost a century. "Because," Duccio observes knowingly, "when you have so much it gets hard to use it all." The couple renovated a small part of the building for themselves, transformed the cellars under the lawn into a restaurant and a shop for their wine and olive oil production, and started arranging visitor attractions such as cooking lessons and wine-tasting sessions.

But the rest of the house stood empty. The decision last year to have the archive moved here from its previous home in the family's grand palazzo in Florence was thus part of a business plan to bring the villa back to life—the papers attract a steady stream of scholars—and place it at the heart of the family enterprise. "In the end," remarks Duccio, "it was mostly about money."

Moving the Corsini papers was itself extremely expensive, the largest operation of its kind since Florence's huge state archive was relocated in 1989. Four thousand feet of steel shelving had to be set up and more than 12,000 files resettled. Since the villa wasn't in any way designed for this purpose, there is no specific entry point, nor any easily apparent order to the rooms. All the same, wherever you come into the archive you are immediately overwhelmed by an intense awareness of *paper*. This is not the experience of an ordinary library where parallel lines of standardized print in neatly bound volumes seem to detach the words from the material they depend on. Here, bundle after bundle of raw papers are tied together with string and squeezed into shelves, from floor to ceiling. There is the thick sepia-toned, slightly porous paper of the 1400s and the ultrathin glossy correspondence paper of the nineteenth century. There are papers with elaborate watermarks, and with tiny cuts made in the sixteenth century to show that the surface had been disinfected against the plague. Some papers have been eaten away by silverfish; others have gotten wet and smudged. Scratchy nibs have poked holes. A name is missing. A date. At every point you are made conscious of the moment in which event was turned into document.

I arrive at Villa le Corti at 9:00 a.m. Clotilde orders coffee and I am soon settled down in a tepidly heated room and introduced to the archivist, Nada Bacic, originally from Croatia. As she pours espresso from a silver pot, we speak Italian, each with our foreign accents, and then set off into the past. The archive is spread through a half-dozen rooms, some little more than cubbies, others as grand as they are cold, one with a taxidermied eagle hanging from the ceiling. Stone stairs and oaken doors abound.

In the bottom left corner of the smallest room are Matteo Corsini's "Recollections" but this is a copy, made in 1475. The difference between a merchant's handwriting and a scrivener's is clear enough, the one scrawled and bold, the other neat and careful. In any event, Italian calligraphy has changed so much since then that both are largely illegible to anyone who isn't an expert. To digitize here would cost a fortune and take an age.

Opening an early tome, I stumble on the last will and testament of Cardinal Pietro Corsini who died in 1403. Written in both Latin and Italian, it fills a thick book eighteen inches tall. The fine clothes he is dressed in for burial, the cardinal warns, must not be removed from his body. Two hundred gold florins are left to a monastery, on condition that the monks recognize a "solemn obligation" to say prayers for the cardinal's soul "in perpetuity."

After various commercial ups and downs the Corsinis consolidated their fortune in the sixteenth century when three brothers, Filippo, Bartolomeo, and Lorenzo, simultaneously ran three merchant banks in London, Lyons, and Florence. Bacic asks my help to shift a fifteen-foot-long bench, behind which the brothers' correspondence is stacked in a dozen mammoth white-and-gold folders. Some of the messages are coded, substituting numbers for letters, to protect business secrets. In 1579, I read, a consignment of wool has disappeared from a ship in Lisbon. In 1583 Bartolomeo in Lyons reports being feverish and sweating through three shirts every night. "But our business in Naples is going well," he assures Filippo in London.

Along with the letters is a slim account book listing Bartolomeo's donations to religious institutions on an almost daily basis.

At the end of each page, the entries are added up and carried over. In the months before his death, the sums are notably larger.

All these Corsini brothers meant to return to Florence in their old age; the family identity was tied to the city. But Filippo didn't make it. His body, his armor, his vast wealth, and his voluminous papers came back from London. Twenty thousand of the 900,000 ducats accumulated were spent on transforming the property in San Casciano into the huge villa it is today.

"And the pope?" I ask Bacic, who is struggling to push a massive folder of letters back onto a high shelf.

In 1730, the family's habit of pushing the second son into the priesthood, so as not to split the estate, paid off when a Corsini was elected pope and chose the name Clement XII. Aside from opening the Capitoline museums and commissioning the Fontana di Trevi, Clement bestowed the title of Prince of Sismano on his nephew Bartolomeo and made another nephew, Neri, a cardinal. Clement also built a chapel in San Giovanni Laterano, dedicated to St. Andrea Corsini. Whether it was business or religion, the goal was always to enhance family prestige. In reality, as princes of the tiny Umbrian village of Sismano, the Corsinis were sovereigns of their own backyard.

By noon, my feet are freezing. Fortunately, Duccio and Clotilde have invited us for lunch in the villa's handsome restaurant. At the table, the sense of continuity between archive and contemporary life is uncanny. Duccio talks about his son, Filippo, who is traveling abroad before hopefully returning to become involved in the family business. The wines on offer are produced by the company Principe Corsini and have such names as Don Tommaso and Sant'Andrea Corsini. The waitress has a Principe Corsini T-shirt.

However, when I ask Duccio if the family continues to add papers to the archive, he answers in the negative. "They ran out of space around 1960 and stopped." It seems strange to me that a family that owns so much property could not find space for more archives if it wished. Something must have changed. Perhaps the perception that everybody keeps business archives these days took the shine off the practice. Or perhaps the strict control the State exercises over the archive, constantly checking its contents and the conditions in which it is kept, has taken away that sense of liberty in secretiveness typical of Florentine families in the past. In any event, as if in enigmatic confirmation that the world is no longer what it was, in this very Italian restaurant both Duccio and his wife order hamburgers and fries.

The afternoon is dedicated to the women of the eighteenth and nineteenth centuries, who were sufficiently emancipated to be regular correspondents. Eleonora Rinuccini (1813–1886) wrote touchingly affectionate missives to her husband and children. Opening a small notebook, I read: "So long as I was in my father's house my existence was like a preparation for life . . . but a life I knew nothing about. Even in my mother's drawing room there was never any talk that wasn't proper . . . When I married my poor husband had to open my eyes, bit by bit."

The near impossibility of keeping these papers in any kind of order, I reflect, or of establishing their exact relation to each other, makes you realize how precarious our interpretations of history must always be, how dense and elusive real life is.

"I've worked in this archive thirty-six years," Bacic tells me, "and I think I have at least leafed through all the hundreds of thousands of papers here. But what does that mean? How much can anyone remember?" Indeed. Back in my hotel after a hair-raising bus ride back to Florence, I find myself hurrying to write down my own record of the day, before it slips away.

SHELLEY PUHAK

Eva, she kill her one daughter

FROM *Black Warrior Review*

1. The Motive

SEVENTY MILES UPSLOPE from my father's village, the sky is almost obscured by fir and spruce; by larch lower down the slopes; and lower still by sycamore, ash, and elm. Here in the remote foothills of the Carpathian Mountains, I'm looking for a village once called Rychwald, so named for "*rich forest*" from the earliest settlers' tongue. Medieval documents refer to "the black forests [that] stretch as far as Rychwald," thick and silent, and even today, over 600 years later, the forest's silence is impenetrable. There is no cell-phone service. And at one point, the asphalt ribbon thins, then becomes gravel, and then just stops. The old road has been swallowed up, reclaimed by the hornbeam and white birches. One of the car's front wheels is caught in a muddy rut; my only option may be to turn back.

I'm here in this black forest because the mountains stand guard over timber-and-thatch homes built along the snakes of streams. I'm here because, at these village crossroads—marked by bridges, cemeteries, and old mills—dwell the werewolves, ghostly babies, ghastly mothers.

In folk tales, the first six weeks after childbirth are a dangerous time—children are consumed by their mothers, mothers are consumed by their children, babies are snatched by spirits and replaced with changelings, mothers are transformed into monsters. One of the Brothers Grimm proclaimed that "women may never be left alone during the first six weeks following childbirth, for the devil then has more power over them." And the things the devil made them do! Measure out the teaspoonfuls of laudanum, paregoric, or milk laced with lime; place the pillow over the baby's mouth.

As it is in folk tales, so it is in genealogies. In fact, the Old English for *genealogy* was *folctalu* or literally, *folk tales*, family stories. One story is scrawled on the bottom of a family tree in my great-grandfather's hand—*Eva, she kill her one daughter.*

A few weeks into my first pregnancy, I was rocked with vertigo and vomiting so constant I hadn't slept for days. I lay flat on my back watching the ceiling rise and ebb, the new Berber carpet grinding into my back, my shirt twisted and stinking of bile: *I wish this baby would die.*

And nine months later, he did. Our first son was unbearably beautiful, seemingly perfect, but ill-equipped for our air. His heart struggled over the oscillator's constant pump-and-suck. He lived for less than a day and died in our arms.

Rychwald, Eva's village, was located on early maps in *Terra Indagines,* or, "the land in-between," and this region is still considered a borderland, between nomad and homestead, between cult and Christianity. I'm also here in this borderland because I've been inhabiting my own borderland, the one between sanity and grief.

There are stories we transmit through folk tales because we can't bear them any other way. One mother beats her infant to death, convinced she is a changeling left by the devil. Another mother so cursed drinks an elixir and it restores her maternal instincts. And another mother goes mourning-mad, sits at a magic rock waiting for her baby to wriggle back out, waiting until moss tunnels into her ears and quail nest in her skirts.

By the medical standards that reigned in Eva's lifetime, Andrea Yates presented with a textbook case of *puerperal insanity*—she was refusing to eat, unable to sleep, losing weight, having delusions, and not wanting to touch her newborn. Yet that infamous June morning in 2001, a very ill Andrea Yates was left in charge of five small children. She systematically drowned them all in under an hour.

People magazine's headline was "Nightmare." The article went on to call Yates "ordinary," and then offered up the following examples: "fresh-baked Christmas cookies [for the neighbors] . . . the whole family pitched in for landscaping chores."

One phobia common to most anxiety sufferers is the fear that they will go crazy, that they will be transformed into what they most fear. Werewolf lore takes the sensation of being uncomfortable in your own skin to its most extreme: you wake in a predator's skin, compelled by brutish instincts. So do contemporary infanticide narratives—the *ordinary* mother suddenly turned monstrous.

There are still days, more than a decade after the Yates case, when I methodically put away any sharp objects left out on the counter or sitting in the sink, fearful that I may suddenly go insane and attack my family with nail scissors or a paring knife.

It didn't help that, during and after my second pregnancy, I was regularly screened for my propensity to snap. I would sit in the beige chair in the beige office, swelling and weary and still grieving—my dearest firstborn, you who smelled of milk and earth and had crystalline eyes that you opened exactly twice—and the psychiatrist would run through the Edinburgh Postnatal Depression Scale (EDPS). I was supposed to respond Yes/No to a series of ten statements about how I'd felt that past week, statements like *I have blamed myself unnecessarily when things went wrong* and *I have been so unhappy that I have had difficulty sleeping* and, of course, *the thought of harming myself has occurred to me.*

The psychiatrist also wanted to know how I was occupying my time, pregnant on modified bed rest, waiting until my second son was born and either died or didn't. I told him I was making a quilt from the baby clothes. I told him I was boxing up all of the hospital bracelets, rereading the autopsy results, and storing the ashes inside an elaborate iron box.

You are still very tearful, the psychiatrist observed.

My baby is still dead.

He suggested yoga poses and breathing exercises I could do in bed. Or a craft of some sort, a project to keep me occupied.

I told him I was going to start researching a great-great-aunt who had murdered her child in the 1880s.

He frowned and leaned forward in his beige chair, but was careful to phrase his disapproval in the form of a question: *Why do you think you feel compelled to do this?*

My search officially begins in a 1970s-style church basement. I unspool microfilm and feed it into the projector, then scroll through amplified hieroglyphs projected onto white construction paper. These are the church records for the village formerly known as Rychwald in a region formerly known as the Kingdom of Galicia in what was once the Hapsburg Empire.

But these microfilmed church records stop at 1849, too early for me to find any evidence of my own great-great-grandfather Peter Zanowiak or his mysterious sister Eva. It takes another year of spinning other microfilm reels and wiring money to translators in remote archives before word comes from the Polish National Archives that there is hard evidence of Eva's existence. She was born in 1866 in a small village with an ornate onion-domed church and grew up in a long, low home plastered and painted white, the youngest of the seven surviving children of a respectable farmer.

On a Thursday after weeks of ceaseless rain, raucous thunderstorms, high winds, and tornado warnings, I first glimpse a copy of her baptismal record. It will soon be the summer of Casey Anthony. Jury selection has just begun in the media circus of a case surrounding a young woman accused of killing her two-year-old daughter.

The contemporary media offers me only two narratives of infanticide: Women who kill their children are either mad or they are bad. They are either perfect mothers who inexplicably snap, like Andrea Yates, or they are defective women, incapable of maternal sacrifice, like Casey Anthony. The tabloid images in the newspapers and flashing across the TV screen show a slender tanned brunette at a nightclub, shot glass aloft. *Monster mom partying four days after tot died* is one headline.

I find even more archival evidence of Eva's existence during the spring that Tonya Thomas shoots her four children and Stacey Smalls suffocates her eighteen-month-old twins, and the cover of *Time* asks, *Are You Mom Enough?*

And so, during the summer that Lisette Bamenga forces her two children to drink windshield wiper fluid, I walk the snake of asphalt that runs along the brook, past the goat and the satellite dish, and ask why she did it, why *did* Eva do it?

2. *The Witnesses*

I suppose my mother, with three little ones already, was simply sick of helping with homework, with elaborate projects—dioramas, posterboard displays—that required more out of her than of me. Fair enough. And maybe she didn't snap as I remember, but something about that family tree project and her reluctance stuck with me.

Besides, who really wants to relive the steamer trunk and the acrid pallet, the watery soup, the cloudy water, the anthracite dust in trouser cuffs, then thread-chaff, then factory gates chained shut, the crescendo of cheap vodka, the slow rusting of the whole town?

And so I told my third-grade classmates I was a Romanoff descendant, the grandchild of a princess. This is early evidence of my flair for the dramatic, but also of my deep uncertainty about my origins. My classmates could say they were Irish, or Italian, or could offer up precise equations to account for themselves: *I am half Turkish, one-quarter Japanese, and one-quarter Native American.* My dream of being a Russian princess was rooted in the ship manifests and census records that listed my ancestors as *Rusyn,* or *Rusynak,* or *Ruthenian.*

I wasn't quite sure what or *where* that meant.

My ancestors hailed from a place that had changed hands so many times, been subject to so many mass exterminations and exoduses, that it was scarcely a place at all. Ethnic Rusyns have never had their own homeland. My father's branch of this ethnic group was ruled by Hungary. My mother's branch lived under Polish, then Austrian, then Polish rule. In the nineteenth century, this northern branch became known as *Lemkos,* a nickname derived from their dialect, which uses the word *lem* to mean *only, just,* or *but.*

I can visit the remnants of Eva's birthplace, a Lemko sheepherding village in what is now southeastern Poland, but there may be no one left to tell Eva's story.

Any ethnic Lemkos left in Rychwald after World War II were

rounded up between March and June of 1947 and marched to the closest railway station. They were then loaded onto many of the same freight cars that had been used to transport their Jewish neighbors to the concentration camps. Those who resisted were shot. Before World War II, there were 140,000 Lemkos living in Poland. Today, that number is around 6,000.

Many villages were set aflame or razed to the ground; others, like Rychwald, were reduced to ghosts of their former selves and given new, more Polish names. According to the 1936 census, Rychwald held 1,050 Lemkos, thirty-three Roman Catholics Poles, and three Jews. By 1949, the village name had been changed to the Polish *Owczary*, and not a single Jew or Lemko remained. It is not just women who have been systematically silenced or erased, but entire peoples. Ghost children. Ghost villages.

My guide, Alicja, folds and refolds the maps while her boyfriend eases the car along in first gear, turning off onto a rutted dirt road that seems promising. This circuitous route into Eva's village is how we acquire Anna, or rather, how she acquires us, for her immediate reaction is that of *babas* everywhere—she enthusiastically adopts us, and then immediately begins to scold us. Alicja translates her rapid-fire admonitions: We will come in. How can we bear to think of saying no to a lonely old woman? We haven't eaten enough. We should not refuse her offer of coffee; that is rude. What will our mothers think of our manners? We should always listen to our mothers. She, herself, was a very obedient child.

The house is a single-level log and stucco home with plaster walls. She settles down on her bed, motioning at the wooden chairs and table for us. Anna's personal style can be best summed up as *Eastern European Utilitarian:* a traditional embroidered kerchief over her hair, but also a man's white undershirt, a man's suit vest, black sweatpants, and orthopedic shoes. If her dress is utilitarian, the rest of her textiles are impractically decorative. Everything possible is embellished: the large tapestry on the wall behind Anna, the comforter on her bed, the hand towel, the tablecloths—embroidered with blond women in blue dresses, spindly trees and near-neon flowers, narrow saints and spring lambs.

Even Anna's speech is embellished, by chortles and snorts, comical faces, emphatic gestures, and bits of song. Alicja can barely keep up with the conversation, and so her boyfriend, when he is not laughing, steps in as translator: *Now she is telling us complaints about her dead husband . . . and now some story about drinking too much, but I am having trouble following . . . Now she would like us to come back and visit in July, when there is a big festival . . .* Complicating matters, Anna's songs are in a nearly extinct dialect neither of them can translate well. I scramble to try to record scraps of this mother tongue on my iPhone. After each song, she waits until we respond with applause. Then she promptly launches into another litany of complaints. *Now she is telling how the cow keeps wandering off. She says she was once robbed by village boys . . . Now she is arguing with Alicja about what day we will come to visit next.*

This is why the summer sky is low and gray with impending rain by the time we arrive in front of the wood-shingled church in the center of the village. The walk over revealed a rural village like most others, rolling green punctuated by haystacks, until this improbable fantasy with its three bulbous copper spires. *Opieki Matki Bożej* or Church of the Protection of the Mother of God, a UNESCO World Heritage site, is one of the oldest wooden churches in Europe, built entirely of larch shingles without a single nail.

Houses have burned and collapsed, fields have been left fallow, but the overall design and property lines are unchanged from when Rychwald was officially chartered in 1417. This means that I see some of the same structures as Eva's parents did—her mother Rozalia in thick white and blue skirts, her father Daniel in his distinctive shepherd's coat—when they left House #27 and trudged across the snowy road on December 9, 1866, to have their four-day-old daughter baptized. The same slant of sky, the same rolling hills. Someone's woodpile; a tilting well; and other long and low wooden homes, stuccoed and lime-washed white or blue. In winter, the animals would have been stabled, but, now, in late June, there are cows in the pasture and sheep on the hill.

The church is surrounded by a low stone wall. A woman from the village unlocks the front gate. To enter, I must duck under a weathered plank with AHO DNI 1653 scalloped out in script. I find myself in a gilded world—icons with their long, flat faces refracted and multiplied by stained glass, illumined in an afternoon light both mournful and terrible. If the fields outside promise an infinity of one kind, the cycles of the harvest and the undulation of the hills, then this church promises another infinity, one that is layered and paneled, vaulted and iridescent. These *simple* country folk had scrimped and saved to create astounding artifice. While they lived in cramped, dark, and smoky quarters, they worshipped in glittering and airy spaces.

The church was built in the Greek Catholic tradition, which means the altar is hidden by an *iconostasis,* an elaborate partition that runs floor-to-ceiling and has been untouched since the seventeenth century, except by termites. This partition is topped by seven panels of somber saints and, at its center, an icon of Christ in the Tomb. Two baroque side altars—carved columns, cherubs, inlays, and more gilt—portray the Madonna with Child and the beloved St. Nicholas. I can sit in the same pew Eva sat in, Sunday after Sunday, I can stare at the same elongated saints, but I can get no closer.

Anna tells how there were no tanks, only vehicles, soldiers. *But we were not lucky like the other villages who had two hours to pack—we were given exactly twenty-five minutes.*

Anna tells how there were 360 Lemko houses here before World War II. In the 1950s, only seven Lemko families returned. She and her husband were the first, and they had to buy back the home that had been in the family for 250 years from its new occupants.

Anna had heard of the Zanowiak family, she could point to where their house once stood, but as much as she wanted to help us, she could conjure no village gossip about any Eva who had killed her daughter.

In the church cemetery, I find evidence of only one Zanowiak: the surname on a headstone, in stout and square Cyrillic, topped with a vaguely Mayan Madonna and child. There are dozens of cracked monuments, dozens of smaller stones, all children, uncounted.

3. The Means

Eva came of age during an epidemic of infanticide.

Folk tales from the period tell of murdered infants who refuse to stay buried, who continue to live stunted and underground. One Lemko villager claims that, when he was eight, he saw the following: "This little boy ran and squeezed under the house . . . He was barefoot and bareheaded and wore nothing but a very small shirt . . . The women told us it was a *zmitca,* that is a baby who never developed because the girl who had it smothered it when it was born." In another folk tale, the *zmitca* lives under one of the porch steps. In a legend called "The Crying Child," a servant girl suffocates her illegitimate child and buries his body under a shed. Now all who pass this shed hear an infant wailing. The folk tales say the babies will keep crying until given proper burials.

Infanticide was so pervasive in the Hapsburg Empire that, by special imperial decree, a specific door of Vienna General Hospital was designated for the use of unmarried women who wished to deliver anonymously. This entrance was in operation for seventy years, and similar entrances were designated in the hospitals of other large towns.

Between 1882 and 1898, when Eva would have been at her reproductive prime, there were 1,658 reported cases of infanticide in the entire Austrian Empire, an average of about 100 reported cases per year.

In Western Europe, especially England, infanticide rates were even higher. Consider that, in less than a year, a single London district reported as many infanticide cases as the whole Austrian Empire. In the whole of London, more than 200 infants were found dead in the streets every year. The press there was often apocalyptic about the epidemic of maternal monsters:

> The metropolitan canal boats are impeded, as they are tracked along by the number of drowned infants with which they come in contact . . . We are told by Dr. Lankester that there are 12,000 women in London to whom the crime of child murder may be attributed. In other words, that one in every thirty women (I presume between fifteen and forty-five) is a murderess.

If English girls drowned their babies, wrapped in newspaper, soggy with sleep, in the Thames, Rusyn village girls did so in forest creeks or family wells. Among the lost Lemkos, drowned infants become a particular ghost, not *zmitca* but baby *rusalki* who haunted these creeks as water nymphs and will-o'-the-wisps.

I came of age during an infanticide epidemic too, the heyday of Dumpster babies, of tiny corpses found behind malls, behind dormitories, in the gym bathroom during prom.

The summer I was planning my wedding and contemplating motherhood, Andrea Yates's descent into psychosis was the first sign that the world as I knew it was imploding. Three months later, the planes would crash into the Towers and the Pentagon and the Pennsylvania field. The next week, the news commentators advised me to buy duct tape and surgical masks, to protect myself from the powdered anthrax being mailed to U.S. senators down the road.

The next month, I would pass men in fatigues with automatic rifles in the security line to board my honeymoon flight to Paris. When we left Paris, an airlines agent unceremoniously dumped out the content of my luggage—my frothy honeymoon lingerie, evidence of the last pleasures I had left—onto a gray foldout table in front of our gate.

When we say mothers snap, it is tempting to think it really is that easy: one morning, one point of impact, one detonation, one genetic switch flicked ON.

I wish I'd finished reading that *People* magazine article back in 2001, instead of waiting until now. While *People* called Andrea Yates an "ordinary" mother and the drowning of her five children "unfathomable," "unthinkable," and "horrific," the magazine also detailed her suicide attempt and subsequent hospitalization, move to a new home, fifth pregnancy against a doctor's orders, and suicidal relapse. The article notes that Yates was abruptly taken off her antipsychotic medication. Her brother is interviewed detailing her further decline into a near-catatonic state in the weeks before the killings.

Even in Eva's lifetime, even in the backwoods, no mother suffering from puerperal insanity was left unsupervised with children. The act of attempting to harm one's child was offered in court as proof of insanity.

Note that Andrea Yates was originally found sane and convicted of capital murder.

Note that, in our time, Andrea Yates could pass for *ordinary*.

On our walk back from the parish cemetery, we first pass a World War I cemetery, then a modern bus stop across from the church in the shade of some trees. Anna breaks away, hobbling, thrusting into the underbrush with her cane. At first it seems she is indignant about the bus stop itself (*no*, Alicja's boyfriend realized, *she is just mad about a bus being late once*), but then we realize she is gesturing to a crumbling stone structure next to the bus stop.

As we step closer, it doesn't appear to be much—a lump of small stones.

But Anna pokes the stones with her cane again and gives me a gummy smile, clearly pleased with herself. This was their old well, the Zanowiaks' well, I am made to understand.

Anna asks a question and looks at me expectantly, eyes shining. Alicja translates: *Maybe your Eva drown her baby here?*

4. The Opportunity

What does it mean to speak of one's *mother country* or *motherland,* when a mother's borders are so permeable? Some things the folk tales got right: women are forever changed by pregnancy. Mother and fetus swap blood during pregnancy. They swap cells too, and this process is called *microchimerism,* after the mythological Chimera, an improbable amalgam of lion, goat, and snake. Maybe you've heard of people absorbing lost embryonic twins that later appear as tumors or cysts. In much the same way, fetal cells live on in a mother's body, found in her brain, lungs, liver, kidneys, thyroid, even skin, sometimes decades after she gives birth. Even weirder, women inherit microchimeric cells not just from our children, but from our own mothers, and thus, our grandmothers, our crazy great-aunts. Scientists are not sure why. These cells may induce autoimmune diseases, or they may be protective, regenerative even.

Maybe it was these microchimeric cells. Or maybe it was the neurochemical cocktail of oxytocin and serotonin and pheromones that rendered me besotted. I still well up just staring at the hollow behind his knee, or the perfect curve of his bottom lip, or his particularly delicious earlobes.

Now, when we snuggle before bed, I snarl, *You're lucky that you're cute. Know why?* He replies: *I'm lucky I'm so cute or else you'd EAT ME!,* and I gather him to me and he shrieks as I pretend to nibble his arms, nosh on his head.

He intuits, in the way that children do, another folk tale, that of the dark mother, the witch in her bone home in the woods who consumes children, who bakes them in a casserole or simmers them into a stew. Mommies are chimera, impossible and incongruous creatures. And yet, he still pats my hand, kisses grape juice on my cheek.

The forest is thick, but it is not silent, as I first wrote. Mountains feed the streams, streams feed the trees. Trees talk via an electrochemical thread, an underground fungal network that transfers nutrients or antibodies, taps out alarms. Threaded with these trees' murmurings, the *zmitca* wailing, the *rusalki*'s teeth chattering. Here, villagers once recited spells, charms, and signs of the cross, carried garlic and wormwood, left gifts of scarves and soup.

In the onion-domed church I lit a candle for my firstborn. Among the hornbeams and white birches, the beech and fir, the spruce and mountain pine, I said a prayer for Eva's daughter.

There is no record of Eva past her childhood in Rychwald. One neighboring parish burnt down during the First World War. Another library was bombed during the second. Any remaining records have been moved to Austria, to Hungary, to Poland, no, to Ukraine. No one knows where the records are. Or everyone knows where the records are but accessing them requires this form, and this form, and a native-born lawyer or an EU passport.

There are possible Evas, probable Evas—glimpses in a port, then a tenement, a warehouse, a factory. Still, finding Eva and her daughter may be like looking at the sun, something I can only attempt slant, through folklore and court records, through genetic tests and midwifery texts. But I know that I have to try.

One Person Means Alone

FROM *The Missouri Review*

BEFORE TAIGU, people warned me: China was a fiercely social country. After I arrived, I rarely went anywhere unaccompanied. I was ushered into crowded noodle stalls and into corner stores stuffed with plum juice, chicken feet, and hot-water thermoses. I often needed help at the post office, with its hundreds of strict regulations and wisp-thin envelopes you sealed with a depressor and paste. Students took me to the White Pagoda and the court-yard of H. H. Kung, the only historical sites in town that hadn't been destroyed during the Cultural Revolution. Eventually, I'd be invited into my Chinese colleagues' small apartments, where sev-eral generations of the family often lived together. I'd be gener-ously served five kinds of dumplings, the bowl full again before I had the chance to set down my chopsticks.

In the unheated, Soviet-feeling building where I taught univer-sity English, I waited in line with other women to use toilets with-out doors or stalls. At first, I tried to turn my face away from the others, demurring. But there was no use trying to hide anything about our bodies here: whose stomach was upset, or who was cry-ing, or who was on her period that day. We saw it all. We offered stacks of tissues when someone had run out of their own supply.

I lived in a tiny brick house, the tiles on my roof painted with evil eyes to ward off badness. I'd often wake to the arguing of an unknown college couple, shouting their insults right in front of my window, just a few feet away from where I had been sleeping. I'd stumble into the kitchen, startled to find a stranger outside the back door, shaking my (was it mine?) jujube tree and picking up the fruits from the ground.

Like most teachers at the agricultural university, I lived on campus, and I wasn't hard to find. My thoughtful students showed up on my front stoop, bearing jars of weird floating grains and fermented vegetables sent by their grandmothers. "If you eat this for six days," they'd say, "you will be well."

The word was out: I was sick a lot. It was my first time living abroad, and the new microbes were hard on my body. In Taigu, there was delicious street food as well as contaminated cooking oil, air, and groundwater. Shanxi province, even by Chinese standards, was an environmental disaster. The coal plants were next to the grain fields, pink and green smoke rising out of the stacks. On a good day, you could see the mountains that surrounded campus. Most of the time, they were hidden by pollution. Particulate matter caked the windowsills in my house.

People were curious about me. I was asked daily by strangers in the market square what country I was from and why I had come to Shanxi province—sort of the West Virginia of China, except that it was on the edge of the desert—as opposed to the more glamorous Shanghai or Beijing. They also asked how old I was, how much money I made teaching at the university, if I'd eaten that day yet, and, if so, what had I eaten? And why was I "a little bit fat," they said, but not as fat as some Americans? How often did I need to color and perm my hair? (It was reddish and was curly on its own, I said.) Was that American living in the other half of my duplex my boyfriend? (He was not.) Well, did I at least have a boyfriend in the States? (Sarah, my girlfriend from college, was teaching in Indonesia, but I didn't explain her, for obvious reasons.) And, occasionally, from students and younger friends: What did I think of the movie *American Pie Presents: Beta House*? Was it an accurate portrayal of American university life?

Eventually, I borrowed my friend Zhao Xin's laptop so I could watch the pirated version with Chinese subtitles. I was horrified. One of the thankfully forgotten sequels of the original *American Pie*, it made me squeamish during scenes of a fraternity's hazing ritual, something about attaching a bucket of beer to some guy's genitalia. There was also one exaggerated fire-hose moment, a sorority sister experiencing female ejaculation for the first time. As for the question of whether this resembled university life in the United States, I told them, in all honesty, I wasn't sure. I had just graduated from a small, studious college in the Midwest. Despite its sex-positive atmosphere, things were, all in all, pretty quiet there, with some nerdily themed parties but no Greek life at all.

In truth, I'd had plenty of sex in college, but that had to be my own business. More specifically, I didn't reveal my lesbian identity to anyone in China, at least at first. I responded to boyfriend questions with a simple "No." I didn't know what the consequences of coming out might be, and I couldn't take the risk. Keeping this a secret, I'd come to realize later, was part of what made me feel so isolated that first year in China, even though other people surrounded me.

As a student in America, my life had been pretty communal. Still, like a number of Generation Y, middle-class, considerably selfish Americans, I thought I was fiercely independent and staged myself as the protagonist in my own life story. Very little prepared me for the level of social responsibility and interconnectedness that came with moving to Taigu. One of the first words I learned was *guanxi*, which can be roughly translated as "social connections," or maybe "relationships." If you had *guanxi* with others, you could count on them for most everything, and they could count on you; if you failed to foster a sense of *guanxi*, people would resent you or think of you as selfish, even though they might not say it out loud. *Guanxi* emphasized — or mandated — the whole you were a part of rather than the part you played alone.

I embraced this idea the best I knew how. My American co-fellow, Ben, and I mounted a disco ball in our living room and started hosting weekly dance parties for our Chinese friends: social activity for the greater good, something students reported as scarce on our small-town, farm-school campus. At these parties, at first, we'd awkwardly stand in a circle. But then the sorghum-alcohol punch we provided began to take effect, and our loopy, arrhythmic movements took over the room. Over time, we perfected our playlist: a mix of American '80s and '90s hits and cheesy Chinese pop songs. By our second year in China, our living room floor was beginning to split from people's dancing enthusiasm.

The Americans got a wild reputation on campus. Our parties were on Thursday nights, but then we got a noise complaint from the university's vice president, who happened to live in a house just thirty feet from our front door. When we showed up on his porch the morning after, with a giant fruit bowl and profuse apologies, he smiled and invited us in, as if nothing bad had happened. Our *guanxi*, the neighborhood harmony, seemed to be restored.

Overall, however, I was not the best at fostering *guanxi*. I often found myself hungry for space between others and myself: a necessary measure to quiet the buzz in my dislocated brain. I'd draw the curtains and hole up in my side of my foreign-teacher duplex, the door to my half closed. This action was usually perceived as hostile or a symptom of possible depression.

"Why is she not coming out here?" I heard someone ask Ben on the other side of my door. "Is she sad about something? Why is she alone?"

The word *alone* in Mandarin can be translated in various ways. The expression I heard on the other side of my door, traveling by myself on a train, or walking down the street solo was *yi ge ren*. *Yi* is "one"; *ge* is a kind of counting word, placed between a number and an object. And *ren* means "person" or "people." The expression "Are you *yi ge ren*?" when translated literally is "Are you one person?" In context, though, I began to understand this as a way of asking, "Are you on your own? Are you alone?"

Of course, I was rarely 100 percent alone, unless you counted when I was asleep or in the single-person bathroom in my apartment. I had come to Taigu paired with Ben, another recent college graduate, and there were two more Americans living in the house next door to us, doing their second year of the same teaching fellowship we'd all received. Most of our life outside of class involved a mixed group of American fellows and Chinese graduate students, with a few older Chinese undergraduates mixed in. We ate dinner together most nights at the hot-pot place, just outside the campus gate, or at one of the noodle stalls at school.

Every once in a while, though, I'd find myself walking alone in public. I was not afraid: not near my house, not on the other side of campus, not even in the bleak brick-and-mud Taigu village alleys scattered with trash and piles of used coal pellets. There were terrible stories, real or imagined, of people getting snatched up around here and having their organs harvested. There was a line of massage parlors, a sort of red-light district, the neon signs flickering on and off.

When I passed another person, I'd see what I came to know as the Look: not threatening but a look more of curiosity or even shock, mostly due to my obvious non-Han appearance. Sometimes they'd ask me where I was from. Some would say nothing. Some would even ask me if I was okay, if I had eaten, and where I was going.

I don't know whether it was the fact that we lived in the ultra-militarized People's Republic or just that Taigu men are not the type to catcall, but I always maintain that China felt like the safest place I'd ever lived. Perhaps my outsider status as a Westerner protected me. Years later, when I returned to the United States, finding myself living in a host of smaller towns, as well as cities like Chicago, Washington, D.C., and New Orleans, I was shocked at how often some stranger on the street would whoop at me or stare for too long or start to walk too close. In my own homeland, strangely, I felt the most unsafe being by myself.

In a country of a billion people, personal space isn't just something that's frowned upon; it's often impossible to find. Even a small town like Taigu—just 40,000 people—was no exception. If you wanted to be alone in the daytime, you could ride your bicycle past the grain fields and the coal- and bauxite-processing plants to the even smaller village at the edge of the mountains, where there were several temples in the outcroppings.

In China, university dorms are not named after famous educators or benefactors but are instead referred to by serial numbers: "26 building," "27 building," and so on. I soon discovered that the undergraduates were living eight to a room: four sets of bunk beds pressed against the walls, one shared table in the barely existent center of the room. The graduate students, thought to be deserving of a bit more space, were also in dorms but housed in groups of four. The first time I entered a dorm room at the agricultural university, it was as if I were entering a unit in a warehouse. I saw schoolbooks, clothes, shoes, packages of dry noodles, and clothes-washing bowls crammed beneath the lowest bunks and around the perimeter. The room's one narrow window was strung with several drying lines for shirts and underwear. It was the middle of the day, so the students were elsewhere.

My friend Wang Yue, a twenty-year-old English major, pointed disapprovingly to one of the lower bunks and told me that a pair of her roommates—two nineteen-year-olds who preferred to be called by their self-selected English names, Sky King and Toni—

always slept side by side in this single bed. They were obviously in the early stages of a romance. "It's like they wish the rest of us weren't here," Wang Yue told me, rolling her eyes.

It was unclear to me where her disdain came from. Was it just homophobia? Was she annoyed because these women had upset the *guanxi* and balance of the group, prioritizing their personal interests over the harmony of the whole? Or was it because they were two women, finding a loophole in the single-gender dorm, the thing that was supposed to keep students focused on school, not on sex?

Everyone on campus was struggling for intimate space. The foreign teachers' houses were adjacent to a small circular garden where the willow and birch trees created a shadowy canopy over a few park benches. This was hardly a hidden place, but it was more secluded than the rest of campus. If I passed by at nightfall, I'd see the flash of someone's limbs wrapped around another body, and then another couple on the next bench, just a few feet away. This was the official campus hook-up area, a kind of twenty-first-century drive-in theater. The students called it the *qingren shulin,* or "Lovers' Forest."

Even the privacy in my half-a-duplex was not a thing I could always count on. My girlfriend, Sarah—who also had a teaching fellowship, but in Indonesia—managed to visit China the first fall I was there, during her Ramadan break from school. We'd spent a large part of our senior year in college in bed together, but coming to teach in Asia, as well as our physical separation, had resulted in an almost celibate life for both of us. Desperate, we tried to cram as many sessions as possible into those two weeks of her visit.

One late Friday afternoon, we were interrupted by Ben's frantic knocking on the door to my bedroom. He warned us that Xiao Zhang, a staff member for the Foreign Affairs Office, had just come over, and she was about to walk in any minute. She needed to see something on my side of the house, and right now, apparently.

A wave of indignation passed through me, which was instantaneously replaced by panic. I didn't have any closets to hide inside. There were no locks in our house, except on the front door. And it was no use to pretend to be out: Xiao Zhang and the office staff members, for all sorts of reasons, regularly came into our apartments when we weren't home and would have no trouble coming into the bedroom. The units belonged to the university, after all; we were just living in them.

Flushed, I pulled on my tossed-off clothes and rushed out into the foyer area, apologizing for my delay. I tried to close the bedroom door behind me, but, like most doors in the house, it didn't fully latch. Xiao Zhang advised me, in the slowest Mandarin she could manage, about getting some sticky paper to try to trap the mice that had invited themselves in just after the weather had turned. "Right," I kept saying, nodding, hoping to make the conversation as short as possible. I stopped understanding her instructions after a while. My language skills were not up to snuff, especially when I was panicked.

But it was clear from her hand motions that she was describing what happens when the mouse actually dies its horrible death inside the adhesive. She even went so far as to mimic a rodent scream, just so I would be prepared. I stood fidgeting. On the other side of the partially cracked door, Sarah was hidden under the duvet, still undressed and trying not to move.

Besides teaching, eating, and the lessons with my Chinese tutor, I spent a few late afternoons a week at the campus's indoor swimming pool. The idea of swimming, especially in a poor, dry province like Shanxi, sounded luxurious in theory. In practice, the pool felt like an environmental apocalypse, so gritty and chemicalized that you could barely make out the T's on the tiled bottom. The water smelled like a mix of spoiled vegetables and bleach. The chlorine powder was dispensed in satchels that looked like giant artificial jellyfish floating just above the underwater jets.

One week, I ran into my student and his friends on their way back from the pool building. He told me they had closed the pool down for a couple of days. "They must change the water this week," he told me assuredly, in English. "It is the first time in seven years they will change the water." I hoped something had been lost in translation.

The pool scene was, despite this, pleasant enough. Of course, if you headed there with the sole intention of swimming a bunch of laps, you'd be frustrated. Like everywhere else, the pool was full of bodies, especially in the shallow end. For every fifteen meters I swam, I'd usually stop to talk to someone: a student, or a friend, or sometimes a complete stranger. If I didn't stop, I'd likely collide with them in the water anyway.

Right away, I noticed that most of the women stayed in the shallow end, trying to develop the basic skills to pass the university's swimming test. The lifeguards/pool keepers, all middle-aged men with beer guts and sagging swim trunks, were impressed with my sessions in the deep end and with my swimming skills. "You have a good *sui jue*," one of them told me, which literally translates to "feeling of the water."

But my sense of the water wasn't intuitive so much as it was another marker of my Western, middle-class upbringing. I thought of the series of photos in my mother's albums back in North Carolina: me at six months, fat and smiling, at baby swim class at the YWCA; me at four, splashing in the waves at the beach; my first swim-team picture at the age of six, posed next to the diving board. In China, however, swimming pools were scarce, and most natural bodies of water seemed apocalyptically contaminated. For most of the Chinese students, the university was the first place they'd had access to anyplace where they could swim.

The women at the pool intimidated me. It was not because of their swimming. It was the locker-room shower scene that I found daunting: an enormous, packed-to-the-gills mob of bodies and steam.

Unless you are very wealthy in Shanxi, most homes do not have their own shower. Chinese towns have public bathhouses. At university, similarly, there were no showers in the dorms themselves; showering was something most people did a couple of times a week in one of the university's provided facilities. Or, if you bought a swim pass, you could take your showers at the pool.

At any given time, the showers at the pool had four or five people gathered around each showerhead, taking turns to rinse. To pass through this shower room, even just on your way to or from the pool, was to push through a crowd of women and soap and hair. Much to my Puritan dismay, it was almost impossible to find unscented anything in rural China, including laundry detergent or maxipads, and the shower room was no exception. The air was overwhelming with its shampoo and soap perfumes, freesia and juniper and lavender. In the fog, it was a humid, scented forest, with limbs reaching in every direction.

I had never seen so many naked bodies together, been close to so many people at once. Most of the women, being students, were in their twenties: their skins completely smooth, their breasts small, their bodies angular and narrow by my own Western standards. Many of them had tied a red string around their hips, with a jade pendant for luck. There were some older women too, who were teachers or lived in the community. Their bodies were considerably rounder, more weathered by time. Some had cesarean scars that had never faded, their bellies divided by the pink line.

The level of intimacy here terrified me. In this shower space, my own shame came from what I couldn't hide: the obvious strangeness of my Caucasian body and its larger proportions of fat, muscle, and hair. It was one thing to walk through Taigu, wearing jeans and a jacket I'd bought in town, and be stared at immediately because of my red curls and pale skin. It was another to enter the shower room, for it to be obvious that the hair in my crotch was as red as that on top of my head.

"Wow," my friend Wang Hui Fang said the first time she got a look at me, not long after we had met. We weren't even showering then; she and I and our other friend were just changing into our bathing suits, stuffing our clothes into a shoebox-sized locker with no lock. "*Name hong!*" she exclaimed, an expression meaning "really, really red."

When she saw my embarrassment, she switched to English and tried to reassure me.

"It is very interesting," she said with enthusiasm. She grabbed, then, at the nonexistent flesh on her own waistline. "I am really getting fat," she said, as if she meant to comfort me.

So I usually rushed through the shower room at the pool, being there only long enough to rinse off, my frantic quality probably causing me to get even more attention than I would have otherwise. Sometimes I avoided the shower room altogether, opting to walk home shivering, with the chlorine eating away at my hair. I was choosing, then, to use my own showerhead in my apartment, which was simply attached to the wall and got everything else in the tiny bathroom wet: sink, toilet, trash can, floor. Even in the privacy of my own bathroom, showering could be a messy, unbounded experience.

*

Once I went with Wang Yue to visit her hometown of Datong in the north of Shanxi province, another cold, dusty, coal-mining city that borders Inner Mongolia. On Saturday afternoon, we went to a public bathhouse near her family's apartment.

The showers were strangely empty that day, much less crowded than the pool building's at school. Several middle-aged women turned to look at me incredulously and then went on with their scrubbing. With all that empty space in the tiled room, I actually felt cold despite the hot water beating down on me.

I admitted to Wang Yue then that I felt embarrassed showering at the pool at school. To make things even weirder, I pointed out, I was a teacher. The shower room called to mind one of those teaching-anxiety dreams, I explained, when you suddenly find yourself naked in front of one of your classes. Wang Yue looked at me, confused. It hadn't occurred to me that the "teaching naked" dream might be specific to my cultural background.

"Like, what if I see one of my students in the showers?" I asked her, reframing my point. "That would be embarrassing."

"Why?" she asked. "I mean, like . . ." she said, her English colloquialisms flawless, "they are also there taking a shower, right? They don't care. They are doing the same thing as you." She offered me her bottle of soap. She had a point.

In this new phase of my life, where I felt exposed all the time, there was still so much in the culture that seemed guarded, so much information I'd never be privy to. At the start of the day's classes, I frequently got notes from missing students who gave vague excuses for their absences. "Dear Teacher," the notes usually read, in English, "I am sorry I will not attend class today. I have something to do."

In Mandarin, the expression *you shi* means you have some kind of business to deal with, the specifics of which might be private and need not be explained in detail. There is no good translation for this phrase, at least in my experience, though my students tried. What these *somethings* were, I never found out.

Despite the communal culture, there was a limit to how much of myself could be seen. I had my own secret. My first year in Shanxi, I felt I couldn't explain to any Chinese person—mostly because of the conservative social mores of where I was living—how much I longed for Sarah and how impossible communication had become, given unreliable Internet access and my crackling phone as well as the unpredictable restrictions from the government in Beijing. We found our Skype calls going silent.

As exhilarating as it was to be living abroad, there was also, for me, the day-to-day panic I didn't know how to explain to others, which came from an accumulation of small things: not being able to read all the characters on the bus schedules or figure out how to send a package. Or what to do when you eat something that gives you violent diarrhea all night and when the water source to your toilet is cut off, in a province with severe shortages, between 10:00 p.m. and 7:00 a.m. When I think back on China, even my good days had an undercurrent of deeper, untranslatable anxiety. It was that dislocation that only comes when you find yourself living, all of a sudden, on the other side of the world and not understanding how anything works. On bad days, I felt that I shouldn't have come to China. As an outsider, maybe I had no business being in Shanxi at all.

At night, I lay awake in my cold little bedroom, listening to the rat inside the radiator vent toenailing his way out onto the dark floor. China is a pretty loud place, but at night in Taigu, there was only this, plus one other noise: a train, about a mile away, from Xi'an on its way to Beijing, sounding its horn into the crisp, landlocked night. I could hear its pitch shift as it grew closer, then farther away. A sort of reverse alarm clock: I heard this every night at the same hour. Years later, when I think of the word *alone,* I still hear this sound.

That first spring, when I'd been in China nine months, Sarah finally broke up with me over the phone, the result of a multi-call argument we couldn't seem to resolve while in two separate countries. Neither of us would back down. "This is impossible," she admitted and then hung up, as if some unknown force in the universe were responsible for what was happening to us. Despite the fact that we were already physically separated, and knowing the unlikely odds for relationship survival—several countries between us, two new cultures to adapt to, no plans to see each other until later in the summer, and being immature, in our early twenties —the breakup blindsided me.

I wasn't out to any of my Chinese friends yet. So the night after the phone call I spent wallowing in the company of the Americans next door, eating, in alternation, seaweed-flavored potato chips and beef-flavored potato chips. (We would eventually start calling them "breakup chips," since hardly any American's long-distance relationship survived while one member of the couple was living in China.) We drank large bottles of Xue Hua, a mediocre Chinese beer. The next morning, I woke at dawn, hungover and disoriented, to the loudspeaker narration of a campuswide exercise routine. I couldn't decipher any of the voice's directions except for the counting parts. "Three . . . four . . . five . . . SIX!" the voice kept saying, the reason for this emphasis unclear to me.

My grief that spring was enormous, maybe even out of proportion. Before China, I had never been particularly weepy, especially not after a breakup. Now I cried anytime I was not in front of a group of students: during dinner, during my Chinese lessons, after I bought vegetables in the square, while sweeping my floor or wiping the black coal dust from the windowsill. In Shanxi, all my usual emotions became augmented in ways I didn't understand, and the boundaries for who should and shouldn't know my feelings became more and more unclear.

Everything I ate made me sick. I started to resent hosting the usual dance parties, giving a thin-lipped smile as twentysomethings flooded my house. It wasn't long before my new Chinese friends put two and two together, even though I had never directly explained to them that Sarah, who had visited in the fall, was my girlfriend. I did not have to spell it out. "Oh! You have *xin shi*," they would tell me, letting my lesbianism be implied rather than stated outright.

When it comes to emotional matters in China, there is a variation of the vague expression *you shi,* the usual "I have business" or "I have something to do." If you say *you xin shi,* it means, more specifically, you have a matter of the heart to deal with, or something is weighing on you, or that you're worried in an all-consuming way. The word *xin,* written 心, is an actual pictograph meaning "heart." *Xin shi* was how my friends referred to struggles with their boyfriends or girlfriends, or, occasionally, even more sensitive matters. (One close Chinese friend, I eventually discovered, had had three abortions in the previous four years, all of which she'd kept a secret from her family and most of her friends at school.) The phrase is useful and can serve as a euphemism if you want it to, allowing you to both guard the details of your situation and also offer the gesture of an explanation.

The first time I uttered the phrase, it was because it was a bad day for me, my eyes still red and swollen when I entered the grain-seller's store to buy a half kilogram of flour. After I asked for the flour, the woman nodded, looked hard at me like an all-knowing mother. "*You xin shi,*" I said, and she seemed to accept that.

"This poor foreigner," I heard her say to her husband, shaking her head, as I was heading out the door. But that was the last time she'd refer to me as *foreigner.* I'd always be one, but the next time I came in to buy something, she called me Luo Yi Lin, the name I'd been given by a Mandarin tutor just after I'd arrived to China.

Not surprisingly, being with other people could sometimes distract me from my breakup. But I preferred to hang out with my friends one-on-one rather than be in the crowd. My favorite thing to do that spring was to sit on my stoop late into the evening with my Chinese tutor at the time, Zhao Xin (or "Maggie," as she sometimes called herself), drinking cheap beer and talking. Maggie had slowly become my closest friend in Shanxi. She was less demure than most of the Chinese women I knew—she cursed and played badminton and got angry at her boyfriend a lot. With the formal hour of the Chinese lesson long past, our conversations tended to get crasser and crasser as the night went on. These sessions, I maintain, are how I finally got conversational in Mandarin.

Maggie showed up at my house one spring night, appearing like a ghost on the dirt path leading up to my porch. She was coming from her graduate program's class party. "I had dry white wine," she kept saying, over and over, in English. Something was off about the translation: there was no dry white wine, at least the kind made from grapes, anywhere in town. Maggie spoke English to me only when she was drunk; it was her secret code to let me know what she'd been up to.

She had missed the dorm curfew, so she stayed with me. We shared my double bed, talking loudly and rudely for a while, scaring off the mice. She kept asking me, in English, with a strange British accent I'd never heard, if I had any beer in the kitchen. I didn't.

Far away, we heard the train pass, its timbre now more muddled than what I remembered in the colder months. Why was that so? We lay on our backs next to one another, our shoulders just barely touching. The ends of her black hair crossed onto my pillow. I could smell her shampoo. The room felt still, big around us. What was this? It was a closeness I hadn't felt in a long time.

I was thinking about what could happen, what would not happen between us. We got quiet. I wanted to know what she was thinking. Finally, she rolled toward me and reached across my arm. I held my breath and froze.

In a teasing, nonsexual way, she grabbed the hem of my shirt and tried to tickle my stomach, the way my sisters would do when we were kids. She stopped suddenly, with the heel of her hand just below my ribs.

"It's strong here!" she said, jubilant and surprised, pointing to my upper abdomen. "I like it."

When I exhaled, it came out as a laugh. She rolled back onto her back. A thin sliver of moonlight was wedging its way through the bedroom curtains. Our chattering thinned out, and the room went still again. I heard her breathing shift toward sleep. Our shoulders were still touching.

Language-wise, I finally gained the confidence to spend a good chunk of that first summer traveling alone. On a warm night in June, I stood beside the railroad tracks outside Taigu Railway Station, balancing my backpack across my feet. Alongside me was a small group of students with tiny suitcases, farmers with burlap bundles across their backs, and a handful of men and women who carried nothing except poker cards and the sunflower seeds and pears they would snack on. When the train to Beijing approached, a red light and a low honking in the dark, it slowed only long enough for the twenty or so of us to climb on: not from a platform but directly from the dusty ground. A train attendant reached her hand out to grab mine.

From Taigu to Beijing, a trip I'd made many times, took nearly eleven hours, meaning we'd wake up just before the train pulled into Beijing Station. And then it was another twenty-four hours to Inner Mongolia, the first new place on my journey, where I'd end up, for several nights, sleeping in a yurt, under quilts and on the floor. A hole at the top of the tent showed the pollution-free, star-spangled sky.

On that train to Inner Mongolia, we passed through a dry mountain range that eventually leveled out against the grasslands: a kind of lush prairie filled with long shadows, the sky enormous and flat and blue. The herds wandered in the distance, a scatter of white coordinates. I sat on a foldout seat by the window, talking to strangers for hours. "Are you *yi ge ren?*" they would ask me, surprised, wanting to know if I was really traveling by myself.

I was, I said. And I wasn't, in another sense. At night, in my train compartment, I slept on the high bunk with my backpack nestled under my head. There were two strangers on the bunks below me and three more against the opposite wall. We were together, if only for tonight. A man across the way snored rhythmically, precise. I could still feel my grief from the past year close to the surface, but it felt good not to be alone as I drifted into an on-and-off sleep. The six of us jostled across the terrain, passing towns and villages in the dark. Occasionally, I woke to the train's deceleration and the *thunk* of a new rider being hoisted aboard.

Back in Taigu, I had finally gotten over the showers at the swimming pool. Because my American co-fellows were men, they couldn't help me with this. I faced my fear by always entering the shower surrounded by my women friends. This is what all the women did; I don't know why it took so long for me to figure out that it was my aloneness, not just my foreign body, that made people stare.

After a long afternoon in the pool, with our hands turned as wrinkly as Shanxi's jujubes, we climbed out of the water and slipped into our plastic slippers, careful not to fall as we headed into the tile corridor. We passed the open toilet stalls, the stench pricking my nose, just before the perfumed smell of the shower room took over. We peeled ourselves out of our suits and wrung them out with our hands. I could feel my breasts swaying a little as I stepped over the tile ledge, the cold air grabbing my bare skin. As I crossed the foggy threshold, I heard, in English: "Teacher!"

I had finally run into a group of my students. They were undergraduate freshmen, English majors. I had only seen most of them when they were wearing their glasses, so I hardly recognized them at first. Luo An, who introduced herself as "Annie" in my class, looked at me in a dreamy, blurry sort of way. She was one of her class's leaders and the most forthright in English, talkative and clear.

"Do you come here often to have a shower?" she wanted to know immediately. "And are you by yourself?"

"I usually shower at my house," I told her. I motioned to my friends in front of me. "We are together today."

The smallest student, who called herself Stella, nodded at me demurely, her wet bangs and bob still hanging in a perfect square around her face. She was less than five feet tall. Undressed, her body seemed to be composed solely of bones and skin, barely pubescent. Her chest was almost completely flat. At this point, I remembered my own shame, that I was also naked. *They must all be looking at the weirdness that is my body,* I thought to myself: my red bush, sturdy thighs, and sizable butt. I could feel my face growing hot, despite the cold air.

But I resisted the urge to turn away. *There is nothing weird here,* I told myself. I was twenty-three years old. The students were nineteen: barely even women yet, but still women, nonetheless. Toward the end of my conversation with my students, it hit me that they were treating me in much the same way they had at the times we'd run into each other in the marketplace, fully clothed. Seeing their teacher out in public was seeing their teacher out in public, regardless of the circumstances.

I slipped further into the steam, the showers' whooshing noise, the clamoring of female voices, their exact words getting lost in the larger din. I placed my plastic caddy at the edge of the room, with the dozens of others, what seemed like hundreds of bottles of shampoo and body wash crammed inside, washcloths draped over the handles. By now I had run out of all of my preferred Western toiletries—my last holdout from my former day-to-day life in the United States—so it was next to impossible to tell my basket from the others.

On the one wall where there were no showerheads, I saw a dozen undressed women lean against the tile, as if poised for a series of painful tattoos. Instead, their friends vigorously scrubbed their backs. The scrubbers wore hand-shaped loofahs, what looked like textured oven mitts, and rubbed so hard—more like scoured —that the top layers of skin began visibly pilling in some places. Of course, I had no loofah mitt of my own, but Wang Hui Fang insisted that she use hers on me. "You first," she said. "Then me."

Eventually I turned, putting my hands on the tile wall. I glanced over my shoulder. There had been a handful of women staring at me since I'd entered the shower room, but once they realized that I was with friends, they went back to their showering, seemingly losing interest.

The scrub hurt almost as much as I imagined it would. Wang Hui Fang worked in long, shoulder-to-butt strokes, the friction so fierce that it felt like my skin was lit. At first I thought this force was unnecessary, but then I remembered the swimming pool's chemicals and what the bottoms of my feet looked like: almost black in the dry, dead parts at the edges of my heel, and the ball of my foot its own dingy plateau. I had made the mistake of trying to go barefoot in my apartment a few times, earlier in the year, and I had paid the price. I couldn't seem to get all the Shanxi dust off my body, no matter how hard I tried under my tiny home showerhead, no matter how many times I mopped my apartment.

Pronouncing me done, Wang Hui Fang handed me the fluorescent pink mitt, and I looked for an open showerhead to wash it out and rinse myself. There were none. "Just push your way through," she suggested. I edged slowly into the crowd, waiting and waiting, my backside getting cold, until finally a woman stepped out from under the spray, and I got my clearance. I rinsed the mitt off first and then myself. The water was hot, and the pressure was good, much better than the lukewarm trickle of the sad shower in my apartment. I was not alone. I was so close to the stranger next to me that when I bent forward, my shoulder brushed hers. The woman and I turned to look at one another at the same time, both of us sort of smiling in acknowledgment. The collision was inevitable; the room was very full. Neither one of us felt the need to apologize.

Citizen Khan

FROM *The New Yorker*

THE FIRST PERSON in Sheridan, Wyoming, to learn that Hot Tamale Louie had been knifed to death was William Henry Harrison Jr. The news came by telegram, the day after the murder. Harrison was the son of a member of Congress, the great-grandson of one president, the great-great-great-grandson of another president, and the great-great-great-great-grandson of one of the signers of the Declaration of Independence. Hot Tamale Louie was the son of nobody knows who, the grandson of nobody knows who, and the great-great-grandson of nobody knows who. He had been selling tamales in Sheridan since Buffalo Bill rode in the town parade, sold them when President Taft came to visit, was still selling them when the Russians sent Sputnik into space and the British sent the Beatles to America.

By then, Louie was a local legend, and his murder shocked everyone. It was front-page, above-the-fold news in Sheridan, and made headlines throughout Wyoming, Colorado, and South Dakota. It traveled by word of mouth across the state to Yellowstone, and by post to California, where former Sheridan residents opened their mailboxes to find letters from hometown friends mourning Louie's death.

That was in 1964. Two years later, the killer was tried, found guilty, hanged, removed from the gallows, then hanged again. Within a few years after that, Louie, his tamales, his murder, and everything else about him had faded from the headlines. A half century passed. Then, late last year, he wound up back in the news.

The events that propelled him there took place in the town

of Gillette, ninety minutes southeast of Sheridan. Situated in the stark center of Wyoming's energy-rich but otherwise empty Powder River Basin, Gillette grew up around wildcat wells and coal mines —dry as a bone except in its saloons, prone to spontaneous combustion from the underground fires burning perpetually beneath it. Because its economy is tied to the energy industry, it is subject to an endless cycle of boom and bust, and to a ballooning population during the good years. The pattern of social problems that attend that kind of rapid population growth—increased crime, higher divorce rates, lower school attendance, more mental-health issues—has been known, since the 1970s, as Gillette Syndrome. Today, the town consists of three interstate exits' worth of tract housing and fast food, surrounded by open-pit mines and pinned to the map by oil rigs. Signs on the highway warn about the fifty-mile-per-hour winds.

A couple of hundred Muslims live in northeastern Wyoming, and last fall some of them pooled their money to buy a one-story house at the end of Gillette's Country Club Road, just outside a development called Country Club Estates, in one of the nicer neighborhoods in town. They placed a sign at the end of the driveway, laid prayer rugs on top of the wall-to-wall carpeting, and began meeting there for Friday worship—making it, in function if not in form, the third mosque in the state.

Most locals reacted to this development with indifference or neighborly interest, if they reacted at all. But a small number formed a group called Stop Islam in Gillette to protest the mosque; to them, the Muslims it served were unwelcome newcomers to Wyoming, at best a menace to the state's cultural traditions and at worst incipient jihadis. When those protests darkened into threats, the local police got involved, as did the FBI.

Whatever their politics, many outsiders, on hearing about Stop Islam in Gillette, shared at least one of its sentiments: a measure of surprise that a Muslim community existed in such a remote corner of the country. Wyoming is geographically huge—you could fit all of New England inside it, then throw in Hawaii and Maryland for good measure—but it is the least populous state in the Union; under 600,000 people live there, fewer than in Louisville, Kentucky. Its Muslim population is correspondingly tiny—perhaps 700 or 800 people.

Contrary to the claims of Stop Islam in Gillette, however, the

Muslims who established the mosque are not new to the region. Together with some 20 percent of all Muslims in Wyoming, they trace their presence back more than a hundred years, to 1909, when a young man named Zarif Khan immigrated to the American frontier. Born around 1887, Khan came from a little village called Bara, not far from the Khyber Pass, in the borderlands between Afghanistan and Pakistan. His parents were poor, and the region was politically unstable. Khan's childhood would have been marked by privation and conflict—if he had any childhood to speak of. Family legend has it that he was just twelve when he left.

What he did next nobody knows, but by September 3, 1907, he had got himself a thousand miles south, to Bombay, where he boarded a ship called the *Peno*. Eight weeks later, on October 28, he arrived in Seattle. From there, he struck out for the interior, apparently living for a while in Deadwood, South Dakota, and the nearby towns of Lead and Spearfish before crossing the border into Wyoming. Once there, he settled in Sheridan, which is where he made a name for himself, literally: as Hot Tamale Louie—beloved Mexican-food vendor, Afghan immigrant, and patriarch of Wyoming's now besieged Muslim population.

When Khan arrived in Sheridan, he and Wyoming were roughly the same age—the man in his early twenties, the state nineteen. At the time, the idea that anyone at all would move to the region was a novelty. Although Native Americans had lived there for millennia, Europeans didn't visit until at least 1743, and they didn't linger. As late as 1870, scarcely 9,000 people lived in the entire territory. The coming of the railroad, which was supposed to solve that population problem, temporarily exacerbated it instead. "Hundreds of thousands of people had seen Wyoming from train windows," the historian T. A. Larson wrote, "and were spreading the word that the territory looked like a barren wasteland."

That was particularly true in northeastern Wyoming. The rest of the state could be daunting, with its successive mountain chains rising like crests on a flash-frozen ocean. But at least it had grandeur, and verdure. In the east, by contrast, you could travel 500 miles and not see a tree. Precipitation was similarly scarce. The Homestead Act offered Western settlers 160 acres—not enough, in that landscape, to keep five cows alive. In winter, the mercury could plunge to fifty degrees below zero. People froze to death in blizzards in May. Frontier Texas, the saying goes, was paradise for men and dogs, hell on women and horses. Frontier Wyoming was hell on everyone.

Perhaps because it so desperately needed people, Wyoming was, from the outset, unusually egalitarian. Beginning in 1869, women in the territory could vote, serve on juries, and, in some instances, enjoy a guarantee of equal pay for equal work—making it, Susan B. Anthony said, "the first place on God's green earth which could consistently claim to be the land of the free." Despite resistance from the U.S. Congress, Wyoming insisted on retaining those rights when petitioning for statehood; in 1890, when it became the forty-fourth state in the Union, it also became the first where women could vote. On the spot, it acquired its nickname: the Equality State.

At statehood, Sheridan was a tiny settlement, just across the line from Montana, just east of the Big Horns, and otherwise very far from much of anything. But two years later, following rumors of coal (true) and gold (overblown), the population began to boom. By 1909, when Khan arrived, around 8,000 people lived there and, on the evidence of the local business pages, the town had developed a kind of frontier-cosmopolitan chic. It had seventeen Blacksmiths, one Bicycle Dealer, and five purveyors of Buggies and Wagons. It had a Clairvoyant—one Mrs. Ellen Johnston—and a great many Coal Miners. Residents could go Bowling, or to the Opera House, or visit a Health Resort. They could get a Manicure from a Mrs. Rosella Wood, who was also available for Massages. They could read two different newspapers—one Republican, one Democratic. They could buy Grain and Guns and Horses, Books and Stationery and Coffee, Camping Outfits, Driving Gloves, Musical Instruments, and Talking Machines.

But perhaps the most striking entry in the Sheridan business directory was the one tucked in between "Tallow and Grease" and "Taxidermists": "Tamales." When Zarif Khan first began selling them, he shouldered a yoke with a bucket swinging from each end and walked to wherever he could find customers: outside the bank at lunch, outside the bars at closing time, down at the railroad depot when the trains came in. Business was good enough that he soon bought a pushcart. By 1914, the *Sheridan Enterprise* was referring to him, inaccurately but affectionately, as "the well-known Turkish tamale vendor." (In fairness, nearly all references to Khan's nationality were inaccurate, including his own. Although he identified as Afghan and official documents pertaining to his life reflect that, his natal village was ceded to British India before his birth, and today belongs to the Federally Administered Tribal Areas of Pakistan.)

In 1915, or maybe the year after, Khan opened a restaurant—a hole-in-the-wall on Grinnell Avenue, around the corner from Main Street. The hand-painted lettering on the facade said LOUIE'S, and, forever afterward, that is what both Khan and his restaurant were called. It had a service window that opened onto the street for customers who wanted their food to go, and a counter lined with stools for those who preferred to eat inside. In addition to the tamales, Khan served hamburgers, chili, pie, and ice cream —any flavor except chocolate, which he avoided because it sullied the cuffs of the white button-down shirts he liked to wear to work.

For nomenclatural purposes, however, none of these other menu items mattered. To the town of Sheridan, Khan would always be Hot Tamale Louie, or Tamale Louie, or, because it sounded best, Louie Tamale. He could have served steak tartare and the name would have stuck. Purists insist that it was apt, because nothing Khan or anyone else ever served was as delicious as his tamales. He made them at home, from chickens he kept in the backyard and killed in halal fashion. Everett McGlothlin, who last tasted one of Louie's tamales when he worked there as a high school kid, in the 1950s, said, "I love tamales, and I still haven't found anything that comes close."

For another faction, however, it was Louie's hamburgers that dazzled. Sixty years on, locals who hear someone talking about Khan will cross the room and interrupt the conversation to say that he made the greatest burgers in the history of burgerdom. Five generations of Sheridan residents ate them, and those who are still around go into a kind of blissed-out cholesterol-bomb reverie when attempting to describe them. Some claim that he used only bull meat, and rendered his own tallow to fry it in. Others say he cooked the burgers in chicken fat, or sizzled bay leaf into the grease, or mixed in hearts and tongues.

Whatever his secret, Khan was particular about how he served his hamburgers. Cheese was unheard of, and woe betide those who requested ketchup. A burger from Louie's came plain, or, if you chose, with mustard, pickles, and onions. (Several former repeat customers, now in their seventies and eighties, pointed an imaginary knife at me and said, "You wan onions, keed?") He sliced the pickles the long way, with a rapidity that mesmerized his customers. On a good day, he went through 150 buns. On a really good day—when the rodeo came to town, say—he would fire up a second grill and bring on an extra high school kid, and tour buses would pull up and order a hundred burgers at a time. By 1919, the restaurant was doing so well that Khan opened a Ladies Annex, "fitted with tables for the convenience of women," as the *Sheridan Post* reported. The place was still a hole-in-the-wall—those tables numbered precisely three—but it was the most popular hole-in-the-wall in town.

It helped that it was always open. Seven days a week, fifty-two weeks a year, Khan began prepping at ten, opened the window at eleven, and served food until midnight or one or whenever the last of the bar crowd went home. It also helped that he would serve anyone. Sheridan in 1919 was still the kind of place where businesses posted signs saying NO DOGS OR INDIANS ALLOWED, but Native Americans were welcome at Louie's. Some of them, in consequence, became strikingly loyal customers. Joe Medicine Crow, the scholar and Second World War hero, who died this past April, at 102, loved Khan's burgers so much that, on his way home to Montana after the war, he hopped off the train during a thirty-minute stop in Sheridan and was still down at Louie's eating when it pulled out again—much to the dismay of his mother, who had organized a town-wide celebration at his home station.

Kids were welcome at Louie's too, as were the women who worked at the nearby brothels and people who were too broke to buy a meal. Khan would hand out a tamale anyway, although the next time he saw you he might say, "Hi, Mr. Ten Cents," and if by then you had a dime you'd pay him back. The only people he refused to serve were the drunk, the foulmouthed, and the brawling, whom he personally threw out on their ears. He was five feet six and weighed 120 pounds, but nothing and no one intimidated him. For one thing, he had got himself all the way to Sheridan from the Khyber Pass. For another, he was the one holding the foot-long knife. Also, he had good aim with an onion.

Khan's egalitarian attitude raised eyebrows among Sheridan's snootier citizens. In the end, though, no one could stay away from the food, and so Louie's gradually became its own little Equality

State—an American kind of place, diverse and democratic, where the staff of the newspaper wolfed down post-deadline burgers elbow to elbow with society ladies, and schoolkids counted out their nickels next to stockbrokers ordering large. Meanwhile, Louie himself had gradually become American as well, and in 1925, after nearly twenty years in the United States, he decided to make it official. The town fathers, all of them Louie regulars, were happy to help; when Khan filed his naturalization petition, it was witnessed for him by the general counsel for the city of Sheridan and one of its former mayors.

The citizenship hearing was held on November 6, 1925. Because naturalization examiners showed up in Sheridan only once a year, the event was crowded with would-be Americans from around the county: seventeen from Poland, six from Austria, four from Czechoslovakia, two each from Greece, Scotland, Hungary, and Montenegro, one from Russia, one from Sweden, and one—Hot Tamale Louie, né Zarif Khan—from Afghanistan. On February 2, 1926, the paperwork came through, and Louie became a citizen. Five months after that, he received a subpoena from the U.S. Attorney for the district of Wyoming, ordering him to appear in court in the matter of the *United States of America v. Zarif Khan*.

The first naturalization law in the United States was passed in 1790, one year into George Washington's first term as president. It established that only "Free white persons" were eligible to become citizens, a constraint designed to exclude Native Americans and slaves. After the Civil War, that law was changed to extend eligibility to people of African descent. As a result, beginning in 1870, those petitioning for American citizenship had to be either black or white.

That left immigrants from Asian nations in the lurch—deliberately, as Congress soon made clear. The 1882 Chinese Exclusion Act prevented anyone born in China from becoming American. The Immigration Act of 1917 established an "Asiatic Barred Zone": a region, encompassing dozens of countries, from the Middle East to Melanesia, whose native citizens could not be naturalized. In theory, such laws were plenty clear. In practice, however, Asians petitioning for citizenship simply contended that they were white. Whether that was true was a matter of heated dispute among ethnologists, anthropologists, political scientists, policymakers, and government officials around the nation.

The courts, brought in to clarify the issue, made a mess of it instead. In *White by Law: The Legal Construction of Race*, the Berkeley law professor Ian Haney Lopez provides a tragicomic list of court rulings on racial identity, together with their legal rationales. Among those rulings: that Hawaiians are not white (based on scientific evidence); that Mexicans are not white (based on legal precedent); that Burmese are not white (based on common knowledge); that Japanese are not white (based on legal precedent); that people who are one-quarter Japanese are not white (based on legal precedent); that Syrians are white (based on scientific evidence); that Syrians are not white (based on common knowledge); that Arabs are white (based on common knowledge); that Arabs are not white (based on common knowledge); that Native Americans are not white (based on nothing).

That is the kind of wild inconsistency that eventually compels the Supreme Court to weigh in, and in 1922 it agreed to do so. Instead of resolving the muddle, however, the Court issued two rulings in under a year that made matters worse. In the first, *Ozawa v. United States*, a Japanese man brought up and educated in Berkeley argued that, for naturalization purposes, he was white. The Court acknowledged that Ozawa's character was irreproachable, and also that he had a paler complexion than many people whose whiteness went uncontested. But it denied him citizenship, ruling that "the words 'white person' were meant to indicate only a person of what is popularly known as the Caucasian race." A year later, the Court took up the case of Bhagat Singh Thind, an Indian man who was, as the justices reluctantly conceded, technically Caucasian. This time, however, the judges ruled that "white persons" was "synonymous with the word 'Caucasian' only as that word is popularly understood."

Like Zarif Khan, Thind had already been naturalized; upon ruling against him, the Supreme Court stripped him of his citizenship. For most of U.S. history, that process, called denaturalization, was used to revoke citizenship that had been fraudulently obtained, or to remove from the ranks of Americans felons, traitors, and war criminals. The former Auschwitz guard Jakob Frank Denzinger was denaturalized, as was the anarchist Emma Goldman and the alleged Communist spy Solomon Adler. But, beginning in the early twentieth century, the Naturalization Bureau (later the Immigration and Naturalization Service) sought to denaturalize Asians who had been granted citizenship by courts that were either ignorant of current immigration law or deliberately defying it. According to the legal scholar Patrick Weil, this process was so far from systematic as to be scattershot. In effect, it came down to chance: an Asian citizen who'd had the good luck to find a lenient representative of the Naturalization Bureau then had the bad luck to be found by a strict one.

No one knows exactly how such a person found Zarif Khan. Perhaps he tried to obtain a passport, or perhaps he was summoned for jury duty, or perhaps someone read about his citizenship ceremony in the local papers and decided to tip off the authorities. Whatever happened, on August 12, 1926, U.S. Attorney Albert D. Walton—best known for helping to represent the federal government during the Teapot Dome scandal—filed a suit alleging that Khan's naturalization was "illegally procured."

Khan's case arrived at a curious moment in immigration history. The year before, an Indian man from San Francisco named Vaishno Das Bagai had been stripped of his citizenship, as had his wife and children—a particularly dire development for a California resident, because, by state law, those ineligible for citizenship could not own property. Sometime later, Das Bagai told his family that he was going on a business trip, booked a hotel room in San Jose, and killed himself. In the note he left behind, he described his suicide as a political protest. "I came to America thinking, dreaming, and hoping to make this land my home," he wrote. "But now they come to me and say, I am no longer an American Citizen . . . Now what am I? What have I made of myself and my children?" Das Bagai addressed the note to the *San Francisco Examiner,* which published it.

Das Bagai's death marked the beginning of a gradual shift in both public opinion and official policy on denaturalization. In 1927, the Supreme Court refused to hear a case against a naturalized Indian man, thereby sending a message to the lower courts to stop revoking citizenship on the basis of race. By then, it was clear that, as a practical matter, no good would come of judicial wrangling over whiteness, and also that attempting to maintain a white population through naturalization policy was a losing battle. Moreover, immigration laws were rapidly becoming ideologically untenable as well. At the start of the Second World War, the United States was the only developed nation other than Germany to explicitly restrict citizenship on the basis of race—a common ground that became increasingly uncomfortable as Nazi atrocities came to light. Midway through the war, Congress repealed the Chinese exclusion laws. Immediately afterward, it lifted all race-based citizenship requirements.

But all that came too late for Zarif Khan. His citizenship was challenged at a time when the courts had consistently held that whiteness was a requisite quality in a new American, and one that Afghans lacked. At some point, his cause must have seemed hopeless; when his case came to court, Khan did not contest it. On December 30, 1926, a judge declared him "forever restrained and enjoined from setting up or claiming any right, privilege, benefit, or advantage whatsoever" of U.S. citizenship. All told, Khan had enjoyed those rights for under a year. Then his naturalization was canceled, and the form on file with the court was emended to read "member of the yellow race." He was ordered to pay the cost of the lawsuit, plus tax.

If Khan was bitter about his loss of citizenship, he didn't show it. He may never even have mentioned it; no one I talked to, including his children, knew that it had happened. Instead, he set his sights on that most American of goals: making money.

It began in the 1920s, with the wealthy men who settled into the stools at Louie's and studied their newspapers. What's so interesting in there? Khan wanted to know. They laughed at him, but they told him. He began buying the paper every day and asking whichever kid was working for him to take a break from peeling onions to read the business pages aloud. Khan couldn't read or write English. He had no formal education to speak of. But he was frugal, focused, patient, and, as it turned out, exceptionally good at picking stocks. The rumor around town was that he'd already made a million dollars by 1929.

Whatever his earnings were, they were wiped out in the Great Depression. But he still had the restaurant, and now he had experience. He began buying up stocks made cheap by the crash —General Motors, for instance, which was then trading at eight dollars a share and had hit ninety by 1960. Also General Electric, Standard Oil, Union Carbide, Northern Pacific Railway, B. F. Goodrich, International Telephone and Telegraph, and Texaco. He favored utilities, the energy industry, and mining companies. He bought thousands of shares in Lucky Friday, a silver and zinc mine in Idaho, for thirty cents each, and sat on them as they rose to thirty dollars.

In 1944, he hired a woman named Helen Ellis as a combination bookkeeper and all-purpose assistant. She worked for him for twenty years, doing everything from handling his correspondence to tying the strings on the ends of his tamales. When his finances got more complex, he hired an accountant—Bill Harrison, of the presidential lineage—and Ellis began working exclusively in the restaurant. Khan himself kept working there too. Very few people knew that he had any other source of income, and his day-to-day life betrayed no signs of improved financial circumstances. He still rented the same house on North Scott Street that he'd moved into in 1909. He still rented the same tiny restaurant space on Grinnell Avenue. He still walked everywhere, and he still worked eighty hours a week.

The only way Khan ever displayed his wealth was through his generosity, which had always been remarkable and eventually became legendary. In the 1920s, for instance, a country kid named Archie Nash began boarding in Sheridan so that he could attend high school there. In the long gaps between visits from his parents, when his money and his tolerance for loneliness ran out, Nash would go to Louie's to soak up the company and gratefully accept free food. After graduation, he took a job at the *Sheridan Press,* and began buying a whole lot of meals at Louie's. Eventually, he and a local woman fell in love; too poor to afford a wedding, they decided to elope. Nash told no one except Louie, who had only one question. As Nash's daughter later told it: "You got ring for dat girl?" Nash did not. Louie opened his register, took out some cash, and told him to go buy one. That girl wore it for nearly forty years.

Stories like that abound. Khan knew everyone's name, never failed to ask after sick children or aging parents, never forgot anyone on a birthday or Christmas. The hungry could count on him for meals, kids could count on him for jobs, overseas service members for money and gifts. Yet, as open as he was toward others, Khan was reserved about his own life, almost to the point of shyness. He was professionally close to Bill Harrison, Helen Ellis, and his lawyer, Henry Burgess. Beyond that, he had no known friends.

Perhaps for that reason, no one ever seems to have asked Khan many questions about himself. Any information that circulated about him was largely rumor and often wrong. He was from Greece; he was from Turkey; he was from Mongolia. He was Buddhist; he was Hindu. He had spent some time in Texas; he once owned a grapefruit farm in Arizona. But, of all the questions that went unasked, the most glaring omission was the obvious one: Why was an Afghan man named Zarif Khan making a small fortune plus a whole lot of Mexican food under the name Louie Tamale?

People floated theories, of course. Some thought that Khan, before arriving in the United States, had worked as a cook in Mexico, then gradually made his way north to Wyoming. Others claimed that he first arrived in San Francisco, where a Latino immigrant taught him to make tamales. In reality, Khan never went to Mexico and was not taught his trade by anyone from Latin America. Instead, in becoming Louie Tamale, Zarif Khan also became part of a curious piece of culinary, labor, and immigration history: an entire network of Afghan tamale vendors who, from roughly 1900 to 1920, sold their wares on the streets of nearly every city in the West, from small-town Wyoming all the way up to Alaska.

Tamales are old, as food goes; they preceded Columbus, and possibly Christ. They originated in Mesoamerica, likely courtesy of the Maya, and were the carryout food of their day, much prized by soldiers, hunters, and other hungry people on the go. By the time Europeans got to the New World, tamales could be found, at a minimum, in much of Central America and throughout Mexico. As late as 1884, however, they were sufficiently unfamiliar in the United States that the Associated Press felt compelled to refer to them thus: "A queer article of food, locally known as 'tamales.'"

Ten years later, tamales were the nation's hottest new food trend, the cronuts of fin-de-siècle America. According to Gustavo Arellano, the author of *Taco USA*, the craze began in 1892, when a San Francisco man named Robert H. Putnam started the California Chicken Tamale Company. Putnam took his culinary cue from the city's popular Mexican tamale peddlers and his fashion cue from, apparently, pharmacists: the vendors he hired wore white from head to toe, with the company's brand emblazoned on their hats and their buckets—mobile chafing dishes, basically, with fire below, boiling water in the middle, and steamed tamales above. Putnam then took his tamales to Chicago, where they became the hit of the 1893 World's Fair.

Like other forms of peddling, the tamale business required relatively little up-front money, which made it attractive to immigrants and the poor. In New York City, tamales were sold chiefly by Irish and Italians, while in the South and the Midwest most vendors were African American. But in the Rocky Mountain West the tamale trade was dominated by men from Afghanistan.

Specifically, it was dominated by men from Afghanistan with the surname Khan. (The men were generally unrelated; the name is extremely common.) In the first two decades of the twentieth century, tamale-selling Afghan Khans could be found in Deadwood and Fargo and Reno; in Seattle and Spokane and Wenatchee, Washington; in Butte, Montana, which boasted eighteen such tamale men by 1913, and all over the rest of the state as well—in Flathead, Fort Benton, Silver Bow, Anaconda, Havre, Great Falls, Red Lodge, Miles City, Chinook, Billings. Starting in 1908, you could buy tamales in Alaska from a Buhadin Khan, a Habib Khan, an M. Khan, and a guy called Tamale Joe, whose real name was likely also Khan.

Not every tamale vendor in the West was from Afghanistan, of course, and not every Afghan vendor sold tamales. A smaller but still significant group, for instance, sold chili, as Zarif Khan later did in his restaurant. (One such vendor, Dollha Jaffa Khan, got his start with a pushcart in Seattle, in 1916, before opening a successful chili parlor there. Later, Jaffa Khan changed his name to Joseph Joffrey; his son Robert went on to found the Joffrey Ballet.) But it was the Afghan tamale vendors who were so common as to become a stereotype—akin to Turkish coffee-shop owners, Syrian rug dealers, and Jewish pawnbrokers.

With that stereotype went another; that tamale sellers were constantly at one another's throat. There was some truth to that, but the problem was not limited to Afghans. Throughout the country, for the duration of the culinary craze, headlines about "tamale wars" were comically abundant. "The hot tamale war which has been raging in this city for the past few weeks reached a climax last evening," the *Colorado Springs Weekly Gazette* reported in 1895:

gunfire had broken out between rival vendors and a boy named Harry Risner was shot in the arm. In Montana, in 1901, a man named Joseph Marino was killed by Salvagora "Bull Dog" Demicilli over "a rivalry in the tamale business." Among the Afghan vendors, the worst of the tamale wars took place in Seattle, where the trade was dominated by a Khan with a mafioso reputation: mean, mendacious, scary as hell. Eventually, he was shot in the back, presumably by one of his fellow-peddlers, but, if the murder was meant to ease tensions in the tamale scene, it failed. Nearly a decade later, the *Seattle Star* was still reporting on "the vendetta of the hot tamale men."

All of this sheds some light on why Zarif Khan ended up in Sheridan. No one there seemed to know about the Afghan tamale trade, but some people recalled hearing that Khan had been treated poorly by other South Asians when he first came to America, and headed for the hinterlands in search of a place with fewer immigrants—a report that comports with the climate in Seattle when Khan arrived. If you were him—new to the country, new to the tamale trade, by all accounts private and peaceable—you, too, might have gravitated toward small-town Wyoming.

Contrary to family legend, however, Khan did not show up in Sheridan alone with his yoke and pails and introduce the town to tamales. He had a predecessor: one Azed Khan, born in 1871 in the Afghan village of Behbudi. Azed was the town's first tamale vendor; when Zarif first appears in the Sheridan business directory, it is as his assistant. Over the next ten years, three more tamale salesmen and one chili peddler set up shop in Sheridan. All were named Khan, all lived in the same modest house on North Scott Street, and by 1923 all but Zarif were gone. By that time, tamales themselves were also on the way out. Between 1900 and 1916, sales fell from 4 million per year to just 40,000, and the once omnipresent tamale vendor began vanishing from city streets.

Among those who left the trade during this decline was a German-born Wyoming man named Louis Menge. In 1910, Menge placed an ad in the *Sheridan Daily Enterprise:* "Wanted: some one to learn hot tamale business." After finding a successor, he moved with his wife and child to Montana to try his hand at farming. Two years later, a return visit to Wyoming found him in dismal straits: the work was brutal, good help was scarce, and drought was destroying his crops. The *Sheridan Post,* which reported the visit, reminded readers that they had known the struggling farmer in better days: "Mr. Menge is more familiarly known to Sheridan people as Hot Tamale Louie."

These days, Mr. Menge is known to almost no one. His farm failed, his wife and child predeceased him, and he died alone at the Yellowstone County Poor Farm. Hot Tamale Louie, however, lived on. In time, the first man to hold that title was forgotten, along with all the other Khans who had come through Sheridan and the entire nationwide tamale craze. Soon enough, only Zarif Khan was remembered, because only Zarif Khan remained. As many immigrants can tell you, sometimes a story about leaving turns into a story about staying.

By the time Zarif Khan applied to become a United States citizen for the second time, he had been living in Wyoming for nearly half a century. He was in his late sixties. On the naturalization petition, his official hair color had turned from brown to gray. His skin color remained unchanged but no longer constituted a barrier to citizenship. On May 4, 1954, the federal government conferred upon Khan the privileges and duties it had once forever enjoined him from claiming.

Meanwhile, Khan's life had changed in another momentous way. The year before, he had traveled to Pakistan and returned home a married man. The marriage was an arranged one; the bride, Bibi Fatima Khan (no relation), was fifteen years old. People in town talked, of course, but the tone was less judgmental than jokey—along the lines of "I wouldn't have thought he had it in him."

He did, apparently; in the course of the next eleven years, the couple had six children. Khan, a doting father, could be seen around Sheridan hoisting his firstborn, Roenna, on his hip, while pushing his infant son Zarif in a carriage. When they got older, they recalled for me, he took them to the restaurant, set them at the counter, emptied the till, and used the money to teach them how to count. Meanwhile, more children kept coming: Fatima, named for her mother, then Zarina, then a second boy, Nazir, and, finally, Merriam. After each birth, Khan flew the whole family back to Pakistan to introduce his relatives there to the new arrival.

In 1963, not long after Merriam was born, the family once again returned to Bara. This time, though, in addition to showing off his baby, Khan had business to conduct. Like many immigrants, he had spent much of his working life funneling money back home: paying to build wells and mosques in areas where travelers would otherwise have no water to drink and nowhere to pray, buying land for his relatives to farm and houses for them to live in. Now he began giving all of that away, distributing deeds to those who were living in his properties and money to nearly everyone.

In the course of doing so, his children told me, he got into a dispute with a ne'er-do-well grandnephew by the name of Sultan Khan. When Sultan was a kid, just sixteen or so, he had been involved in a violent crime; rich Uncle Zarif in America had helped bail him out and got him into private school, but the kid had not shown signs of reforming. Now Sultan was thirty years old, and rich Uncle Zarif was no longer inclined to be generous. Sultan screamed and threatened; Khan held his ground.

The next day, Khan and a different grandnephew left Bara early in the morning to run an errand in a neighboring town. In keeping with Khan's lifelong habit, they went by foot. Partway along the route, Sultan was waiting with a knife. It was June 23, 1964. Khan was roughly eighty—one of the few eighty-year-olds of whom it could be said that he still had most of his life ahead of him. In a picture taken earlier that year, he is holding the toddler Nazir on his lap, surrounded by his wife and other children. The oldest is barely ten, the next one eight, the next one seven. The others are too young to have begun salting away memories of their father, and they would never get to make new ones. Sultan Khan killed his cousin, then stabbed his uncle seven times. Zarif Khan died in the dirt in a place as important to his life as any other: the road out of town.

The shock of Khan's death was followed by the surprise of his will. Other than his accountant and his lawyer, no one, not even his wife, had known that he was rich. When the will was probated, his estate was worth around half a million dollars—almost $4 million in today's money. Supposedly, he had an equivalent amount back in Pakistan. Apparently worried that someone would marry his wife for her money, he had placed most of the estate in separate trusts for the children, leaving Bibi Fatima just $10,000 plus a monthly allowance. Under Wyoming law, she was entitled to more, and, with the guidance of a lawyer, she sued for it. Eventually she was awarded half the estate.

Thus began the afterlife of the Wyoming Khans. At the time of Louie's death, Fatima was twenty-six years old, responsible for six children under the age of ten, uneducated, illiterate, unaccustomed to so much as leaving the house on her own. She brought a brother and a nephew over from Pakistan to help, and then, in an act of self-creation that rivaled Khan's, set about figuring out how to thrive in Sheridan under radically changed circumstances. She hired an English tutor, learned to read and write, and joined the PTA. She got her driver's license the same day as her oldest daughter. In 1970, she became an American citizen, Two years later, she bought the J. E. Motel and Café in Sheridan. Ever since then, the Khan family has been in the hospitality business—which, in a sense, Zarif was too.

In time, the relatives whom Fatima brought over to help with her children married and had children of their own. Some of them brought over other relatives, who also married and had kids. Many of those kids now have children as well. As the family multiplied, it also dispersed. In 2003, the brother Fatima brought to Sheridan moved to Gillette to open a hotel; these days, his branch of the Khans owns eleven hotels in the area, and his grown children have young kids of their own. In total, there are now some 150 or 200 Khans, mostly in Wyoming, though also in South Dakota, Colorado, and beyond. As with most families, there have been fallings-out, about the kinds of things families fall out over: who got more money, who got more affection, who slighted so-and-so at such-and-such a time. Still, most of them get along, and they try to get together—at Eid al-Fitr and Eid al-Adha, at births and weddings and funerals.

Many of the Khans contributed money to fund the mosque in Gillette, and the threats against it came as a shock to them all; none had ever personally experienced such vitriol in Wyoming. Zarif Khan's children, in particular, seem to have been shielded from whatever racism and xenophobia they might have otherwise encountered in nearly all-white Sheridan by their father's standing. "Growing up here, it was great," Zarina, who now owns Sheridan's Holiday Lodge, said. "We had friends. No one asked about our skin. No one asked about our religion. No one would say,

'Where are you from?'" Instead, the community recognized the Khans as its own; immediately after 9/11, Zarif told me, his Jewish pediatrician showed up to make sure the family was all right. Even in those tense times, Zarina said, "we had no troubles, no friction, no fight."

The fight, when it arrived, came in the form of Bret Colvin, the founder of Stop Islam in Gillette. Colvin, who is forty-nine, grew up on a Wyoming ranch, left after high school, and spent the next decade in the Marines. Later, he worked in private security, in crab fishing, and in the oil and methane fields of the West. But these days oil is down, Gillette's economy is suffering, and employment is hard to find. "You can't even get a fast-food job in this town," Colvin said; to get by, he'd been doing some computer and cell-phone repair.

That left him with a lot of time to stare at the Internet, which is how he learned about the mosque. Colvin was the one who organized the protests against it, and, according to the Khans, threatened to train a scope on it as well. He also menaced the town's Muslims more generally; when he heard about a public lecture on Islam being held in Gillette, he used a podcast he produces to announce his plans to attend and "fuck some shit up," and urged his listeners to come help him "run the ragheads out of town." At some point, the threats grew sufficiently serious that the FBI got involved.

Like the Khans, Colvin's family has been in the West for a long time, though it represents a very different strain of the American character. "There's been Colvins in Wyoming since the wagon-train days," he told me. "My great-grandfather used to shoot Indians for the cavalry for five dollars a head." That conduct—the effort by a group of newcomers to subdue or eradicate their predecessors through violence—is precisely what Colvin fears from Muslims. He believes that they are planning a violent invasion of America, and considers himself personally responsible for trying to stop it. That is why, he told me, he went to investigate the mosque after it opened. "I'm one of those people that just does stuff, okay?" he said. "I went down there and beat on the door and asked them who the hell they were and where they came from and what they were doing. They said, 'We're the Khan family.' I said, 'Well, that doesn't mean anything to me.'"

Who the Khans are and where they came from and what they're

doing here is a long story, and a quintessentially American one. The history of immigrants is, to a huge extent, the history of this nation, though so is the pernicious practice of determining that some among us do not deserve full humanity, and full citizenship. Zarif Khan was deemed insufficiently American on the basis of skin color; ninety years later, when the presence of Muslims among us had come to seem like a crisis, his descendants were deemed insufficiently American on the basis of faith.

Over and over, we forget what being American means. The radical premise of our nation is that one people can be made from many, yet in each new generation we find reasons to limit who those "many" can be—to wall off access to America, literally or figuratively. That impulse usually finds its roots in claims about who we used to be, but nativist nostalgia is a fantasy. We have always been a pluralist nation, with a past far richer and stranger than we choose to recall. Back when the streets of Sheridan were still dirt and Zarif Khan was still young, the Muslim who made his living selling Mexican food in the Wild West would put up a tamale for stakes and race local cowboys barefoot down Main Street. History does not record who won.

WELLS TOWER

No Amount of Traffic or Instagrammers or Drunks Can Take the Magic Out of (Semi-) Wilderness

FROM *Outside*

THE WELCOME SIGN is not entirely legible, because a large tourist stands in front of it with her selfie stick. The real tip-off is the river of brake lights past her shoulder. We have entered Great Smoky Mountains National Park.

Park rangers meander through the traffic jam. To what purpose? To exact a foliage-season surcharge? To search the block-long motor homes for undocumented domestics? In fact, they are here to warn us that elk are visible in the field to our right. To prevent astounded drivers from crashing, the rangers have set up a pull-off area, where motorists are discovering what distant ruminants look like on a smartphone screen.

The local elk count is lower than the minivan count, slightly higher than the roof-mounted-GoPro count, and, if the quantity of Florida license plates means anything, far short of the south-migrating-snowbird count. Though perhaps the plates mean nothing: we three are North Carolinians, from four hours east of here. I had reserved a Jeep for the trip, but the car-rental clerk had his own feelings about what is proper for a weekend in the Smoky Mountains and instead assigned us a Chrysler Town and Country minivan with Florida tags.

But to visit Great Smoky and complain that it's choked with out-of-staters and Winnebagoists is like going to the Grand Canyon and complaining that it's a large hole. Great Smoky is America's most heavily trafficked (if not necessarily trodden) national park. Close to 11 million people come here annually—nearly twice the Grand Canyon's tourist haul—and all the houseguests are taking their toll. The park's fog-cloaked valleys resound with Harley pipes. Smog has cropped the ridgetop views. Acid rain has killed off brook trout in some high-elevation streams and is threatening red spruce. Thanks to industrial, vehicular, and coal-power emissions, air quality in Great Smoky has been among the worst in the eastern United States, though, fortunately, ground-level ozone has decreased in the past fifteen years due to tighter air-quality regulations. For these reasons, although I've spent most of my life within a half-day's drive of the park, I've never once been tempted to make the trip.

But then one day, life finds you with a three-month-old son who, so far, has practiced his enthrallment with trees mostly through windowpanes. Curating a child's preferences is, of course, a doomed endeavor. Still, we'd like Jed to be fond of wood smoke and galaxies, to grow into a knowledge of books but also splitting mauls, the bowline, the taut-line hitch. Yet winter is on its way. Wait until spring to take him camping and he may already have become a version of his dad, a sluggish, indoorsy type who stores against his own father memories of Chef Boyardee warmed over Sternos and interstate-side KOAs, where firelit drunks at the next site over cast frightening shadows on the walls of the tent.

Now is the time to get him out-of-doors. But where? Somewhere lovely but close. (At about the four-hour mark in his car seat, our boy gets purple and loud.) Somewhere not too far from a 110-volt outlet to keep our breast pump humming. Somewhere with trees, mountains, online campsite booking, and enough human clamor to keep the bears at bay. No use resisting: Great Smoky is the place. You hate to add your family to the burdens of America's most put-upon national park, but then it may be wise to let the boy tick Great Smoky off his list while there's still park left to enjoy.

A mile into the park, the traffic thins. The dusk is upon us. The roadside is astrobe with foliage the color of goldfish, carrots, and scab. Our home for the next two days is Smokemont Campground (and RV dump site), near the park's southern access at Cherokee, North Carolina. Yes, our campsite is smaller than our old New York City apartment and surrounded by about as many people, a proportion of whom are not our sort of folks. Two of our neighbors' pickup trucks fly Confederate flags. Another bears a decal of an AR-15 under the antibiotic slogan ASSAULT LIFE. But it is a handsome campground, in the deep shade of sycamores and tulip poplar fed stout by a chuckling brook. If there are toxins in the air, they are undetectable beneath the scent of damp earth and ferns.

My goal for our weekend is modest: to provide Jed with a camping experience less grubby and miscarried than those my old man arranged for me. Breakfast with him was peanut butter sucked off a spoon, dinner cold spaghetti between two slices of Roman Meal. His tent was a frail, magical device whose special power was to summon storms so that it could collapse beneath them. I remember few nights that did not end with a sudden flight to the station wagon, where mosquitoes expected us, whetting their swords.

Seeking to avoid my father's organizational shortfalls, I have packed the Town and Country to the rafters with gear. Courtesy of corporate donors, we have: a Coleman tent that sleeps six, four different models of infant tents and sleeping pens from KidCo, a wearable sleeping bag from Selk'bag, another wearable sleeping bag from Poler, two camp chairs, and a compact wood-burning camp stove from Biolite that can cook food and charge an iPhone if not download kindling from the World Wide Web.

It falls to me to set up camp while Erin feeds the baby. Unpacking our tent and other equipment is a swift return to childhood. But the Christmas-morning ecstasy of uncrating new toys disintegrates under the problem of their assembly. In my defense, the tent is barn-size and best raised with a team of Amish powerlifters. For more than an hour, I bash stakes into a graveled earth whose revulsion for aluminum is vehement. At last I build something resembling two fat men in a nylon donkey suit. Then there is the rain fly to deal with. The problem of draping it does not drive me to tears—just wrathful, high-pitched squeals and a glossolalia of curse words. The tent keeps slipping the shroud. It's like putting silk pajamas on a bull.

After a time, I repair to the Town and Country, panting and fuming. I venture the sullen claim that the tent is unusable due to factory defects and suggest we all sleep in the minivan. Erin, now soothing two babies at once, reaches out and wipes my brow. "It's strange," she says. "Generally, I feel like you handle stress really well, and then some little thing comes up and you just snap and can't handle . . . dick."

The campsite next door is home to a quartet of Australians, which we know because they speak to one another as though across a crowded stadium. Judging from their supply of beer, they'll have no cause to stop yelling until 4:00 a.m. or so.

Erin, a preternaturally sunny person, sighs grimly. "I love you," she says, "and I mean this in the gentlest possible way, but this camping trip is bullshit. We get all this stuff and drive all this way so we can listen to these people party? We'd be more away-from-it-all if we'd pitched the tent in our yard."

But the night is on us, and there's nothing to be done. We put the baby in his crib inside the tent. We get the rain fly sitting right —or sort of right, given the rhomboidness of the thing beneath it. "It'll be fine," I say. "I don't think it's going to rain." The darkness deepens. We bed down. The rain begins.

The rain fly reports for partial duty. Inside the tent, it's not a downpour so much as a sifting Britishness. We position Jed's crib in the driest corner. Except for the maternity ward, Jed has never passed a night anywhere but our house. Yet he settles easily into sleep, grunting over the depth of his slumber.

His mother and I are doing less well. We have brought a brand-new queen-size inflatable mattress. But the manufacturer forgot to label the box in giant, hazard-orange letters: "Pump not included but very much required! Mattress cannot be inflated orally! Unincluded pump is the difference between comfort and misery! Without pump, mattress will give your ass a PhD in gravel! Without pump, you will lie awake wondering why you made your family leave your warm and pleasant house to spend a chilly night listening to RV generators and an Australian beer party! Without pump, you will pass eight moist, black hours conceiving the proper torment for the Coleman employee who left WARNING! PUMP REQUIRED off the mattress box! Habanero seeds tamped beneath the fingernails with an ice pick is what you'll settle on around dawn or so!"

All night long, the rain falls outside and inside the tent. A cheerful little brook runs past my cheek, swells the butterflied diapers I'm using to cushion my pelvis, forms a pond near my toes. Just as the sky is bluing, it lets up. The baby is gurgling. His parents are sore and sad. We determine that some sort of stroll might lift our spirits and disperse the bruises on our hips. A campground official happens past. I ask her if she knows of any good trails around here. "To be honest, I don't know," she says. "I'm just up here from Florida."

By 8:00 a.m. the rain is again pelting down. There is nothing to be done but drive to the nearest big-box store to buy a mattress pump. After, we loiter in the parking lot while the shower swells to grapeshot. The sky, an opaque whey, will not be running out of water anytime soon. If asked, I would have a hard time naming a place I'd less rather spend a rainy day than a Walmart parking lot, but it beats our wet tent by a mile. "I'm not often in a situation I'm really bummed about, but I don't want to go back there," Erin says. "I suppose it's good for us, but I don't see how. It's like being forced to go to church."

But we must go back. And what's more, owing to the seasonal crush at Smokemont, I was unable to reserve the same site for two consecutive nights. We have to move the tent to new digs, some 300 yards away. Erin's opinion is that the tent must be broken down, dried, repacked, and rebuilt. But pitching the tent was such a conniption-inducing experience that I am resolved against full dismantlement.

Over Erin's prophesies of injury and failure, I collapse a few load-bearing members and hurl the wet, leggy mess onto the roof of the van. With Erin at the wheel and me standing on the running board while holding the thing in place, we manage the relocation. Tilting the tent upright takes me the better part of an hour. I am drenched beyond all caring, but it's on its feet again. This time I get the fly taut enough to bounce a nickel. "Dry" would be overstating the condition of our shelter, but it is no longer raining within.

Under a tarp, calmly strung, I get a fire roaring. I scorch some burgers, boil some water, and sterilize a batch of bottles for the boy. We chow hastily and retreat to the tent, which now contains a mattress that doesn't hurt to lie on. Jed finishes his dinner and does the postprandial performance that I love. He wobbles on his haunches and goes into a gourmandizing pantomime, sculpting in the air the ecstasy of milk enjoyed and recalled. His mouth works in O's and beaklike shapes. It is a silent song and dance about the miracle of nourishment. In time he comes to the awareness that the milk he celebrates is milk that was, not is. This causes him to weep and sue for reapplication to the breast. He eats some more, grunting with a contentment that his mother and I are surprised to find we share. "Babe, I'm proud of you," Erin says to me. "You got the camp all fixed up. You were totally the man of the family, and you had ideas that actually worked."

On the face of it, car camping of this sort should deliver none of the pleasures of actual camping. It brings you among throngs, not away from them. You climb nothing, push no physical limits, interface with no wildlife that could not be seen in Central Park. Perhaps the car camper is a special sort of idiot. At considerable expense and inconvenience to himself, he contrives a burlesque in which the provision of food and shelter becomes a minor pain in the ass he can congratulate himself for coping with.

Or perhaps the car camper is a practical genius. He understands that adventure's pleasure principle is scalable, that one need not lose his nose to frostbite to taste the joy of survival. Tonight, in the crowded Smokemont campground, I am as satisfied with life as I lately have been. We are dry and full of beef. Our delight with our inflated mattress is worth the night we spent on rocks. In a puny sort of way, I've spent today being necessary. I cannot recall a day apart from the birth of my son that I have glanced less at my phone.

All across the campground, amid the RVs, travel trailers, and multi-room nylon chateaux, scores of campfires spark and crackle in the dusk. The night gives off the congregational feeling of cigarette lighters at concerts or paper lanterns set afloat. We have, of course, done nothing very great in coming here. In fact, given the air-quality issues in Great Smoky, one wonders if shuttering the campground wouldn't be the best thing for the park. But it's somehow moving that with so much to do indoors these days, people still believe that existence may be enriched simply by sleeping in a wet and crowded stretch of woods.

By morning the clouds have left a sky of propane blue. We can finally get out into the park. A helpful fellow at the rangers' shanty gives his recommendations of spectacles that are accessible to people encumbered with babies and diaper bags. Clingmans Dome, the park's highest point, is the main thing to see. This we already know by the steady stream of automobiles flowing that way. The drive winds through vistas whose beauty is nearly grandiose. Red and orange bosk-oramas. Lemonscapes mallow-topped with roiling mist. Announcing every scenic overlook is a queue of folk bearing iPads, tripods, and Nikons with bazooka zooms.

The scene at Clingmans Dome confirms Great Smoky's transformation from an actual place to an abstract pop phenomenon. Up at the summit, dense fog has shrunk the valley view to about four feet. But here, too, dozens stand with selfie tackle, though the vista could be perfectly reproduced by a gray flannel bedsheet. The park, it seems, now shares a status with the Statue of Liberty or the *Mona Lisa*. Sheer numbers insist it is a thing to be experienced before we die. One need not climb it, touch it, or even see it necessarily. A picture of a grinning head before a white monotony still serves its purpose in a photo album so long as the location tag reads "Clingmans Dome."

Away, away from Clingmans Dome, through the calico mutt-pelt hills, out through Cherokee, past the moccasin dealers, the gem flumes, the retailers of "moonshine souvenirs," past the minigolf courses and go-kart tracks, past the Teddy Bear Motel, the Hiawatha Park and Cabins, and the Gear Head Inn (WELCOME BANGSHIFT FORUM FREAKS), and onward to our first actual hike in the park: the Juney Whank Loop Trail, near Bryson City.

The Juney Whank, we've been told, offers three separate waterfalls, all easily accessible to the infant-laden and infirm. We are not the only people come to savor the trail's convenient wonders. The parking lot is full, but after a ten-minute wait a spot opens up.

"Where you from in Florida? We're from Bradenton," a genial lady tells me as I'm fitting Jed into our ventral baby holster. I explain that the Town and Country is the only Floridian among us, with apologies that she drove so far to be confronted with such crowds. "This is nothing," she says. "The other side of the park? Gatlinburg? It's bumper-to-bumper for miles. And this isn't even the real foliage season. This ain't even peak."

Say what? This ain't peak? The newspaper told me that this would be peak. In some abstract sense, I do understand that the Great Smoky Mountains are not the same thing as the Gregg Allman show at the Harrah's Cherokee Casino, yet I do feel as though I've learned, after shelling out for my ticket, that he will not play "Ramblin' Man." This is the trouble with Great Smoky: the park is so encrusted in its own celebrity that you come here not as a human creature encountering earthly terrain, but as a ticket holder to a spectacle annually endorsed and certified by 22 million eyes. You feel cheated when the flora isn't turning in the performance of its life.

Up we go to Waterfall Number One. Humanity on the foot trail is no less dense or international than on a moving sidewalk at LaGuardia. Ahead of us is a pair of young Chinese aristocrats, he in Prada shoes and a lustrous pompadour, she in a red floral dress with a Coach purse and a Borsalino hat. Behind us is a South Asian American family whose vanguard is a boy of nine or ten in a *Duck Dynasty* T-shirt, rapping fiercely and treading on my heels when my pace flags.

Ten minutes later, we're standing on a bridge beneath which the waterfall spills into a steep, gold-greenness of mountain laurel, tulip poplar, and fern. The landscape seems no uglier or realer than a painting by Bob Ross. Beside the falls is a big mossy rock. By some undeclared agreement, we all understand that we have not really fulfilled a visit to Waterfall Number One unless we have been photographed sitting on that rock, our smiles suspended by invisible hooks. The photo boulder is a close relative, I think, of the section of plastic log, bolted to a chair, on which we were told to fold our arms by the man who snapped our senior portraits back at Chapel Hill High School.

Honestly, I am not trying to be a snoot about those of us who cannot see the park but through a viewfinder or a screen. The general problem of how to experience nature's seasonal beauty is not easily solved. What to do with the spasm of desire and memory that dying leaves summon in the human beast? They have me thinking of a bygone fall when I was seven. Under the season's influence, my brother and I broke into our friend's house and burgled his toys. Our thinking was that he was better off than us and would get new stuff for Christmas. When, fleeing with the loot, we bumped into our pal and his mother coming up the street, we threw his things into a leaf-strewn ditch and said, "What toys?" I am thinking, too, of a pretty girl at an autumn yard party many years ago. She was chilly. I draped my corduroy jacket around her, and she fell into the bonfire. Steal stuff. Be horny. Get your last licks in, says October. Get on in years and the purchase of an overpriced leaf blower is how you answer the season's call. Or you take up splitting firewood by hand. Or you come out to Great Smoky for the plenary experience of autumn, just as shivering in Times Square is the plenary experience of New Year's Eve. But getting close to autumn's soul is tough spiritual work. Gaping at a ripening leafscape, one is haunted by the question: Am I getting it? Am I feeling enough? How does one consummate the beauty of the natural world? A big Nikon kills these questions. Take a picture of the mossy rock. File the photographic evidence in its mega-pixel envelope and decode it later.

But, to be fair, the photomaniacal family ahead of us is having a lot of fun. They bustle along the path with all the purpose of a media gaggle, logging a snapshot every ten feet or so. The duties of model, photographer, and editor circulate among them. It appears to be good for the parents' marriage. Their favored pose is an open-mouthed makeout, reenacted with equal ardor whenever the path winds past a suitable backdrop.

Down the grade to get a gander at Waterfall Number Two, the Tom Branch Falls. A steep blackness, silvered with falling water. A flotilla of young people in tanks and cutoffs are gamely trying to tube the brook while holding coozied beers. The water depth is about nine inches in many places, so tubing involves a close, scooching survey of the creekbed with one's butt. The operation looks more painful than pleasurable, but one nonetheless envies the tubers. They are the only people along the Juney Whank, myself included, who seem to be experiencing the park as mammals and not as clientele.

Correction: my son seems to get the place. His eyes blink and swivel at a canopy the color of blood and Gatorade. The strangeness of it thrills him. His tiny heart beats pertly against my ribs. I kiss and sniff his fontanel. He squeaks and biffs me in the jaw. I'm spoiling the view.

To reward my family for two nights spent in the woods, and because Jed is in need of a scrub, I have booked for this evening an electrified and climate-controlled accommodation at a place I will call the Very Adorable Kuntry Kabin, a short drive from the park. At the main house, a stolid woman greets me through a screen door, parted no wider than necessary to transmit the Kabin key.

The Kabin, one of six identical twins, is nice. Or rather it is "nice," a modern, modular cottage to be appreciated by that guy

with the ASSAULT LIFE sticker on his truck. It is made 100 percent of chemicals: plastic flooring, enameled-tin doors, marble-
print wallpaper, nylon window bustles, etc. An apple-spice Air
Wick so powerfully suffuses its interior that in two breaths flat your
insides are coated with a holiday glaze. Other amenities include
three TVs, a cornsilk scarecrow, an earthenware cartoon frog, and
a guest book with kitties on the front. It is the sort of mountain
getaway where salesmen of puffy stickers come to break their marriage vows.

A note from the proprietress tells us that the scarecrow, the
frog, and the rest of it have been inventoried against theft. A numbered list of Kabin facts advises that "breakfast does not come with
a cabin stay." Also: "Do not feed the ducks" and, the last command-
ment, "Have a good time and enjoy the mountains as we do."

"This place is so much worse than camping in the rain with no
mattress," Erin observes. We put the Air Wick on the porch, probably risking a serious fine. Then we sleep as quickly as we're able
and lead-foot it for home with the rising sun.

So that was it. That was Great Smoky Mountains National Park.
That was our first family trip. What did we really do? We pitched
a tent, moved a tent, saw some traffic jams, some water, and some
pretty leaves, and milled about with the throngs. I suppose it
was all fine, but in my heart I know that we've fallen short of the
Kuntry Kabin's directive to enjoy the mountains, and for this we
should rightfully be pierced with candy-coated pitchforks wielded
by teddy bears.

Is there time to give Great Smoky one more chance? Just barely.
Before getting on the highway, we set a course for the closest
lobe of the park. It is a place called the Cataloochee Divide Trail,
and if we hurry, we may stroll forty minutes of it and still return
the rental car on time. The Cataloochee is up a suite of hollows,
past the roadside corpses of washing machines, pickups, and ex-
cavators, past a country church whose sign this week reads FALL
LEAVES, JESUS DOES NOT.

No one is on the trail this morning. The Cataloochee doesn't
lead to the park's uppermost vista or greatest quantity of waterfalls. It simply goes into the woods. The forest is dark, belichened,
wetly ticking. Other sounds are the lowing of an owl and the howl-
ing of a dog that, if Jed were older, he would insist was a coyote

or wolf. The park's air may be more polluted than in some cities, but here it feels better, cleaner, unbreathed by other human lungs. In spots the trail hits the ridge, but unpruned brush obscures the views, and anyway the opposing mountainsides are too far off to show their colors to advantage.

By silent assent, Erin and I tromp along without speaking. I jot no notes. She takes no photographs. There are no marquee attractions for the Instagram feed. No cataracts or geysers or faces in the rock, just tall hardwoods with no people around. But after three days of hordes, traffic, and spectacle hunting, we are stunned mute to find a beautiful semiwilderness free of selfie-ists and three-wheel Gold Wing motorbikes.

In the end, what do we want from the woods? Primitively put, we want the woods to put in us a feeling that doesn't happen indoors. Its symptoms are looking around, shutting up, and greedy respiration. It's a feeling that has something to do with our helplessness before nonhuman splendor and geologic time, a feeling one can't describe without risking language best left to the druid grove or the kitty guest book back at the Very Adorable Kuntry Kabin. To profess registering this feeling while not twenty minutes down a path a mile from the blacktop may strike the reader as meretricious and unearned. That's okay. Whatever it is, we are glad to stay dumb with it for ten full minutes more, until the baby starts to cry and we head back to the car.

My Father's House

FROM *BuzzFeed*

I REMEMBER FEELING GRATEFUL that we never said "Merry Christmas." We didn't say it on Christmas morning when we awoke in Virginia, during a layover at the world's most desolate Hampton Inn & Suites, and took long showers and poured too much batter into the waffle machine. Or at Washington Dulles International Airport, 1,400 miles from our cul-de-sac in Houston, where, at 8:00 a.m., bright, deserted corridors seemed to me pleasantly indifferent to the calendar. Near midnight on Christmas Eve, we had wished for a shuttle in lieu of a sleigh, making our plea with a dead-eyed driver who we'd been told could take us to the Hampton Inn. His broad white vessel didn't have a ramp for Dad's electric wheelchair—the one that chirped like a repair droid (*meep murp*) whenever you turned it on—and was too far above the ground for us to maneuver him out of it and into a seat. The driver suggested that my sister Adaeze and I ride the shuttle with our bags while Mom and Dad follow in a taxi. But Mom threw me a look that even I understood meant "I don't want to be alone," and so Adaeze rode with the bags while the three of us stayed behind, waiting by the curb at passenger pickup as the cool black night ticked into morning.

We were traveling to Nigeria in an ostensibly holiday-themed edition of a pilgrimage my family has made infrequently since 1991. But I hardly thought of Christmas once and called it mercy. That it was the most wonderful time of the year didn't cross my mind at the boarding gate at Dulles, where we waited for one in a series of progressively smaller airport wheelchairs that would deliver Dad to his seat on the plane. Nor when the chair eventually materialized, bringing with it the special airline staff that assists you when your body is broken and uncooperative and the experience of standing on your own feet, let alone walking, is an unapproachable memory. These people, distinguishable by their self-serious demeanor and uniform of dreary polo shirts and Dockers, are well trained to minimize airline liability and flight delays; less so, it became clear, to mitigate the routine suffering and indignity of the humans in their care. Mostly, they shared the grace and tact of their counterparts in bag handling, and whenever one seemed intent on wrangling Dad and his chair like an obstinate mattress, we intervened and took care of him ourselves, using all the little tricks and techniques each of us knows but never wanted to learn.

When we were finally in our seats, belts buckled and seat-back trays securely fastened in front of us, I focused my mind and vanished stubborn memories of our cul-de-sac, and the lit Christmas tree, and the framed photo of my younger brother, Chidi—not more than ten years old in a baggy T-shirt and white high-tops —that he had fashioned into an ornament with glue sticks, green and red glitter, and yarn. I steered my thoughts away from The Last Good Christmas two years ago when Chidi was twenty-one and Adaeze and I spoiled him like we usually did with a flight to visit me in New York, a trip that marked both his first time flying alone and the last time I would ever see him alive. And I allowed myself to forget the Christmas the year after, when I had insisted (to be normal? to be "strong"?) on trotting out the tree, and the lights, and the glitter-encrusted ornament, and quickly, tearfully, pitifully regretted all of it. We never said "Merry Christmas" as the plane arced fitfully over the Atlantic and then Africa for fifteen hours and across six time zones, while day bled into night and into day again. And I was grateful for that.

I.

I wish I could tell you this was a story with a silver lining, that the trip to the country of my parents' birth was ultimately restorative for my mom, dad, sister, and me. If I could make the illusion stick, I'd say it was a trip worthy of the movies, a cathartic, third-act coda that brought our lives full circle and filled our hearts with sober gratitude. And the house that greeted us there? Dad's decade-long obsession that we'd been building (in keeping with tribal tradition) in the lush, sun-baked village of my late paternal grandfather? It was finally completed, standing even as I write this as a shining monument to triumph over adversity and the immortal legacy of mankind's struggle on earth, or something. Yes, we had fallen on hard times, to be sure. But somehow, during those two blistering weeks together, all of the ordinary and devastating tragedies that have fractured my family in ways both sudden and inexorable were put in proper perspective, their greater meaning climactically revealed as we held each other and wept under a mighty acacia tree. I would not be above telling a story like that if only any of it were true. But, of course, that's not the way it happened.

After a transfer in Addis Ababa, our plane began its descent toward Enugu, capital of Enugu state, the Seattle-sized southeastern city where my father was born and with which my family shares both historical and etymological bonds. (In Igbo, "enu" = "top," "ugwu" = "hill.") By random coincidence, we discovered that we were sharing the flight with the gallant Nigerian-British actor Chiwetel Ejiofor, star of *12 Years a Slave*. Adaeze and I spotted him across the aisle chatting and laughing with what must have been a brother or cousin. We poked each other and spent idle minutes furtively guessing at the reason for his travel. (A later Google search solved the mystery: a sister's wedding.) It was the kind of imaginary kinship with a celebrity that is customary in America, but all too rare when you're the child of immigrants, born into the wrong color skin with a wrong-sounding name. It was exciting. But if I harbored any hope that Nigeria's most famous living international movie star was an auspicious omen, it was extinguished before we left the Enugu airport.

My sister is shorter than me with long, glossy black hair. At thirty-two, she's three years older, though her unreasonably faultless skin makes people think I'm the older one. At baggage claim—a Darwinian gauntlet even in countries with space programs—we were sentries, each standing watch at one of two carousels in a hot, un-air-conditioned room. We stood shoulder to shoulder with dozens of flustered-looking men from the plane, all of them sweat-soaked and combustible after a long flight. They erupted into shouting matches in Igbo and broken English whenever a foot was smashed or an elbow jammed. A stifling aroma of dust and body odor lingered in the room like burnt rubber at a stock race.

Given the length of our trip, Dad's suite of medical equipment, and the assorted small gifts Mom brought for very extended family, we were traveling with so many bags that a Kardashian would have blanched at the excess. Even though on an intellectual level we recognized a certain recklessness in checking so much luggage across three flights and 7,000 miles, we had never dwelled on airline operational efficiency, just as we had never dwelled on the lack of cultural or infrastructural accommodations for disabled people in Nigeria, or on the vague assurances from relatives that our house in the village was in a habitable state, more or less, despite the fact that construction had been beleaguered and none of us had seen it in person in over six years.

You could say that we were delusional, that we weren't sufficiently cautious or fearful. And I guess you'd be right. But the truth is that we *were* afraid. In fact, we were terrified. But our greatest fear wasn't to do with luggage, or transportation, or housing, or any of the real and upsetting consequences that could and did await us for being reckless with such things. Our fear, the one that we couldn't live with, was of what would happen if we weren't — if we were sensible and stayed home, or waited for more convenient flights to present themselves, or for the house to be perfect. We were afraid of failing to act with appropriate urgency, of not pulling together even in all of our brokenness before it was too late. "I don't want to die in this country," Dad had said when he first showed us the blueprints of a house he hoped to retire in, before the stroke had robbed him of the chance. No. It was too risky, we decided, to be sensible. So we chose to be reckless.

After several minutes, the carousels at baggage claim whirred to life. Dad's electric wheelchair was among the first wave of luggage to round the circuit. I exhaled. We had broken the chair down into three parts, which cumulatively weighed about 110 pounds. I plucked the black leather office chair–like seat from the track first, then the race car–red base, which was emblazoned with a manufacturer name that I had never noticed before. The name, "Pride Mobility," struck me as both patronizing and a little on the nose, like a nightclub called Sad Dark Sex Preliminary. I set the base aside and noticed that the battery, a ten-pound brick with a handlebar that drops into the base, wasn't with the other two pieces. Maybe it would come out later. Adaeze and I focused on retrieving the rest of our bags, quietly rejoicing whenever one would turn up, as if our number had been drawn in the Powerball. But after everything else had been accounted for, after we had searched the baggage claim area corner to corner, we were forced to accept the simplest conclusion. The battery was lost.

When I think of my dad walking, I think of his shoulders. They're broad and slice purposefully through the air on a course just a couple degrees shy of George Jefferson. I see him and his aviator eyeglasses coming through the door of our brick house on the cul-de-sac after a long day of work, wide print necktie and white dress shirt exposed by a freshly unbuttoned suit jacket. The suit is gray and slightly oversize—the kind that has somehow never gone out of style in the South, with billowing fabric at the ankles—and he clutches a boxy leather briefcase firmly in his right hand. I see him at his gym, where he used to take me when I had hoop dreams and was in urgent need of bigger calves, pedaling relentlessly on a stationary bike in his white singlet and striped white tube socks. Beads of sweat accumulate on his hairy chest and on the top of his head, which is shaven so smooth that a reflective glare clings to it always like a tiny cap. I see him making the rounds in the church foyer after service—the only true extrovert in our family—smiling and gregarious while talking with the Greggs about their new car, or the Kobiljaks about their boy in Iraq.

In 1967, when he was sixteen or seventeen, Dad lied about his age and ran away to fight for the Republic of Biafra in the Nigerian Civil War. He went through the hell of basic training and worked his way up to lieutenant. He became acquainted with death—the way it looks and smells and sounds when life leaves the body. Men were razed like ripe sugar cane to his left and right. Once, in a firefight, a bullet struck his rifle and thwacked it right out of his hands. More than a million were killed or starved to death before the Biafrans were defeated, but, somehow, Dad made it home and his story continued. He finished secondary school with distinctions in math, or, as they called it in the Queen's English his late parents never learned, "maths." Through an application mailed from the U.S. embassy in Lagos, Dad won a chemical engineering scholarship to Michigan Tech, of all places, and was overjoyed. He bought a plane ticket in 1974, using money he had earned by convincing his brothers and sisters to sell one of the family's plots of land. When he arrived in Michigan, with about $100 to his name, it was winter. He got clobbered by the cold; gobsmacked by the snow.

Dad went back home to Enugu the summer after graduation triumphant, a job offer in tow from the chemicals manufacturer Union Carbide in Indiana. That summer, he met Mom and vowed to make her his wife. He was a golden child, blessed by God Himself. Dad worked as many side jobs as he could get in preparation for a family, and to put Mom through school. They would both become PhDs ("Dr. and Dr. Ugwu"), but first he was a part-time ice cream truck driver, and semitruck driver, and door-to-door textbook salesman. My older brother Chiugo was the first of the kids, in 1980. Adaeze came along three years later; and then me, six hours into her third birthday (she still razzes me for crashing the party). Chidi was the last of us, in 1992—born with sickled blood cells and a bum liver, but ridiculously cute. By that time we were in Elyria, Ohio, a suburb outside Cleveland, living early '90s Midwestern childhoods: Huffy mountain bikes and Super Soakers and *Mario Kart* for days.

Dad got an administrative job at Galveston College, but moved us all to Houston, a thirty-minute commute away, which had better school districts. The weather was amenable, much better than the Upper Peninsula, and there were other Nigerians around—the highest concentration of any city in America. Life was good. Dad and Mom bought us boomboxes and put us in YMCA leagues and took us to Rockets games to see Hakeem "The Dream."

In 2000, when I was thirteen and finishing middle school, Dad announced a grand plan to send me back to our homeland for a year, to get a sense of where we'd come from and, perhaps, some discipline—tricky to teach in the Land of the Free. He hadn't been able to afford to send his other children back when they were still young and pliant, but he'd be damned if he didn't send at least one. I fought like hell but returned from the experience with my world a little larger. I told myself I'd leave Houston on my own odyssey one day. By then Chiugo had moved out, following an epic dispute with our parents over college and the direction of his own life. He rarely spoke to them for fourteen years; didn't set foot in the brick house on the cul-de-sac again until after Chidi died. It was a dark sort of symmetry. One son taken, one returned.

II.

We left the airport in search of a hotel that might accommodate us. The house was still being cleaned. Dad and I were chauffeured in a small Peugeot sedan by my cousin Obiora—thirtysomething, tall and clean-shaven with black, rectangular glasses—while Mom and Adaeze rode with another cousin, Emeka—even taller and albino with sherbet-tinted skin and light hair. Both had been among a familial welcoming party that warmly received us after we emerged battery-less from baggage claim. It had been over six years since Dad and I last visited home, nearly a decade for Mom and my sister.

I didn't remember there being so many hotels in town the last time I had visited. Now they seemed to have sprouted up everywhere, especially in Independence Layout, the prosperous capital district that was home to Ifeanyi Ugwuanyi—the newly elected governor of Enugu state. His fat cheeks and stilted, gap-tooth smile beamed from a legion of billboards as we drove around the city in ninety-four-degree weather on a December afternoon.

"Day by day, we are making Enugu state better."

The billboards were imprinted with a fine layer of rust-colored dust—a side effect of red, iron-rich soil—as is everything in Nigeria during the dry season: roads, cars, buildings, palm trees . . . even the air. The entire visible world often took on a red-orange tint, as if someone had replaced my contacts with blue-light filters.

We drove to four different hotels before we found one that could work. This wasn't a matter of pools or Wi-Fi or complimentary breakfast. It was the stairs. Each hotel telegraphed its suitability to wealthy foreigners with grand staircases at the entrance framed by Greek columns, or stone sculptures, or manicured hedges—ostentatious displays that suggested aspirational if not literal distance from the poorer, less developed sectors that composed most of the city.

But to us the stairs were an intractable, inescapable menace. Able-bodied people are not inclined to consider the stark tyranny of stairs. How a single step—invisible when the body is cooperative—can be a wall between a disabled person and the basic comforts of civilization: shelter, bathrooms, air conditioning. In Nigeria—where, despite decades of oil-backed anti-poverty initiatives, even the healthy and gainfully employed do not enjoy easy access to simple conveniences like reliable electricity and potable water —there is no national disabilities legislation. So our expectations that any of the buildings we encountered would be wheelchair accessible in a meaningful way were extremely low. We aimed instead for accessible-ish, which, in the case of a sixty-five-year-old, five-foot-ten, hemiplegic man in a 100-pound, semi-functional wheelchair, meant fewer stairs than Jay Gatsby's imperial ballroom.

We settled on Dmatel Hotel and Resort in Independence Layout, a midscale, two-story residence with gray and tan exteriors and rooms available on the first floor. I counted six tiled steps between the parking lot and a set of steel and glass double doors that led to the guest quarters. Foot-long agama lizards, their black bodies capped with red heads and tails, flitted in and out of the brush.

Dad can no longer move the right side of his body, the consequence of a weak blood vessel in the left hemisphere of his brain that ruptured one ordinary summer night in 2010. In the years since, my family has devised an ad hoc catalog of precise, multipoint procedures to help him do many of the things he can no longer do for himself. In America, when it comes to getting around, this generally consists of picking up where the Pride Mobility chair leaves off: maneuvering him from the chair to his bed, or from the chair to the toilet, or from the chair to the car. Some procedures are more involved than others, but none typically require more than a moment or two of strenuous physical exertion: lift, support, pivot, place. None of our procedures account for stairs.

Obiora parked the Peugeot at an angle, the passenger-side door as near to the stairs as he could get. I bent at the knees, hoisted the wheelchair out of the trunk, and lugged it up the steps and through the glass doors. One of the back wheels was stuck, but if you switched the chair to manual mode and shoved hard, the skidding wasn't exactly terrible. Mom came around the passenger side to help. Dad trusted her to hold him. She was soft but strong; had never shied from the hard things. She unbuckled him and pulled his legs toward her so that he was facing the car door. He reached with his left hand and grabbed it for support. As a boy, he'd been taught to scorn the left hand; he'd never used it for eating or shaking. But since 2010, none of that had mattered, or could. Left was all there was.

Six steps. Dad didn't want to be carried. His pride, now as ever, a blessing and a curse. I chose to be empathetic. I told myself he could ascend the stairs with our help, if we folded our bodies into his and made him strong. If we supported him like he had taught us to support each other. Mom grabbed him by the waist and lifted him up to his feet. He rested his hand on her shoulder. She crept backward slowly while drawing him with her, as if they were slow dancing and she had taken the lead. The right side of his body slumped at the shoulder. Dad stepped forward with his left leg, trailing Mom's momentum. I grabbed hold of his right leg and made it follow. Obiora helped prop him up from the back. We were moving. Mom climbed the first step and then the second and Dad lifted his left foot and I lifted his right. I thought that the three of us must look like marionettes, except we, too, were puppets made of patchwork cloth, and the show wasn't a show to us but all that we could know of life.

Something happened and Dad slipped, stumbled. His left hand dropped from Mom's shoulder and clutched at the hem of her blouse. Then he cried out "Jesus!" and gave voice to despair. His body was bent ninety degrees, like a cheerleader forming an "R." Obiora and I grasped him from behind, didn't let him fall, didn't let him fail. Mom repositioned. She guided his arm back to her shoulder and he was standing again, or as close to standing as he had ever been, as close as we were capable. Two more steps. First Mom, then the left leg, then the right. Once more and we were at the top of the stairs. Now we needed the chair. "Are you holding him?" I asked Mom, searching for her brown eyes. "I'm holding him," she said. And I let go and ran to grab it, pushed hard and made it skid toward them with its missing battery and one stuck wheel. Mom and Obiora lowered him into the seat gently, folding his right arm into his lap and lifting his right foot onto the footrest. We mopped the sweat from our brows with the backs of our hands and breathed. Finally—after fifteen hours, and 7,000 miles, and four hotels, and six steps—we had arrived.

III.

There's a taxonomy of looks we get when we're out in public with Dad. As a venue for genuine human feeling, I've found the face of the rubbernecker to be raw and dependable. The sudden and transitory nature of their encounter with us prohibits polite composure, the curtains drawn at an uncharitable hour. We'll get common pity in a crowded restaurant, or morbid curiosity while browsing a department store. Among close friends, extended family, or the rare empathic stranger, you might catch a glimpse of genuine sorrow, a slight quivering of the lip. Most of these looks I ignore, unfazed. The voyeur feels at a great remove from me, as if we are on opposite sides of some unbridgeable chasm. The only look that ever really penetrates, can make me hot with contempt, is relief. The look that says, with a whiff of revulsion, "Thank God it's not me."

I recognized that look on the plane to Addis Ababa as I worked with the airline staff to roll Dad down a cramped aisle. I saw the averted eyes, the pursed lips, the chins tucked into necks. I felt the spike in my blood pressure long after I had settled in my seat. In those moments, I could take no solace from any sense of self-righteousness or moral superiority—I was sure I had been guilty of similar looks in the years before the stroke. But I was soothed by something that felt more useful and harder to earn, an awesome awareness that began to bloom in 2010.

I could see clearly that the comfort in "Thank God it's not me" was a delicate self-deception. A lie that warms and embraces us like swaddling clothes. A mirage in the desert. I knew that just as God had not spared us, He would spare no one in the end. That infirmity and death await each of us and each of the ones we love. That everything can change in an instant. I knew this and was soothed because of the blind justice of the cosmos—the timeless balm of all grieving people. And I felt neither shame nor self-pity, but a powerful kind of peace. At least, at last, I was living in the truth of life, in all its frailty and impermanence—the truth of weak blood vessels and bad livers and mortality itself. The lie had been vanquished and I was free.

In the morning, Adaeze and I ordered room service, something we had never done before in Nigeria. I asked for an omelet with a side of sausage, but when it came, something about the sausage looked a little off.

"Is that . . . a hot dog?" Adaeze asked, clamping one between her thumb and index finger.

"No way," I said. "It's a sausage . . . Right?" Adaeze took a tentative bite and chewed.

"Definitely a hot dog."

Our cousin Nwachukwu picked us up in his black Nissan Pathfinder to take us to the house. He's barrel-chested, bald, and boisterous with a high-impact voice and mischievous laugh. "Ochinawata!" he blared, greeting Dad by his ceremonial name. He reached for his right hand before clumsily accepting his left. Loosely translated, the name means "Man Who Was Crowned Chief at a Young Age."

After our Waterloo on the stairs the previous day, Dad agreed to let Nwachukwu carry him to the car, piggyback style, which went totally fine. Mom, Adaeze, and I squeezed into the back.

My father is from a village called Umuatugbuoma, about a thirty-minute drive outside of central Enugu, or twenty minutes when Nwachukwu is driving. We zipped through the city like a rabbit through a briar. I noticed there were traffic signs on the roads—another change from the previous times we had visited— some of which were commonly observed (stop lights) and others of which were apparently decorative (stop signs). The roads themselves were touch and go, with no marked lanes and the occasional trenchlike pothole that would send us swerving. In Nigeria, driving is like double Dutch: half-steppers are best left to the sidelines.

The city was a riot of extreme wealth and extreme poverty, provincialism fading feverishly into modernity. Our route took us by men in tattered T-shirts herding white oxen down a main thoroughfare, and by giant LED billboards advertising Glo Mobile wireless service. We passed decrepit, windowless buildings with tin roofs and doors dangling from the hinges; and gorgeous, gated compounds with villa-style mansions and new Mercedes parked out front.

The houses have always been exceptional. Those who can afford to build homes do so with gusto. Hulking cement domiciles with separate servant quarters and elaborate landscaping are common, as are barbed security walls and live-in gatemen. The house is the essential luxury, less a building than a vessel for perpetuating foundational values in Igbo honor culture: family, resilience, work ethic, and hospitality.

I don't remember exactly when Dad initiated construction on our own house in the village. No one in my family does. I know that I learned of it at some point between 2001, when I returned from teenage repatriation, and 2006, when Mom and Adaeze surveyed the site after groundbreaking. What I remember most of all is Dad's unsinkable pride in the very notion of the place. I remember the satisfaction in his voice as he gave us progress reports in family meetings where Adaeze, Chidi, and I flopped listlessly into couch grooves. I remember the palpable urgency of his regular international conference calls in the family room (the last landline standing), one of vanishingly few activities he managed to continue after the stroke. I remember the framed *Sims*-like computer rendering of the house—resplendent with a little black car in the driveway—that still sits on his bedroom dresser.

In actuality, Dad's plan to build the thing proved only barely tenable. He had little choice but to personally oversee construction by phone from Houston, having forsaken the help of expensive professional contractors on the ground. Given that most of the project was conducted before the recent surge of camera phones and broadband Internet access in Nigeria, this meant that messages to and from the site—care of a cousin or family friend or whomever Dad could cajole into playing envoy—arrived effectively as hearsay. Accounting and supply chain management were constant headaches. Project managers were hired with enthusiasm and fired with bitterness. But I think the greatest challenge of building the house, what ultimately allowed it to spiral—like a bad episode of *Fixer Upper*—from dream home to albatross, wasn't the fault of technology but of physics.

Aside from the trip he and I took in 2009, when he could swing it and get time off work, Dad was rarely physically present at construction. He wasn't able to look the project managers and masons and carpenters in the eye and make them understand the greater meaning of their labor that could only ever be lost in translation by phone or third party. He couldn't make them see the house as it was in his mind when he lay still in bed at night and the dream was real. And they never did. It never mattered to anyone like it mattered to him.

We exited the highway and pulled into Umuatugbuoma. The main artery that leads to our village, formerly a red dirt road, had been paved with craggy asphalt. It carved through thick, waist-high brush and scattered patches of yam and cassava plants, with throngs of towering palm trees just beyond. Nwachukwu honked with glee at a group of schoolboys playing football in a clearing, their bodies elastic and glistening in fierce sunlight.

Our house is at the top of a hill surrounded on three sides by undeveloped grassland. Even behind four cement walls that form a perimeter, you see it long before you reach it—the intricate tan shingles of the cascading, cross-hipped roof; the two sets of brilliant white rectangular columns that face south and west. The scale of the place is genuinely stunning. It seemed large enough to contain our Houston house on the cul-de-sac two times over.

As we got closer, the extent of the work yet to be done became clear. The security walls were unpainted and unfinished, with ragged edges and exposed bricks that had gone dingy and gray. The entrance gate was at the lowest point of a sharp incline, and the terrain beneath it was so jagged that the Pathfinder's undercarriage took a loud beating on the way in—much to Nwachukwu's displeasure. The land leading up to the house was a sweeping scar of red gravel pocked with weeds.

The house itself, viewed up close, would have been exquisite were it not for a handful of unnerving flaws, like an ill-fated romantic prospect you'd never text while sober. When Dad and I visited in 2009, it was essentially a pile of bricks, with gaping holes where windows would go and no roof. Now it had those things, and many other things that generally make a house look like a house, but nothing was as finished as it should have been. A planned two-tone paint job—white on the second story, apricot on the first—had dried unevenly, and the exterior was covered in gray blemishes where rough spots had been sanded down. Some edges of the building itself were misshapen. Doors fit awkwardly in doorways that either had warped, were poorly constructed, or both. The kitchen was a pile of rubble. Stairs were of inconsistent width and depth. Roof panels sagged. Floor tiles were missing or misplaced. The floor plan itself occasionally tested logic, with superfluous walls creating puzzling alcoves. And that's to say nothing of plumbing (nonexistent) or electricity (on in some rooms, off in others).

We had no reason to be surprised at the discord, but I couldn't imagine what Dad must have been feeling—what it must have been to lose the veil. The house, like everything we love, was a mirror in which he hoped to glimpse a better version of himself. He stared for a long time at the blotched paint. "It's an eyesore," he said, wrenching his face.

With some effort, I pushed Dad up a slick tile ramp that had been set just that day and into the house through a side door. Post-stroke, ramps needed to be installed throughout the house, including, hypothetically, a system long enough and shallow enough to safely reach the master bedroom on the second floor. The war against stairs would start at home. Our cousin-in-law and acting project manager for the past year had been waiting for Dad in a spacious first-floor living room with ornate tile floors and an arched entryway. I left the two of them to their business.

Mom, Adaeze, and I probed the house in all its fractured beauty, canvassing room by room, trying to imagine the possibilities. For all its imperfections, it was incontestably lavish, and we acknowledged how absurd it was that it belonged to us. Even if all six of my original family members had been able to inhabit the house at once, even if Chiugo had never left and Chidi were alive and healthy, there would have been too many rooms to fill. We picked out guest bedrooms, a game room, an office—each with floor tiles of different styles and colors.

As we walked up the stairs and down the halls, I felt something —dimmed but discernible—that I hadn't felt since I was a kid: a particular kind of wonder, the recognition of potential not previously imagined. On the second floor, we rounded a corner into a bright room with a forest-green floor and two windows adjacent to a balcony.

"This is my room," I heard myself say.

I recognized the words from a previous life, when my siblings and I were young pioneers, freshly arrived in some new town where Mom or Dad had found a better job, a better *future,* and we were good at the beginning of things. By reflex, I had claimed the room as if something urgent were at stake, as if I were calling dibs. No one put up a fight.

IV.

The morning of New Year's Eve, Mom's younger brother Nnaemeka came to the hotel to give her a ride to the market. He was visiting from Onitsha, where Mom and her siblings grew up, about two hours west of Enugu. The cousin-in-law had been relieved of his duties as project manager, and, in his stead, Mom volunteered to buy building materials, paint, and small furnishings for the

house. The goal was to get it as close to finished as we could before flying back to the States on January 9. We had resolved, once
more, to be pioneers.

In Mom's absence, the responsibility to care for Dad during the
trip fell to me. The reason for this was never put into words, as far
as I can recall, but it didn't need to be. We had all made incalcu-
lable sacrifices since the stroke: plans changed, dreams deferred.
But there could be no comparison between how Dad's condition
altered the course of my life and how it altered my sister's.

In the summer of 2010, Adaeze and Chidi were home in Houston. Chidi had just graduated high school, and Adaeze was entering her third year of law at Vanderbilt. She had always been the
gifted child, the most likely to succeed. My brother and I were
partners in crime since before he could talk, but my friendship
with my big sister cooked more slowly, through heated rivalry in
adolescence and into a tender allyship in young adulthood. When
I was naive and selfish, she was wise and giving—the one phone
call I'd make from jail.

I had left home the winter before the stroke to try to make it
in New York. *Making it* in my case meant a second postgraduate
internship and dates financed with overdraft protection money. It
was Adaeze who called and told me, her speech faltering like foal
knees, that something had happened. I can still only imagine it.
Dad had gone numb the night before, she said. An ambulance was
called. The doctors were running tests. By the time she called, they
were all at the hospital and I was alone in a windowless room in an
apartment I shared with a woman who had four cats.

At some point Adaeze put Dad on the phone, but he was too
emotional to speak. At first I heard nothing, and then an odd
sound. I'll never forget it: a heaving, sorrowful croak. It sounded
strangely anachronistic, like the preverbal cry of some marooned
hunter-gatherer. I heard Dad start weeping, and I was weeping too.
I had never thought much about his diabetes. He had gotten a
stent in his heart earlier that year without even telling me. I found
out days after the procedure, when he was already home. "It was
nothing too serious," Mom had said, dubiously. "We didn't want to
worry you."

They never wanted to worry me. And I never called enough to
be worried. That was the way things worked.

After the call I made myself small on a mattress and box spring.

It occurred to me, as tears dampened my dollar-store sheets, what a profound waste I was, unable even to afford the flight to Houston. It would be over a month before I made it home, a month when the reality of who we were and could conceivably be was shifting irrevocably beneath us.

In the years after, when I had returned to New York, it was Adaeze who propped our family up. Even after she'd started at a law firm and made more than enough to strike out on her own, when it was her turn to be naive and selfish, she did the opposite. Became more generous in spirit. Moved back home and stayed there, helping Dad, yes, but also Mom and Chidi, who needed moral support. And when Chidi got sick for the last time, she was there for both of our parents. Screamed bloody murder by his hospital bed as he was dying. Drove Mom home when it was over and not over at all. No one ever asked her to do these things—she would never make them ask. But she was there when they needed her anyway. She cooked meals, cleaned messes, and DVRed *The Good Wife*. She put our family before herself. That's the kind of person she is.

The kind of person I am is the kind who shows up twice a year and spends most of the time in his room with the door closed. The kind who makes you dredge up Christmas decorations when the pain is still fresh. So though it's true I did my best to take care of Dad in Nigeria, stood by his side and generally tried to make myself useful, I didn't do this because I was a good son, or because I was selfless. It was the opposite. I did it because I'm the selfish one.

To everyone's surprise, Obiora, Mom, and Adaeze had returned to the airport the day before New Year's and recovered the battery to the Pride Mobility chair, which apparently arrived on the flight after ours. Dad was sitting in the newly functional chair when someone from room service knocked at the door. We were in my parents' room, across the hall from the one I shared with my sister, which had tangerine-colored walls with mundane paintings of flowers on them.

I opened the door and tipped a young woman in a navy blue vest a few hundred naira, which amounts to a couple of dollars. I was never quite sure if this was a good tip or a bad one. I cleared space on a table beneath a mirror and set a plate of fried plantain with tomato stew. I poured a bottle of water into a glass and plopped a blue-and-white striped bendy straw inside. Dad clicked his chair on (*meep murp*) and cruised over to the table.

In accordance with our usual procedure, I tore off a paper towel and tucked it into his shirt collar like a bib. I've never tried eating exclusively with my nondominant hand before, but given that I can barely hold chopsticks with my dominant one, I can only think of Edward Scissorhands eating peas.

I had served Dad food, begrudgingly, countless times before the stroke. When we were kids, it was one of the main ways my parents taught us respect for elders, along with requiring us to greet them before school in the morning and when they came home from work at night. I remember being eleven or twelve and ladling ogbono soup, bubbles bursting on its swampy surface, from massive metal pots on the stove in our open-ended kitchen. When Mom wasn't looking, Chidi and I would climb onto the bar opposite the stove and do death-defying stunt dives across the living room, crash-landing on a plush gray three-seater. I remember taking Dad's favorite cup, a giant gray mug with a green handle from Mr. Gatti's Pizza that was bigger than my head, and filling it with water at the ice dispenser. I'd press the button and wait for an eternity as the water gurgled toward the brim.

Dad was the stoic and intimidating type, changing the air of whatever room he walked into. Whenever he was around, we sat up a little straighter, made ourselves less wild. I was in awe of him and the great things he'd accomplished, and I dreamed of becoming a PhD too—buying a nice car and a big house and starting a family in my own corner of the world. But as I got older and my desires changed, so did our relationship. Awe turned into resentment; his life story began to sound like an outdated fairy tale. Rather than following in his footsteps, I started to feel like being myself meant running as far away from the things he had done as I could.

"Check the suitcases, it's around here somewhere," Dad said. He had finished his plantain and wanted to check his blood sugar. He had done this every day, more or less, since I'd been in college, and yet somehow I had managed to remain completely ignorant of what it entailed. "It's in a small black pouch," he said. "Look in your mommy's bags."

After a few minutes of erratic searching, I found the pouch in a plastic tote and brought it to the breakfast table. Dad asked me to open it, and I pulled out a black stopwatch-like meter, a bundle of tiny strips of litmus paper with circuitry on one end, and a long white tube that looked like a pen you'd get from a doctor's office. I spread them out carefully.

Dad asked me to cock the tube, which I discovered was a lancing device, and I pulled the top half back until it made a satisfying click. Then he held out his left index finger, pink side up, and asked me to press the narrow end of the device against it. "Push the button," he said after he had made contact, and I pushed an oval green button.

The tiniest speck of blood appeared on the tip of his finger. I was surprised at how small it was, a red bead hardly wider than a hair. To take a sample, it would need to be bigger, Dad said. He told me to massage the finger, push more blood to the surface. I pressed my thumb and index finger above his first knuckle and pinched, rolling gently. It was the smallest gesture. The bead grew steadily, and when it was large enough, I let go. I inserted the circuitry end of a litmus strip into the black stopwatch meter. Then Dad dabbed the paper end with the blood, which plumed like dye on cotton. The meter read "75."

"Is that good?" I asked, and he said it was. I threw out the strip and put the equipment back in the pouch.

I imagine things work differently in other families with a sick parent, depending on the sickness and depending on the parent, but in my family, being on Dad duty is mostly following orders. Some days, I am better at this than others.

Before the stroke, Dad was about as exacting as you'd expect an army-trained, self-made engineer and academic man from an extremely patriarchal society to be. He was particular about the air conditioning filters in our house in the same way he was particular about the grades we brought home. If he believed in tattoos, the ancient Dad proverb "If something is worth doing, it's worth doing well" would go right around where Tupac had "Thug Life."

When his body stopped cooperating, Dad's need to hold everything and everyone around him to a certain standard only became more dire. He lost his autonomy but concedes no loss of control, directing us on how to dress him and prepare his food and put him to bed as if he has declared war against oblivion and each task performed to his liking marks a tactical victory. Crudely speaking, I know that the power he has to conscript us in this scheme is purely psychic, that by the ignoble laws of nature, our roles have been reversed. But taking dominion over a parent's body is an awful test. What rung of hell is reserved for those who fail it? What are my desires weighed against his suffering? How can I not show his body every ounce of love, and compassion, and fanatical attention to detail that it showed mine, when it was puny and soft and nothing at all but an extension of his own?

I put Dad to bed. Unfastened his black Velcro shoes and set them aside. I grabbed him by his waist, transferring him from the chair to the mattress: lift, support, pivot, place. And when he asked to be moved closer to the center of the bed, I moved him. And when he asked for the pillows to be adjusted four times, I adjusted them. And when I felt the bitterness swell in my throat like a knot, I swallowed it back down again. I was the parent then, and isn't that what parents do?

That night, the plan was for a twentysomething cousin of ours named Chinedu to take Adaeze and me to a nightclub. We would get away from our parents, and the hotel, and the house for a while and ring in the New Year with other Nigerians our own age. The only thing was we weren't exactly sure when Chinedu was supposed to arrive. Our WhatsApp messages confirmed only that he would be coming by "later." This, we remembered, is the way things work in Nigeria. Time is relative. There weren't even clocks in our hotel rooms. In New York, you can't get a cup of coffee with someone without a calendar invite and two weeks' notice, but in Nigeria people lead much less hurried lives. It occurred to me that this signaled two different strategies for contending with the disorder of the universe: resistance versus acceptance.

We got dressed around ten and sat on the bed watching my favorite channel in the hotel's satellite bundle, M-Net Movies Action Plus. From what I could gather, M-Net Movies Action Plus is a near-constant stream of terrible movies starring incredibly famous people that were never widely released in America. Watching it was like watching TV in some alternate reality where the faces were familiar but all the titles and story lines were new and much, much worse. This particular night we were engrossed in a mystifying 2013 gem called *Devil's Knot*, in which someone encouraged Colin Firth to play a working-class investigator with a prominent Southern twang.

At 11:53, we got a message from Chinedu that he was pulling into the parking lot. We climbed into his soft gold SUV and headed to meet more of our cousins at a club in town called eXtreme. From the road, scattered fireworks ignited the black sky, announcing the stroke of midnight. "Happy New Year!" we all yelled and erupted into laughter.

Given the changes I had already seen in Enugu, perhaps I shouldn't have been surprised that the nightclubs there were nearly indistinguishable from the ones you'd find on any booze-soaked promenade in a midsize Western city. And yet, when we arrived at eXtreme and I saw a young woman in a form-fitting outfit delivering bottle sparklers of Moët, I couldn't help but think of mornings fifteen years earlier when I had to fetch bathwater from a well. We peeled through a dark, crowded room skewered by roving laser lights and posted up at a banquette near the bar.

The most remarkable aspect of the club experience was the music. In recent years, Nigeria's music industry, based out of Lagos, has rivaled the Nollywood Industrial Complex for the mantle of most essential cultural export. Contemporary Nigerian pop is both proudly local and pleasantly porous, a fizzy brew of dance hall rhythms, hip-hop triumphalism, and post–T-Pain R&B. The country's hottest young stars, like Wizkid, whose incandescent "Ojuelegba" was remixed last summer by Drake, and Ycee, whose hit "Jagaban" packs more ferocity than anything Maybach Music has put out in years, enjoy the status of royalty and lucrative sponsorships from companies like Glo Mobile and Guinness, maker of Nigeria's beloved stout beer.

"Duro," by Tekno, a crowd favorite with a similar tempo to "Tempted to Touch," the 2004 slow wine anthem by Barbadian singer Rupee, blasted from the speakers as Adaeze and I caught up with our cousins Chinedu, Kanayo, Chukwudi, Nonso, and his new wife, Lota. Adaeze laughed diplomatically when the conversation inevitably turned to the subject of marriage—specifically, when she planned to settle down with a respectable Igbo man. But soon we were debating Donald Trump ("Horrid"), the merits of sushi ("Raw fish?" Nonso said and sucked his teeth. "*Raw. Fish?*"), and Jay Z versus Nas.

Later, we went upstairs to a less crowded area and Nonso ordered a bottle of Hennessy for the group (no sparklers). I let my mind go blank as we danced until four in the morning.

V.

The nucleus of all my extended family in Enugu is a house in Umuatugbuoma my late paternal grandfather, Ugwu Nwamba, built in 1957. It's a sturdy, low-slung bungalow—just a fraction of the size of my father's house—with cream walls, a squat brown roof, and green wooden shutters. Out front is a rust-red gravel yard tromped by a small herd of dairy goats—residents on the property since not long after it was erected. Every time I've been to Nigeria, we've gone to this house for family meetings that follow a typical pattern: my uncles arrange themselves in an egalitarian circle, commence a vociferous airing of grievances, and swig palm wine until the stars hang like tinsel and my eyelids get heavy.

I've heard sketches of Ugwu Nwamba's story countless times since I was a kid. How he was orphaned as a child, was robbed of his birthright, and grew up vagrant and illiterate. How he rose out of penury and became a yam farmer and commodities trader, sometimes walking twenty hours to do business in far-flung towns. How everywhere he went he was known for his honesty and fair-mindedness, always believing that you reap what you sow. And how he eventually flourished, taking four wives and siring six sons and eight daughters, Dad being the youngest of the boys.

I'd heard this legend and admired my grandfather, who died before I was born, the way you admire Great Men you read about in history books—my own personal Founding Father. As with the men in those books, this admiration was more notional than tangible. His life and struggles were too different from my own to have real force, abstracted through semipermeable layers of culture, time, and geography. But one afternoon in the village—when Dad, Mom, Adaeze, and I were visiting the house of my cousin Chinedu's mother—I overheard a darker, more obscure chapter of my grandfather's story that made it suddenly and unexpectedly resonant.

In the story that I'd known, my grandfather was a superhuman figure—unbroken though he'd been born a wretch. He had shaken off profound anguish and alienation as if they were rocks in his sandals, mere pebbles on the road to redemption. It's exactly the kind of story we tell all the time about survivors of tragedy, without pausing for questions, even though we suspect the truth is more complicated.

It would be harder to internalize and impart stories like my grandfather's in their fullness. We don't want to acknowledge that anguish and alienation might never fully leave someone, let alone someone we think we know. We can't accept that a person could feel so hated by the world that he would find himself desperate for escape; or that he would attempt to achieve that escape not once but over and over again in the prime of his life, before things ever had the chance to get better, when better was the end of a rope hung hastily from a kitchen cabinet. The hard story to tell is the story that suggests suffering is not a pebble on the road but the road itself, extending ceaselessly before us into the horizon.

My aunt was openly reviewing this chapter of my grandfather's story because she, too, had been destabilized by tragedy. Her husband, father to Chinedu and five other young children, had recently died suddenly after being taken to the hospital for an asthma attack. In the shadow of grief, Ugwu Nwamba's attempted suicides, once too confounding to contemplate, sprang to the front of her mind. She no longer wondered how someone could covet their own demise.

Like my aunt, I recognized myself in my grandfather's encounters with existential despair. I have never been suicidal and hope to live a long and full life. But in the weeks and months after Chidi died, still engulfed in darkness, I felt ready to die too; by which I mean that losing the person I loved most in the world seemed equivalent to losing the world itself. In truth, like many who experience what is sometimes called catastrophic loss, I felt like the world had actually ended, but for some reason I was left behind, expected to do laundry and respond to emails within a reasonable time frame.

On an ordinary day some decades ago, a few threads of twine and the miraculous timing of a good Samaritan are all that stood between my grandfather and annihilation. That is a part of his story and a part of mine. A shift in the wind and everything that came after, everything I have ever known, would never have come into being, lost to the currents of reverie like so many passing thoughts in an anxious mind.

Had I discovered this fact years ago, in 2009 say, I might have

recoiled in shock, or, duly disquieted, pushed it from my mind
entirely. But at my aunt's house in the village that day, I found that
there was room within me to receive it. I had already been learning to dwell on the imminence of my withdrawal from this world,
to let go of the lie that my life here is inevitable and unending.
This did not mean that I was not afraid of death or that I understood it. But I had begun to make room for it, like an heirloom,
handed down at first breath.

VI.

On our last night in Nigeria we were having a party. Mom had
spearheaded a heroic sprint on the house, which now had a fresh
coat of paint, a new entrance gate, two additional ramps, curtains,
sofas, and beds with linens in each of our rooms. It still was not
finished—the old gate needed to be sealed up, for example, and
the kitchen was still a mess—but it was habitable, which by then
felt like a miracle. We were finally going to be sleeping in our own
home, for the first and only time of the trip, and we planned to
celebrate.

We invited our relatives to a housewarming, for which a cow
and goat were being prepared in the manner of a traditional feast.
This, I had learned, meant slaughtering and roasting them on the
property. "It's organic," Nonso joked.

With Nwachukwu's help, we checked out of our hotel in the
afternoon, making eager use of a ramp that had felicitously been
installed days earlier. The manager—and the guests, and the
cleaning staff—had taken note of our dramatic productions on
the stairs, which apparently put him in mind of a previous visit
from the department of safety.

"Day by day, we are making Enugu state better," the billboards
had promised.

Nwachukwu's Pathfinder, packed like a clown car with all of our
luggage, made it through the house's new gates unscathed. It was
the hottest day yet, at 102 degrees, and my collar wilted on my
neck as I hauled my bags up the stairs to the room with the forest-
green floors.

Even as Dad toiled over the years, seemingly willing a house
into existence by sheer force of vision, I'd made a habit of avoid-

ing the obvious question of who would live in it. It had been introduced, innocuously enough, as retirement planning on the part
of my parents, who, having achieved the impossible in a world far
away from the one into which they were born, sometimes dreamed
of returning home. "I don't want to die in this country," Dad had
said.

But I knew the house was also a scheme of my father's, like
sending me abroad when I was young, to engrave Nigeria on
the hearts of his remaining children—to keep us coming back.
After his stroke, when the exigencies of his condition muddied
the dream of a radiant final homecoming, this second meaning
overshadowed the first. The house, if we chose to accept it, would
become ours; Dad's hope and blood and treasure embodied in
one flawed place.

After nightfall, our relatives descended on the party in droves.
People who had helped us over the past two weeks—Obiora and
his sister Ifeoma, Emeka and his brother Chijoke, Nnaemeka,
Chukwudi, and many more—came with their children and parents, generations of Ugwus assembling in our absurdly large yard
in front of our absurdly large house. Nigerian pop was played,
Guinness and palm wine imbibed, and rice with fresh meat served
to bursting.

In a quiet interlude amid the clamor, sitting between Adaeze
and me on the patio, my dad made one last proposal.

"Come for vacations," he volunteered, tactfully. But what he
really meant was: "Don't forget."

The Currency of Moons

FROM *Creative Nonfiction*

WE WEREN'T SUPPOSED to be stuck in Christchurch. We were supposed to be driving around New Zealand's South Island, in the camper van we had rented. The trip was a gift for Mike's fiftieth birthday, our first significant time off in years, and the first time in a long time we had traveled together. We had both been traveling alone a lot—too much—for work, and in the parlance of currency, our marriage was overdrawn. The only place we met was to fall into bed after long days or weeks apart, and we were simply too tired to tend to each other. We knew there were problems, but we were never together long enough to work them out.

It was a save-your-marriage vacation. We were looking forward to spending long days and nights together, hiking, wine tasting, and fly-fishing. But on the second day, camping near Kaikoura, Mike fell and rolled down a small embankment, breaking his ankle in two places.

We went to a country doctor, who left his Boxing Day dinner to take X-rays and wrap the ankle in a plaster cast. He told us to go to The Bone Shop at Christchurch Hospital for follow-up care.

And so I drove the camper south, along a sheer cliff on the left side of the road, with my husband's foot, elevated, in the rearview mirror. I didn't consult a map; for over 100 miles, I just followed the signs to Christchurch and, once there, followed the giant *H* or cross signs, hoping they meant *hospital*.

The next morning, The Bone Shop buzzed with the sound of saw blades cutting through plaster. They gave Mike a split cast suitable for the flight home and took another series of X-rays. Nurses and physicians apologized profusely for making us wait, for taking so long, in spite of the constant stream of patients. "We always fill up after a long weekend," said the jolly ward clerk, acknowledging the active Kiwi lifestyle.

A surgeon told us that Mike would need to be off his foot for at least six weeks and that he should elevate the foot until the swelling went down before flying home. "Good luck," she said. "Sorry about your holiday."

It would be a week before Mike's ankle was airplane-ready, so we were confined to our hotel room. Our hotel, like the hospital, was at the outskirts of the "Red Zone," a pile of rubble the size of a city that had been cordoned off after a series of earthquakes that had started in September 2010 and were still ongoing when we visited more than a year later, in December 2011. Inside the Red Zone, 600 buildings had been demolished, with 600 more to go. There were disagreements about how and what to rebuild. The thirteen-story central police department was still standing and structurally sound, but people who worked there were taking early retirement because they couldn't bear going into the high-rise, with its view of devastation. It, too, would be demolished.

The Red Zone was littered with broken glass, tile, and bricks that continued to tumble from buildings. The aftershocks continued, sometimes a dozen a day. In our hotel the first night, the room shifted hard from left to right and back in just a few seconds, like someone correcting a sliding stack of books. There was no sense that the seismic activity was over, but one woman said cheerfully to me, "What's going to fall has already fallen." On a bus on the outskirts of town, I saw a mansion half-hanging from a cliff.

It looked to me as if things could get worse.

Each day, after checking Mike's ankle, I feed him pain pills and breakfast then set out to explore. I walk the Red Zone's perimeter. I skirt piles of bricks and buildings cracked in half. Behind the cyclone fence separating the safe from the not-safe are memorials: plastic flowers stuck into the concrete, commemorating some of the 185 people who died in the strongest of the aftershocks, on February 22, 2011.

On my second day out, I glance down a side street and see brightly colored shipping containers attached to each other near what used to be the center of downtown Christchurch. It takes me

a few minutes to realize they contain shops—cafés, clothing boutiques, a bookstore, even a bank with a security guard—and are
stuffed with people: the Cashel Mall. The shipping containers sit
amidst sunflowers, in front of the crumpled and abandoned buildings the businesses once occupied. Concerned that the devastated
city would lose business and its sense of community if the rebuild-
ing didn't come fast enough, its property and business owners'
group had set up the temporary shops.

Twenty-seven of the stores destroyed by the quakes had re-
opened inside the shipping containers—lime green, orange,
turquoise, and yellow boxes that were attached to each other
horizontally or stacked on top of each other. The site was designed to be temporary and recyclable, able to be moved to another part of the city as needed. But already, people wanted
it to stay; they'd become attached to it, the phoenix rising. It was
one thing that had become another, capturing their hearts in the
process.

Slipping into Scorpio Books, I buy *The Sheltering Sky*. I intended
to buy the latest Man Booker Prize–winner, but instead pick up
Paul Bowles's mid-twentieth-century tale of a couple, Port and Kit,
who take their shaky marriage on a trip to the North African desert. An interesting choice, certainly. Perhaps I thought I'd channel
my disappointment through the novel. Perhaps I'd find renewed
gratitude for my marriage after reading Kit and Port's bitter rep-
artee.

I had to admit I was feeling depressed about the turn our vacation had taken, unhappy at being a nursemaid on the other side of
the planet, checking my watch to walk miles back to give Mike his
next round of pain pills and lunch. I feared I would return to our
home uninvigorated, to even more work since my husband would
be off his foot for five more weeks with only me to care for him.

Like the Buddhists advise, I decided to let myself feel the sadness and then watch as it passed and turned into something else,
as things always do.

I was afraid, however, of what it might turn into.

We had both waited until we were in our forties to marry for the
first time.

When I met Mike at a New Year's Eve party, I couldn't say why I was attracted to him, only that I was. On paper, he was all wrong: a Corvette-driving football coach who listened to classic rock. A man.

I was a lesbian. A butchy lesbian who rode a mountain bike and read poetry. My iPod party was bluegrass.

But I could see right away that he had a heart as big as a mountain, and I have always been attracted to kindness. And in truth, his penis didn't bother me. It was just another organ, a bunch of nerve endings, the least mysterious part of the man. In panels or workshops on gender identity, I had often talked to college students about the fluidity of sexuality. My motto, inherited from my father, was: *Who cares? Love who you love. We are lucky if we find it.*

In practice, falling in love with a man was difficult. My years as an out lesbian, especially in Alaska, had taught me that male privilege, and heterosexual privilege, was a dangerous thing. I was afraid of losing myself to a world in which I took for granted that I could hold my partner's hand in the grocery store and not be followed or beaten up or even killed. I was afraid I would become safe and comfortable, and forget how the world really works. And I was afraid I would lose my friends, a group of women so feral and free that I wouldn't want to be on this planet without their company.

So I came up with all kinds of reasons that I couldn't be with Mike, but mainly my objection was that he was part of the power structure, a pillar of the patriarchy. And that Corvette! Stepping into the Stingray with its furry red interior, I felt as if I was in a ZZ Top video, only wearing Doc Martens instead of Daisy Dukes.

Each day, I came up with a new set of reasons it would never work, but he continued to be kind, fixing my snowblower and considering me seriously with blue eyes the color of the lake where we lived. After a day apart at work, he would call to say good night.

I was confused.

My closest friend, Beth, a lesbian, asked me how I felt in my body when I was with him.

"Forget your head; you can convince your head of anything," she said. "The body doesn't lie. How do you feel when you're with him?"

"I feel happy," I said.

"Well, there you have it."

By the time we got to New Zealand, we'd been together eight years.

Christchurch. Suburbs that look like Marin County. Long city blocks that could be Fresno. A downtown that's a pile of bricks. I walk and walk since there is nothing else to do while my husband rests and elevates his foot in bed, doctor's orders. He watches rugby and cricket.

I walk.

Things that make me gasp: buildings missing their backsides, the rooms and their furnishings hanging out like entrails; restaurants, yet to be demolished, that still contain the tableware exactly as it was at the moment the lunchtime patrons fled. I peek inside one window, my hand shading my eyes so I can get a good look. I see dirty plates and cups, a pair of eyeglasses on a table. A hat on a hook. Coats and forks and upturned chairs, a still life in a ghost town.

Things that make me smile: benches fashioned out of earthquake rubble, a greenbelt along a river that never lost course. Flowers: magenta, fuchsia, lemon yellow. Lily pads.

Each night in our hotel room, while my husband watches rugby, I return to *The Sheltering Sky*. Something the character Port says sticks with me, and on my rambles through Christchurch, I return to it. Essentially, it's this: we act as if we have forever, but we don't really know how many sunsets, how many moons we have left.

I look at the man next to me in bed, with his foot elevated, and think about the full moons we have spent together, in the desert camping under a night sky or toe-to-toe in the Maui tide. Or pulling to the side of the road in our own town because of the moon rising from behind the mountains, so large and luminous we are struck blind.

I think about the full moons I have spent with women, doing pretty much the same thing.

What if I have only one full moon left? Do I want my remaining moons to be with this man? With any man?

In college, I had a teacher who was turned on by math. She'd throw her hands to the sky, pacing the front of the classroom, exclaiming that everything in the universe could be explained by math. If we understood math, she'd beam and sweat, we would understand everything!

Say I have thirty years left to live. That means I have approximately 360 full moons. Looking at it this way, it doesn't seem so dramatic or risky to spend another six or eight or twelve trying to repair my marriage. But what's the tipping point? A hundred moons?

I return to the hotel room throughout the day, bearing gifts: savory pies, chocolate, things I find on my travels that I think will please my husband, though he will remember little of it. I'm surprised to find that I'm an angry gift-bearer. How can I be so annoyed with a man drugged in bed with his foot up on pillows because of an accident? In the morning, I leave early to walk it off before he can see it, before it seeps out in my voice and body language. I help him bathe with too much roughness, my mouth set in a grim line.

My husband is a good man, a generous man. Solid. But it's there, like the bone chip on his ankle, which we saw in the X-rays: the idea that our marriage was fractured before we got on the plane. By our time apart and by my struggle to accept being in a heterosexual relationship. And our currencies differ: his currency is not of moons, but of dollars and what they buy. He works hard and knows the exact day he will retire to maximize his benefits. And he will have another job lined up the next day. He values work and how it translates into a good life.

I have often told Mike that I would rather spend time together when we're healthy than work until we drop into retirement. Let's figure out a different way to do things, I have said. Let's have more fun. He has smiled at me as if I'm dim.

"I could get hit by a bus tomorrow!" I say.

"Look both ways," he replies.

"I could get hit by a bolt of lightning!"

"Don't go out in a thunderstorm."

A woman, I think, would understand the moon.

As I walk, my sadness over our ruined vacation is eclipsed by the devastation of Christchurch. Buildings with rooms full of stories and life have gone to dust. People have died.

From the street, I pick up a piece of blue tile from a mosaic that slid off a wall during a good shake, and I hold it in my hands. I think I might pocket it and, at home, make some sort of crafty monument to Christchurch, to resiliency or something. Staring at the ceramic chip, it strikes me that the problem with my marriage isn't simply a lack of time together: it's me. Although I love my husband, I have treated our marriage like a shipping container —sturdy and sometimes beautiful, but a replacement for the real thing, like the Cashel Mall. I believe I will end my days with a woman.

Perhaps I treat this marriage as temporary. Mike doesn't.

My face burns at this realization, and I look around. I see other tourists with cameras, peering through the cyclone fence, sitting on park benches under gray skies staring at the wreckage, chatting. No one is looking at me; no one sees a woman going to pieces.

I let the tile drop back onto the rubble, as if evidence I want to hide. As I walk away, I look back at the crumbling wall with the pile of blue glass amassed at its base like sand in an hourglass.

Five days pass. My husband has become addicted to cricket. I finish *The Sheltering Sky;* it ends with Port dying. Only nearing his death-bed do he and his wife briefly reconnect.

This can't happen to us.

After too much New Zealand wine, I grab a piece of paper and ask my husband to recall his top ten memories from our marriage, and I do the same. The list surprises me: nine of our favorite memories are identical, and they all occur outside, in nature. Not one occurred inside our home.

Perhaps we do share a currency.

Walking Christchurch, my heart opens and I want to ease the suffering of the man who can't walk with me, but it shuts tight when I am back inside, when I close the door to our motel room on the edge of a disaster zone, and, later, when we're back at home. And when I do the work that has been women's work for generations: preparing food, straightening the wrinkles from the bed, placing a cool washcloth on his brow. Am I feeling the collective anger of womanhood or the limits of marriage between a man and a woman? That seems like a stretch, and it's unfair to cast my husband as a man who reinforces gender roles: he broke his ankle, ending his vacation too, while he was doing our breakfast dishes.

There was no negotiation; I didn't even see him go, just heard when he crashed to the ground and our plates and cups shattered.

And he married a lesbian, even though he knew who I was.

He tells me from his sickbed that he's disappointed we didn't get to stargaze in the Southern Hemisphere.

I find a wheelchair and push him out under the moon. I don't know why it makes a difference, but it does.

Contributors' Notes
Notable Travel Writing of 2016

Contributors' Notes

Elif Batuman is a staff writer at *The New Yorker*. Her first novel, *The Idiot*, was published earlier this year.

Tom Bissell was born in Escanaba, Michigan, in 1974. He is the author of nine books and a winner of the Rome Prize and a Guggenheim Fellowship. His most recent book, *Apostle: Travels Among the Tombs of the Twelve*, was published in 2016. "My Holy Land Vacation" marks his fifth appearance in *The Best American Travel Writing*. Currently, he lives in Los Angeles with his partner and daughter.

Catrin Einhorn is a journalist at the *New York Times* who reports and produces narratively driven work in a variety of media, including print, audio, video, and interactive pieces. She has covered urban violence, Americans' complicated relationship with firearms, veterans' issues, and some very special tennis courts. In 2016, Einhorn and Jodi Kantor reported and wrote Refugees Welcome, a yearlong series about everyday Canadians adopting Syrian refugees, exploring the question: can regular citizens successfully intervene in one of the worst problems on earth? A few years earlier, she was part of a team that examined President Obama's troop surge in Afghanistan by telling the stories of one battalion's yearlong deployment in a multimedia series called Year at War. Her work has been recognized with awards from the National Academy of Television Arts and Sciences (the Emmys), Alfred I. duPont–Columbia University, World Press Photo, and Picture of the Year International. Before joining the *New York Times*, Einhorn was a public radio reporter and a Fulbright scholar in anthropology.

Stephanie Elizondo Griest is the award-winning author of three travel memoirs (*Around the Bloc: My Life in Moscow, Beijing, and Havana; Mexican Enough: My Life Between the Borderlines;* and *All the Agents and Saints: Dispatches from the U.S. Borderlands*) and the best-selling guidebook *100 Places Every Woman Should Go.* She has written for the *New York Times,* the *Washington Post,* the *Believer, VQR,* and the *Oxford American* and also edited *The Best Women's Travel Writing 2010.* An assistant professor of creative nonfiction at the University of North Carolina–Chapel Hill, she has lectured across the globe, including as a U.S. State Department Literary Ambassador to Venezuela. Her awards include a Henry Luce Scholarship to China, a Hodder Fellowship at Princeton, and a Margolis Award for Social Justice Reporting. Visit her website at StephanieElizondoGriest.com.

Peter Frick-Wright is a contributing editor at *Outside* magazine and the host of the *Outside* podcast. He received notable mentions in *The Best American Sports Writing* in 2012 and 2013, and a Lowell Thomas Gold Award for travel writing in 2016. He has reported from Bosnia, Burma, Burundi, and Bolivia, but most of the time lives in Portland, Oregon.

Jackie Hedeman holds a BA from Princeton University and an MFA from The Ohio State University, where she served as reviews and interviews editor for *The Journal.* Her work has appeared in *Entropy, The Offing, 1966, Argot Magazine,* and elsewhere. Find her on Twitter @JackieHedeman.

Leslie Jamison is the author of *The Empathy Exams,* a *New York Times* best-selling essay collection, and a novel, *The Gin Closet,* a finalist for the *Los Angeles Times* First Fiction Award. Her work has appeared in *Harper's Magazine, Oxford American, A Public Space, Boston Review, Virginia Quarterly Review,* the *Believer,* and the *New York Times,* where she is a regular columnist for the *Sunday Book Review.* She lives in Brooklyn and is an assistant professor at Columbia University.

Jodi Kantor specializes in long-form, deeply reported stories. Her investigations into working conditions at Starbucks and Amazon prompted policy changes at both companies. Her article about Harvard Business School's attempt to change its climate for women provoked a national conversation about women in business schools. Kantor's report on working mothers and breast-feeding inspired two readers to create the first free-standing lactation suites for nursing mothers, now available in airports and stadiums across the country. In 2016, Catrin Einhorn and Kantor reported and wrote Refugees Welcome, a yearlong series about everyday Canadians adopting Syrian refugees, exploring the question:

can regular citizens successfully intervene in one of the worst problems on earth? For six years, Kantor wrote about Barack and Michelle Obama, delving into their ideas, biographies, family, marriage, faith, and approach to the White House, and covering the 2008 and 2012 presidential campaigns. A new edition of her 2012 book *The Obamas*, detailing how they adjusted to the jobs of president and first lady, is forthcoming in early 2017. Before becoming a reporter, she was the New York editor of *Slate* and the *Times*'s arts and leisure editor. Kantor is a contributor to *CBS This Morning*. She lives in Brooklyn with her husband, Ron Lieber, and their two daughters.

Randall Kenan is the author of a novel, *A Visitation of Spirits;* two works of nonfiction, *Walking on Water: Black American Lives at the Turn of the Twenty-First Century* and *The Fire This Time;* and a collection of stories, *Let the Dead Bury Their Dead*. He also edited and wrote the introduction to *The Cross of Redemption: The Uncollected Writings of James Baldwin*. Among his awards are a Guggenheim Fellowship, a Mrs. Giles Whiting Award, the North Carolina Award, and the American Academy of Arts and Letters' Rome Prize. Kenan is a professor of English and comparative literature at the University of North Carolina–Chapel Hill.

Saki Knafo is a freelance journalist whose work has appeared in *Men's Journal, GQ,* the *New York Times Magazine,* and many other publications. He is a reporting fellow with the Investigative Fund at the Nation Institute. He lives in Brooklyn, not far from where he grew up.

Gwendolyn Knapp is the author of the memoir *After a While You Just Get Used to It: A Tale of Family Clutter*. She currently resides in Houston, Texas, where she tends to her dozen plumerias, dreams up crazy stories, and is food editor for the *Houston Press*. Her work has appeared in the *Oxford American, Cornbread Nation: Best of Southern Food Writing,* and elsewhere.

David Kushner is the author of several books, including *Masters of Doom* and *Alligator Candy*. A contributing editor of *Rolling Stone,* he has written for *Outside, The New Yorker, Vanity Fair,* and other publications.

Gideon Lewis-Kraus is the author of *A Sense of Direction,* a writer at large for the *New York Times Magazine,* and a fellow at New America. He lives in New York.

Robert Macfarlane is the author of a number of award-winning and bestselling books, including *The Wild Places, The Old Ways,* and *Landmarks*. His work has been widely adapted for television, film, and radio, and he is a fellow of Emmanuel College, Cambridge. He was the 2017 recipient of the American Academy of Arts and Letters' E. M. Forster Award for Literature. He is presently finishing a book about underworlds, darkness, and knowledge called *Underland.*

Ann Mah, a frequent contributor to the *New York Times* travel section, is the author, most recently, of *Mastering the Art of French Eating.*

Alexis Okeowo is a staff writer at *The New Yorker.* She is also a fellow at New America. Her book *A Moonless, Starless Sky: Ordinary Women and Men Fighting Extremism in Africa* will be released in October 2017.

Born in 1954, **Tim Parks** moved to Italy in 1981. Author of fifteen novels, including the Booker short-listed *Europa, Destiny,* and *In Extremis,* he has written three highly acclaimed travel books on his adopted home: *Italian Neighbours, An Italian Education,* and *Italian Ways.* He has also translated works by Moravia, Calvino, Calasso, Machiavelli, and Leopardi. Parks lives in Milan.

Shelley Puhak is an essayist and poet. Her essays have recently appeared in *Creative Nonfiction,* the *Iowa Review,* and *Salon.* Puhak is also the author of two books of poetry, the more recent of which is *Guinevere in Baltimore.* She is writing a book about genealogy, genetics, and motherhood.

Elizabeth Lindsey Rogers is the author of the poetry collection *Chord Box,* which was a finalist for the Miller Williams Prize and a Lambda Literary Award. Her poems and essays have appeared in the *Missouri Review, Boston Review, FIELD, Prairie Schooner,* and elsewhere. A former *Kenyon Review* Fellow, she is the Murphy Visiting Fellow at Hendrix College and a contributing editor at the *Kenyon Review.*

Kathryn Schulz is a staff writer at *The New Yorker.* She won the 2015 Pulitzer Prize in Feature Writing and a National Magazine Award for her article on seismic risk in the Pacific Northwest, "The Really Big One," which was anthologized in *The Best American Science and Nature Writing* and *The Best American Magazine Writing.* Previously, she was the book critic for *New York Magazine,* editor of the environmental magazine *Grist,* and a reporter and editor for the *Santiago* (Chile) *Times.* Schulz's writing has appeared in the *New York Times Magazine, Rolling Stone, Time, Foreign Policy,* and the *New York Times Book Review,* among other publications, and she has reported from Central and South America, Japan, and the Middle East. Schulz received the Pew Fellowship in International Journalism (now the International Reporting Project) in 2004. A graduate of Brown University and a former

Ohioan, Oregonian, and Brooklynite, she currently divides her time between the Eastern Shore of Maryland and New York's Hudson Valley.

Wells Tower is the author of the short story collection *Everything Ravaged, Everything Burned.* His short stories and journalism have appeared in *The New Yorker, Harper's Magazine, McSweeney's,* the *Paris Review, The Anchor Book of New American Short Stories,* the *Washington Post Magazine,* and elsewhere. He received two Pushcart Prizes and the Plimpton Prize from the *Paris Review.* He lives in North Carolina.

Reggie Ugwu is a features writer for *BuzzFeed News* and is based in New York.

Kim Wyatt is the publisher of Bona Fide Books in South Lake Tahoe, California. She holds an MFA in creative nonfiction from the University of Alaska–Anchorage and has worked as a bunny girl, deckhand, and nurse. She currently teaches incarcerated students and is writing a memoir.

Notable Travel Writing of 2016

SELECTED BY JASON WILSON

DOMINIQUE BROWNING
The Days of Reveille and Taps. *The New York Times,* July 17.
AMY BUTCHER
Flight Behavior. *American Scholar,* Summer.
BRIN-JONATHAN BUTLER
Farewell, Champions of Havana. *Roads & Kingdoms,* September 30.

ALEXIS COE
Striking Out. *The New Republic,* April.
CHRIS COLIN
Pay Pal. *AFAR,* March/April.
TED CONOVER
On the Rails. *T: The New York Times Style Magazine,* November 13.

BRONWEN DICKEY
Climb Aboard, Ye Who Seek the Truth. *Popular Mechanics,* September.

DAVID FARLEY
A Path to Peace. *AFAR,* March/April.
KEVIN FEDARKO
Losing the Grand Canyon. *National Geographic,* September.
WILLIAM FINNEGAN
A Failing State. *The New Yorker,* November 14.
DOUGLAS FOX
Antarctic Dreams. *Virginia Quarterly Review,* Spring.
PORTER FOX
Everything Is Different on an Island. *The New York Times,* May 22.
MARK FRANEK
Soccer with Vikings. *Roads & Kingdoms,* June 24.

THE BEST AMERICAN SERIES®

FIRST, BEST, AND BEST-SELLING

The Best American Comics

The Best American Essays

The Best American Mystery Stories

The Best American Nonrequired Reading

The Best American Science and Nature Writing

The Best American Science Fiction and Fantasy

The Best American Short Stories

The Best American Sports Writing

The Best American Travel Writing

Available in print and e-book wherever books are sold.

Visit our website: *www.hmhco.com/bestamerican*